364

INFORMATION SOURCES
FOR RESEARCH AND DEVELOPMENT

Use of
Criminology Literature

INFORMATION SOURCES
FOR RESEARCH AND DEVELOPMENT

A series under the General Editorship of

R. T. Bottle, B.Sc., Ph.D., F.R.I.C., M.I.Inf.Sc.
and
D. J. Foskett, M.A., F.L.A.

Use of
Criminology Literature

Editor
Martin Wright
The Howard League for Penal Reform

London Butterworths

THE BUTTERWORTH GROUP

ENGLAND
Butterworth & Co (Publishers) Ltd
London: 88 Kingsway, WC2B 6AB

AUSTRALIA
Butterworths Pty Ltd
Sydney: 586 Pacific Highway, NSW 2067
Melbourne: 343 Little Collins Street, 3000
Brisbane: 240 Queen Street, 4000

CANADA
Butterworth & Co (Canada) Ltd
Toronto: 14 Curity Avenue, 374

NEW ZEALAND
Butterworths of New Zealand Ltd
Wellington: 26-28 Waring Taylor Street, 1

SOUTH AFRICA
Butterworth & Co (South Africa) (Pty) Ltd
Durban: 152-154 Gale Street

First published 1974
© Butterworth & Co (Publishers) Ltd, 1974

ISBN 0 408 70548 5

Printed in England by
Northumberland Press Ltd
Gateshead

Foreword

Thorsten Sellin, Professor Emeritus,
University of Pennsylvania

On my return home in 1926 after two years spent mainly in Paris, Rome, Berlin and London 'reading' criminology, and because of the absence of suitable bibliographical aids, having had to waste much time in the mere labour of finding and locating the pertinent literature, I decided that no student, who wished to read criminology in the United States should lack the guidance I had failed to find abroad. The result was *A bibliographical manual for the student of criminology* (Philadelphia, 1935) with J. P. Shalloo as my co-author. It had the limited purpose of calling attention to the most important published sources of references to titles or analyses of the contents books and articles and other writings; topical bibliographies; ongoing criminological research; organisations promoting or conducting research, and organisations interested in the application of criminological knowledge or in promoting the professional interests of criminologists. The Manual also gave lists of journals or other serial publications containing criminological material and offered information about centres for training in criminological research. A new edition, with L. D. Savitz as co-author, appeared in 1963 (see p. 6).

The editor and the authors of the *Use of Criminological Literature* have greatly improved the formula on which the Manual was based. The present volume does not only supply the kinds of information contained therein but does so for both the United Kingdom and the United States. It furthermore gives titles of important English and American books and articles relevant to a dozen specialties within the field of criminology. Its usefulness to the student is therefore greatly enhanced and its success assured.

Preface

Looking up information seems at first sight to be a straightforward task, but there are pitfalls. The most deceptive of these is that an inexperienced enquirer does not know what he is missing; he may have the impression that he knows of all the references on his subject, when perhaps he has not come within a mile of several of them. Conducting a search requires a sequence of methodical steps; if these are not followed, information may be missed, or extra work created later on.

Conversely, it is as well for librarians to remember that not every reader requires all the information that can possibly be unearthed. A research student embarking on his doctoral dissertation may want everything remotely related to his theme; but the chances are that, say, an applicant for a post in the prison service, or an undergraduate or journalist with a deadline to meet, will want information that is readily available, recent, and in English. It is hoped that this book will be useful for both quick enquiries and comprehensive ones.

Its main aim is to help those who are developing an interest in criminology, including academic social scientists, practising social workers, and students, by providing a guide to the major literature and reference tools, and encouraging them to make themselves familiar with search procedures at an early stage, so that they know how to find information when they need it. It may also be used by librarians working on their behalf; but whereas natural scientists are often glad to ask librarians to make literature searches for them, in the social sciences this is not always considered a good idea, since the process of looking up and assessing references can itself be an aid to thought. Most librarians would accept this approach, provided that the social scientist is familiar with the appropriate reference works and knows how to use them, for it takes time and practice to learn the arrangement of the major bibliographies and abstracting journals, and the relative reliability of periodicals' indexes—to say nothing of the complexities of library catalogues. The present volume may help them to familiarise themselves with the resources available. Those who have not acquired this expertise may feel that it would be worth consulting a trained librarian.

The specialist chapters of the book list sources on the various aspects of criminology, and attempt to indicate their scope. These chapters can be used in conjunction with the index; but it is obviously impossible to enumerate all the contents, and so the user should guard against assuming that, because his subject is not mentioned in the index, it is not to be found in any of the works mentioned. To take a simple example, an individual penal reformer will not be named in the index unless a biography has been devoted to him; but the sections on finding biographical and historical information (in Chapters 1 and 11) contain suggestions which may yield results.

If enough information has not been found after exhausting all lines of enquiry in one's own library, and if the enquiry is of sufficient importance, one can ask a specialist library for help; some relevant ones are listed in Chapter 1 and particulars are given of information services which can help in certain areas of criminology.

When the references have been found, the next stage is to see the originals. If the enquirer has access to a specialist library, he should find many of them there, and some guidance is given on locating materials in libraries. For some material, however, it may be necessary to look elsewhere. Here again, a librarian should be able to help.

Readers may hanker wistfully for an ideal library in which one could look up in a single master index everything from the titles of books on crime among the Iroquois to the library's lending rules. It is true that many bibliographical reference works, and for that matter some libraries, are less helpfully arranged and signposted than they might be. Often the compilers and the librarians, respectively, are well aware of the deficiencies, but are denied the resources of money and manpower to make improvements. Meanwhile enquirers will have to face lists, cross-references and uncumulated abstracting journals. But perhaps there is consolation in the fact that, since no one system will ever be perfect, the existence of alternative routes improves the chance of success—and, for those so inclined, of making refreshing detours along the fertile avenues of serendipity.

M.W.

Contributors

N. HOWARD AVISON, Senior Lecturer and Acting Head of Department of Criminology, University of Edinburgh

A. E. BOTTOMS, Senior Lecturer in Criminology, Faculty of Law, University of Sheffield

DENNIS T. BRETT, Librarian, UK Police College, Hartley Wintney, Basingstoke, Hampshire

TIMOTHY COOK, Director, Alcoholics Recovery Project, Camberwell, London

DAVID P. FARRINGTON, Senior Research Officer, Institute of Criminology, University of Cambridge

CELIA HENSMAN, Department of Health and Social Security, London

S. D. M. MCCONVILLE, Lecturer, School of Cultural and Community Studies, University of Sussex

JOHN E. PEMBERTON, Librarian, University College at Buckingham

A. F. RUTHERFORD, Academy for Contemporary Problems, Columbus, Ohio

CLARE M. SHERIDAN, formerly Assistant Librarian, Institute of Criminology, University of Cambridge

T. G. TENNENT, Director, St Brendan's Hospital, Bermuda

DAVID A. THOMAS, Assistant Director of Research, Institute of Criminology, University of Cambridge

P. WILES, Lecturer in Criminology, Faculty of Law, University of Sheffield

V. C. WILES, Librarian, Faculty of Architectural Studies, University of Sheffield

J. H. WILLIS, Consultant Psychiatrist, Department of Psychological Medicine, Guy's Hospital, London

MARTIN WRIGHT, Director, The Howard League for Penal Reform

Editor's Note

The text of this book was completed by late 1972 and early 1973; in some cases it has been possible to insert references to material published during 1973.

A full survey of standard bibliographical reference works, the use of libraries, US Government publications, and similar subjects has not been included, as these have been well described in other guides to the literature such as John Fletcher's *Use of economics literature* which forms part of the present series.

Abbreviations have been kept to a minimum. The chief are: J. for Journal (of), P. for Press, U. for University, ISTD for the Institute for the Study and Treatment of Delinquency, HMSO for Her Majesty's Stationery Office, and US GPO for United States Government Printing Office.

Places of publication can be found in a directory of publishers such as *British books in print* or, for the US, *LMP* (*Literary market place*).

I am grateful for the help of many librarians in verifying references, and particularly to Miss Rosina Perry, my successor as Librarian at the Institute of Criminology, Cambridge, for suggestions relating to Chapter 1.

Contents

CONTENTS

1

Conducting a search for information in criminology

Martin Wright

DEFINING THE SUBJECT

Criminology is a complex subject which draws upon psychiatry, sociology, criminal law and other fields. It may also be regarded as embracing penology—the study of the treatment of offenders. This complexity is often reflected by specific subjects within, or close to, the field, and the first step in making a search must be to define the area to be studied. Make a list of terms under which to look in indexes, thinking especially of:

(1) Synonyms or near-synonyms, e.g. non-custodial treatment, community treatment, alternatives to imprisonment.
(2) Sub-divisions of the subject: hostels, day training centres, community service orders.
(3) Wider, more general terms: penology, penal policy, rehabilitation.
(4) Related topics: probation, social work.

When the purpose of the search is to compile a bibliography, many of the sub-divisions (2) and a few of the related topics (4) will probably form the headings by which it is arranged.

Some synonyms or related topics are much less obvious than the above examples: learning theory, operant conditioning, behaviour therapy, aversion therapy and token economy are all aspects of the same subject. Beware especially of international differences of usage: preventive detention in French, and sometimes in American, means 'remand in custody'; in England it meant a long sentence imposed on recidivists (until the *Criminal Justice Act 1967* replaced it by the 'extended sentence').

Methodological note 1

You will probably think of other terms as the search proceeds; this means going back to the sources you have already examined. In a lengthy search, it is therefore worth keeping a checklist of works consulted, and the terms you have sought in their indexes.

This is the stage at which, logically, one should decide on the practical limits of the search: How far back in time (but exceptions may be made for important earlier works)? What countries? Any languages other than English? Should research, descriptive accounts, expressions of opinion be included? If the search is on someone else's account, how much specialist knowledge has he? If it is intended to produce a bibliography, is this to be comprehensive—for specialists—or selective—for the general reader? In practice these limits can often be left undefined until the search has progressed far enough to give some idea of how much material exists: this, in conjunction with the time available, will help to determine the degree of comprehensiveness to be aimed at.

To help in defining the area to be covered, it is often worth consulting one or two encyclopaedias. Some contain articles by leading authorities, and several give bibliographical references, which will form a starting point. In addition to the well-known general works such as *Encyclopedia britannica* (continuously revised) and *Chambers' encyclopaedia* (Pergamon, 1965), there are a number of specialist ones. The 17-volume *International encyclopedia of the social sciences* (New York: Macmillan, 1968) does not entirely supersede the same publisher's *Encyclopedia of the social sciences* (15 vols., 1930), which was reprinted in 1957. Single-volume works, which could be described as encyclopaedias despite their titles, are J. Gould and W. L. Kolb's *Dictionary of the social sciences* (Tavistock, 1964) and G. D. Mitchell's shorter *A dictionary of sociology* (Routledge, 1968). All these contain medium-to-long signed contributions, and include references. *A modern dictionary of sociology* (Methuen, 1970), by G. A. and

A. G. Theodorson, contains long definitions rather than short articles. More specifically criminological is V. C. Branham and S. B. Kutash's *Encyclopedia of criminology* (Philosophical Library, 1949), which includes references but is all-American.

THE LIBRARY CATALOGUE

When the territory to be covered has been marked out, the next stage is to make a search in your library's catalogue. If the search is to be a comprehensive one, or is on a subject on which little has been written, you can go on later to consult bibliographies, which list material not necessarily available in your own library; but unless there is a highly developed inter-library loan service, it is generally convenient to begin with what is on the premises. In the absence of a satisfactory subject catalogue, of course, there is nothing for it but to embark on the somewhat cumbersome two-stage process of looking in bibliographies (or asking people) to find out what exists, and then checking the author catalogue to see which items are in the library.

A good library generally has one of two kinds of subject catalogue.

The first is a *classified catalogue*, arranged by a system which attempts to group related subjects. For example, the general section on Penology will be followed by types of punishment and treatment (physical, non-institutional, institutional), each of which in turn is subdivided into more specific topics (capital, corporal, surgical; probation, fine, restitution; and so on). This is done by allocating a code, called a class mark, to each subject. The most widely used scheme in public libraries is the Dewey Decimal Classification, which uses a numerical notation: the number 360, for example, is allocated to Social pathology and social services, and its sub-class 364, Crime and its alleviation (criminology), is further subdivided into subjects of increasing specificity, such as

364·1   Offences
364·15   against the person
  ·152   homicide and suicide
  ·1523   murder

Other examples are:

364·2   Causes of crime and delinquency
  ·3   Offenders

·4 Prevention of crime and delinquency
·6 Correction of crime and delinquency [other than institutional]
365 Penal institutions
·7 Reform of penal system

Another well-known scheme, found in some specialist libraries, is Bliss's Bibliographic Classification. This works on the same principle but uses letters for its main class marks, which are consequently shorter: three figures give up to 999 permutations, whereas three letters give over 17 000. Thus Penology is represented by the class mark QP; this in turn is subdivided into QPA ... QPZ. One of these sub-divisions is Capital punishment, QPP, and the more specific category Hanging is QPPG. A second edition is being prepared on behalf of the Bliss Classification Association by the School of Librarianship of the Polytechnic of North London, which will permit of greater flexibility in constructing class marks for compound subjects. In these and other schemes, each subject may finally be subdivided by additions to the class mark denoting countries, historical periods, and forms of publication such as encyclopaedia, bibliography, conference.

A good classified scheme will often reveal aspects of a subject which the enquirer had overlooked, because it places them nearby in the catalogue, and there should be guide cards to catch the eye. Similarly, if there is not enough information on the exact topic required, the classification can lead the user to a more general one which may include some mention of it. Often the next step in the hierarchy can be found simply by removing the last digit of the class mark; e.g., if there are not enough references under

QOVS b Criminology—offences against property—shoplifting
—USA

try

QOVS   Criminology—offences against property—shoplifting
and then

QOV   Criminology—offences against property
and finally there may be a chapter, and some further references, in a textbook under the general heading

QO   Criminology

But classifications do not always express the structure as clearly as this; consult the librarian about the special features of the scheme used in your library.

Consulting classified catalogues is a two-stage process. It is necessary first to look up, in the Alphabetical Subject Index, the various terms you have listed, to discover their class marks, and then to look for those class marks in the classified catalogue. (Note that some libraries have more than one catalogue: government publications, say, or periodical articles or older works may be catalogued separately.) But the alphabetical index has the compensating advantage that it may bring together subjects which are placed in different parts of the classified scheme, suggesting new lines of search: thus someone looking under Child guidance clinics might find it useful to be reminded that there were also entries under Child cruelty, Child development or Child psychology.

As a short cut one can go straight from the Alphabetical Subject Index to the corresponding shelves in the library; but this is inadequate for a thorough search, since it will lead the enquirer to overlook books on complex subjects which are shelved elsewhere but cross-referenced in the catalogue, books on loan or at the binder's, theses or oversize books, pamphlets, and other material which for any reason is not shelved in the main sequence.

The second main type of catalogue is the *dictionary catalogue*, arranged alphabetically by subject headings. This has the advantage that there is direct access to the terms sought, but related topics are often scattered through the alphabet, as in the case of Burglary, Housebreaking, Shopbreaking, etc. Some, of course, are brought together by the alphabet, but there is no second stage for those which are not. The catalogue will normally include a system or cross-references, '*see*' or '*see also*' as the case may be, but following them up can be laborious, and sometimes they leave the user to think of his own, with such directions as '*see also* names of specific crimes of violence'.

There are other ways of organising subjects in libraries, ranging from optical coincidence cards to computers, but they are not yet widely used in social science libraries, partly because they presuppose an adequate level of staffing.

BOOKS

When the catalogue has been checked, the next step is to refer to the books themselves, many of which will contain their own bibliographies, and to follow up the references listed there. It is also advisable to ask the librarian concerning the possible whereabouts of any books not on the shelves—and also of those which may not yet have been catalogued!

One type of book which can be particularly useful is the

collection of papers: proceedings of conferences; Festschriften (collections published in honour of an eminent man); and the proliferating 'books of readings' which bring together a variety of articles, excerpts from other books, judgments in leading cases, and sometimes material not previously published. Unfortunately, these volumes have often been published without indexes, which saves the compilers' time but wastes everyone else's. Some libraries make analytical catalogue entries for them, and some abstracting services record the items that have not previously appeared. A few may be traced when other authors cite them. Otherwise the only way to plumb this class of publication is by flair: one goes to appropriate sections of the library, picks the volumes off the shelf and looks through the tables of contents.

BIBLIOGRAPHIES

The emphasis so far has been on discovering material in one's own library, and especially items classed as books. This category may, depending on the library's arrangement, include some research reports and other unpublished or 'semi-published' literature, but so far few periodical references are likely to have been found. In some subjects the most recent, most detailed and perhaps even the only information is in periodical articles and research reports: for these the search will depend to a considerable extent on bibliographies, and on abstracting and indexing services and research guides, which will be referred to below.

The best-known list is T. Besterman's five-volume *A world bibliography of bibliographies*; but it is restricted to separately published bibliographies, which do not tend to be the most specialised, and the fourth and positively the final edition appeared in 1965–66. It is in effect kept up to date by the H. W. Wilson *Bibliographic index* (1938–   ), which includes bibliographies published in periodicals also. The only major listing of bibliographies specifically relating to criminology is T. Sellin and L. D. Savitz's *A bibliographic manual for the student of criminology* (3rd ed., New York: National Research and Information Center on Crime and Delinquency, 1963; reprinted from *International bibliography on crime and delinquency*, **1** (3), 1963). This includes a useful and extensive annotated list of general reference works for historical and modern materials, and a section on American official publications, followed by a somewhat American-orientated classified list of bibliographies on specific types of crime, etc. There are indexes of authors and titles, but not of subjects.

Bibliographies on particular subjects will be mentioned in their respective chapters; a few series may be noted here. One is published by the Cambridge Institute of Criminology, whose subjects have included *Deprivation of liberty for young offenders* (1966), *Soviet criminology* (1969), *Education in penal institutions* (1971) and *Parole* (2nd ed., 1972). All are arranged by subject subdivisions, and within each section in chronological order; there are author and subject indexes. There are several American sources. The Institute of Governmental Studies, University of California, has issued a long series compiled by Mrs D. C. Tompkins, including *The Offender* (1963), *Probation* ... (1964), *Juvenile gangs* ... (1966), *White-collar crime* (1967) and *The prison and the prisoner* (1972). Useful lists are often appended to the *Accessions list* of Yale Law Library, and are by no means confined to narrowly legal topics: examples are *Conscientious objectors* (1967), *The battered child, Compensation for victims of crime, The Warren Commission's report* [on the assassination of President Kennedy] and *Riots* (all 1968), and *Recidivism* (1969). Other agencies which produce bibliographies at intervals include the US Children's Bureau, which produced one on juvenile delinquency in 1964 and on the battered child in 1969, among the extensive range of booklets on all aspects of child care which it has published over the years. An example of an international body is the International Union for Child Welfare, Geneva, which has compiled lists on such topics as *Problems posed by unmarried mothers and their children* (1966) and *Planning ... to prevent ... juvenile maladjustment and delinquency* (1967).

Methodological note 2

Note down the *full* particulars of any items that seem likely to be useful, as soon as you have examined them. You will save yourself time later if you write them fully and clearly on separate cards, using a consistent form of citation. Otherwise you (or your secretary) will eventually have to waste a lot of time going back to the library to verify and complete them. Much time is also saved, if it does become necessary to check a defective reference, by noting the source of each item. Use block letters for proper names and for technical terms with which a typist may not be familiar.

For older works there are a few bibliographies specialising in this subject. The main English one is Sir J. G. Cumming's *A contribution towards a bibliography dealing with crime* (3rd ed., 1935). American compilations include A. F. Kuhlman's extensive *A guide to material on crime and criminal justice* (1929), continued in Mrs D. C. Culver's *Bibliography of crime and criminal justice 1927–1931* (1934) and ... *1932–1937* (1939), all published by H. W. Wilson; all are arranged by subject, but the latter two benefit by having author as well as subject indexes. H. K. Spector's *Bibliography on criminology and penology* ... (New York: Rikers Island Penitentiary, 1944) gives the impression of having been produced against heavy odds, but can provide useful references. Apart from these it is necessary to rely on more general bibliographies that are arranged by subject or have indexes, notably the catalogues of certain great libraries published in book form. A leading example is the *London bibliography of the social sciences* (1931–   ), listing the holdings of the British Library of Political and Economic Science at the London School of Economics. Originally the LSE published it, but the most recent instalment, relating to 1962–68, was published by Mansells in seven volumes in 1970. It is arranged by subject headings which are not always obvious, and since the original edition in 1931 the author and subject indexes have been discontinued. More general are the *Catalogue of the London Library* (1913–1955), which also has a *Subject Index*, and the catalogues of the great national libraries, such as the *British Museum subject index of modern books acquired since 1881* and the equivalent, covering the years from 1945 onwards, published by the Library of Congress. Recent British publications, including those of American publishers with British offices, are recorded in *British national bibliography* (1950–   ), which is well indexed and cumulated.

This list is far from exhaustive: general guides to the use of libraries list the other principal bibliographic tools. For the social sciences specifically, see a concise article by C. A. Crossley in *Applied Social Studies*, **3** (1), 137-149 (1969) and two books: C. M. White and associates' *Sources of information in the social sciences* (Bedminster P., 1964) and *A reader's guide to the social sciences*, ed. B. F. Hoselitz (rev. ed., Collier-Macmillan, 1970).

The researcher should know of the main tools of the book trade and of librarians for tracing publications. The *Cumulative book index* (Wilson, 1898–   ) lists books by author, title, subject, etc., thus helping to identify works of which only incomplete details are known. It includes books in English, wherever published. To discover which books are currently in print, *British books in print*

(Whitaker, annual) may be used; the American equivalent is *Books in print* (Bowker, annual). Books available in paperback are recorded in Whitaker's *Paperbacks in print*.

ABSTRACTING AND INDEXING SERVICES

The next main source of references, and for periodical articles the most important, is provided by the abstracting and indexing services. Sellin and Savitz, in their *Bibliographic manual* ... cited on page 6, provide an extensive guide, especially for older (including historical) material; they list services of universal scope as well as specialist ones.

Like library catalogues, the good ones are arranged either in classified order with subject and author indexes, or alphabetically by subject headings with author indexes. If they are to be conveniently usable, they should have indexes annually as well as in each issue, and if possible every 10 years or so; in the H. W. Wilson series the entire entry is reprinted in cumulations which appear in a planned sequence, such as quarterly, annually and triennially. This firm, incidentally, has a special pricing system designed to benefit smaller libraries; to obtain the advantage it is necessary to order direct, not through an agent.

None of these services is really up to date, and those which include abstracts are usually at least 6–12 months behind. *Abstracts in Criminology and Penology* (formerly *Excerpta Criminologica*, 1961–), published—in English—by Æ. E. Kluwer, of Deventer, has reasonable world-wide coverage of periodicals, though for books it is less comprehensive. It has a detailed index based on a computer (which sometimes gives unusual sub-headings) in each bi-monthly issue and at the end of each year; a 10-year index is hoped for. *Crime and delinquency literature* (1970–) is produced by the National Council on Crime and Delinquency, Paramus, N.J. 07652: it is somewhat American-orientated and highly selective, but useful for current awareness and for literature reviews on well-chosen topics such as 'Strategies for decreasing jail populations' (March 1971) and 'Treatment for the violent offender' (March 1972). The promisingly titled *International bibliography on crime and delinquency* was for long a disappointment: the first three issues (1963) were arranged in inconvenient form, but redeemed by appendices containing bibliographies of Greek, Ceylonese and Japanese criminology (the latter supplemented in Vol. 2, No. 3). After changing the title to *Crime and Delinquency Abstracts and Current Projects* (published by the US Government

Printing Office) it improved, though the articles were in almost random order and the index was not cumulated. A computer was introduced in 1967, with unusually severe teething troubles, but the publication has now ceased.

On subjects closely related to criminology the main services are *Psychological Abstracts* (American Psychological Association, 1927–), with about 20 000 abstracts a year from 650 journals, indexed monthly and half-yearly; and *Sociological Abstracts* (S.A. Inc., 1952–), with about 6000 abstracts from 700 journals. The International Committee for Social Sciences Documentation edits the annual *International bibliography of the social sciences—sociology* (Tavistock, 1952–), attractively produced, selective, but rather slow to appear; it is arranged under broad subjects and has a good index which is, however, based only on the titles of the items listed. *Abstracts for Social Workers* (Albany, N.Y.: National Association of Social Workers, 1965–) has a useful coverage of American periodicals, but the few British entries are seldom less than a year old. It is indexed quarterly and annually.

Anglo-American law is indexed in *Index to Legal Periodicals* (H. W. Wilson, 1888–). This has very broad subject headings, so that specific topics such as Sentencing or Bail are buried in general sections such as Criminal procedure—but there is no guide to tell the reader under which heading to look. It covers some 300 journals (including their book reviews) and lists them annually with their addresses. As an interesting, and rare, example of co-ordinated publishing, it is complemented by *Index to Periodical Articles Related to Law* (Glanville Publications, 1958–), which limits itself to journals—specialist legal ones and others—that *Index to Legal Periodicals* does not include. It has yearly and 10-yearly cumulations, with author indexes. The law of other countries is recorded in *Index to Foreign Legal Periodicals* (Institute of Advanced Legal Studies, 1960–). For social science literature the leading foreign guide is *Bulletin Signalétique, sections 19–24 Sciences Humaines* (Centre de Documentation du CNRS, 1947–). Section 20 covers psychology and education; Section 21, sociology and ethnology. There are subject and author indexes; but within each issue there are separate indexes for each section, so the arrangement needs studying before use.

There are also some services which, while including some of the main academic or specialist journals, often index periodicals for the informed layman such as the intellectual weeklies and the 'quality' newspapers (but only feature articles in the latter, not news items). The relevant British service is *British Humanities*

Index (Library Association, 1962–   ), with a fairly up-to-date coverage of some 400 journals; the L.A. also publishes *British Education Index* (1954–   ). The American equivalents of these are all from H. W. Wilson: *Social Science and Humanities Index* (1965–   ), *Education Index* (1929–   ) and *P.A.I.S. (Public Affairs Information Service)* (1915–   ).

Methodological note 3

Some frustration can be avoided by study of the compilers' notes on how to use the indexes, their system of arrangement, the categories of material deliberately excluded, and so on. But some things the compilers do not disclose, and it is up to the user to deduce them or discover them by chance. They do not always use the entry word which seems obvious. Sometimes the indexer partly classifies his index, so that, for example, all offences are listed as sub-divisions of the heading Crimes, instead of under their own names; or all book reviews may be grouped together. When a name is changed, as from 'reform schools' to 'approved schools' and then to 'community homes', indexers may continue to use the old term concurrently, and the searcher, on discovering this, will have to go back again to earlier volumes of the index to discover when the new one began to be used.

To cover any gaps left by the abstracting and indexing services, the annual indexes of some of the principal periodicals should themselves be checked. Many of these are not of a high standard: some are little more than title lists, or contain entries only under the words actually used in the titles. (Authors might do well to remember this: an epigrammatic title may lead to the article's being overlooked, unless amplified by an informative subtitle.) Some journals have annual lists of contents as well as, or instead of, an index. A few, more conscious of their value as sources of information, have issued cumulative indexes covering many years, such as *British Journal of Criminology* (formerly *of Delinquency*) (1950–1970), *British Journal of Sociology* (1950–1969), *Law Quarterly Review* (1885–1964) and *Modern Law Review* (1938–1970). It is also, of course, necessary to check the issues since the last annual index.

Mention must also be made of two new developments. One is the weekly *Current Contents: behavioral, social and educational sciences* (Institute of Scientific Information), which simply reproduces the contents pages of over 1100 journals. Coverage for criminology is not complete, but the editors are open to suggestions. The same firm will publish, from 1973, *Social Sciences Citation Index*. This type of index is based on the fact that earlier authors are commonly cited by later ones writing on related subjects; thus, by looking up the books and articles he already knows the user is led to new ones, where, very often, he will find relevant ideas. This bypasses the vagaries of terminology; but to overcome authors' equally erratic bibliographic habits, a subject index will also be provided.

The references are stored in a computer, which can provide a current awareness service and retrospective searches; copies of original articles can be obtained.

The other mechanised literature searching service available in the United Kingdom is MEDLARS (Medical Literature Analysis and Retrieval System). This is based on the abstracting journal *Index Medicus* (1960–   ), which includes a far wider range of, for example, forensic and social medicine, psychology and psychiatry than its name might suggest, although naturally it does not extend to purely sociological aspects of criminology. The basis for searches is a complete list of Medical Subject Headings (abbreviated to MeSH), issued annually. Straightforward searches on a well-defined topic may be relatively easily made by going through the published volumes of *Index Medicus*; the computer comes into its own when the subject becomes more complex, when greater depth of indexing is required, or when the number of references is very large. It is important to compile the search instructions as precisely as possible, in order to obtain as much as possible of the relevant literature and to avoid being overwhelmed by unwanted references. Guidance on doing this can be obtained from the UK agent for MEDLARS: the British Library, Lending Division (BLL), Boston Spa, Yorks., LS 23.7 BQ. An experienced librarian with some knowledge of classification theory should be able to resolve difficulties. The print-out can be arranged by author, date or subject, as required. As an example of subjects covered, the Cambridge Institute of Criminology holds the print-out of a search on the general theme of Violence.

Lists of the periodicals are contained in the abstracting and indexing journals, usually once a year. For a comprehensive, classified guide, regularly updated, see *Ulrich's International periodicals directory: Vol. 2—Arts, humanities, business and social sciences* (Bowker). R. Rank compiled an international list of 320 periodicals relating to criminal law and criminology in *Law Library J.*, **60**, 249–271 (1967).

> *Methodological note 4*
> By now the search in library subject catalogues, abstracts and indexes should have produced enough references to indicate some of the leading writers in the field. It is worth consulting the *author* catalogue and the *author* indexes of periodicals and abstracting journals, to discover other work which these specialists may have published on the same subject. This method can be especially useful with the more poorly indexed periodicals.

RESEARCH

It is vital for anyone undertaking research to know not only what has already been published but also what is in progress. Criminology is no longer such a small, specialised subject that everyone who is anyone knows everything that is being done. Moreover, research is often very expensive, which makes the waste of scarce resources all the more serious if unintentional duplication takes place. (Deliberate replication is, of course, another matter; but it still requires complete knowledge of what has gone before.)

The only list of research in progress specialising in criminology is published by the Council of Europe Division of Crime Problems, and it is limited in the main to the Council's member countries: the *International exchange of information on current criminological research in member states* (Strasbourg, 1966–   ). Each issue contains a section reporting progress of projects listed earlier, especially publications which have arisen from them.

British academic research is recorded in the annual *Scientific research in British universities and colleges: Vol. 3—Social sciences* (HMSO), which includes also some Government and non-university research, but is somewhat slow in appearing. It is oddly arranged, partly by broad subject, partly by university; the index is extensive but not exhaustive.

American research is listed in *Crime and delinquency abstracts*. The US Children's Bureau has issued, at intervals, lists of research relating to juvenile delinquents and to children; the latter series is now produced by the ERIC Clearinghouse on Early Childhood Education, University of Illinois, Urbana, and published by the US GPO. The Institute of Education, London University has links with ERIC.

The Home Office Research and Statistics Department issues a

Summary of research in progress and of research supported by grant, and the Prison Department lists its own projects separately. Other registers of research on specialised topics are issued from time to time, but their value is limited if they have no regular system for updating. An example is A. Sivanandan and S. Bagley's *Register of research on Commonwealth immigrants in Britain* (3rd ed., Institute of Race Relations, 1968). It would also help users, and the researchers who are repeatedly asked to fill in questionnaires, if the latter were standardised in the form suggested by the Aslib Social Sciences Group.

The recording of research in progress, especially non-academic projects, is thus very incomplete; even for completed research the position is not much better. If it results in a doctoral thesis, it will be recorded in *Dissertation Abstracts International* (University Microfilms, 1969–), which succeeds *Dissertation Abstracts* (1952–1969). It appears in two parts, of which Part A is for humanities and social sciences. The BLL is building up a collection of theses, in microfilm. British theses are also listed in *Index to theses accepted for higher degrees in the universities of Great Britain and Northern Ireland* (Aslib, 1953–). The only British list including research reports, as well as theses from 15 British Universities, is *BLL announcement bulletin* (1971–), with a section on behavioural and social sciences and the humanities. The main comparable listing of American reports is limited to those based on government-sponsored research: the *US Government research and development reports* (*USGDR*) (1965–). Here the few reports relating to social sciences are vastly outnumbered by scientific and technical ones, but to make sure nothing is missed it is worth making a regular check. Much of the major American criminological research is done by relatively few agencies, such as the California Department of the Youth Authority, California Department of Corrections, and the Divisions of Corrections in Florida, Wisconsin, and a few other states, which may be contacted direct.

LIBRARIES

It remains to locate the publications themselves, when they are not in the enquirer's 'home' library. This is essentially the responsibility of the librarian. His task has been made much easier, as regards periodicals, since the British Library, Lending Division (then the National Lending Library) extended its scope to include the social sciences: any library, by becoming a registered borrower, can obtain periodicals on loan or photocopies of individual articles. A list of *Current serials received ... March 1971* is available, but the rate of new acquisitions is rapid, so it is worth requesting titles not listed there. For earlier periodicals, and any others which have escaped the BLL net, the *British union-catalogue of periodicals (BUCOP)* (Butterworths, 1955–) and its supplements list some 140 000 periodicals and libraries which hold them.

Books can usually be obtained by inter-library loan. The BLL has a union catalogue of many libraries' holdings, and has begun to extend its own stocks considerably; for example, it acquires all publications of British and American university presses.

Not all libraries, however, are prepared to lend to outsiders, and in any case it may be more convenient to visit a large library where much of the material will be accessible (although the literature of criminology is liable to be scattered among its constituent disciplines). Serious researchers can obtain permission to visit the British Museum and major university libraries, including the British Library of Political and Economic Science at the London School of Economics, and the only considerable library in this country specialising in criminology, that of the Cambridge Institute of Criminology. There are collections in the libraries of the Home Office in Whitehall and the Prison Service Staff College in Wakefield; it is difficult for outsiders to gain access, but they are usually willing to make inter-library loans. The Howard League for Penal Reform and the Institute for the Study and Treatment of Delinquency both have small collections which their members may use; but the former has transferred its historical material to the library of the University of Warwick, and both suffer from the lack of a full-time librarian.

SPECIAL TYPES OF INFORMATION

The foregoing has dealt principally with the subject matter of criminology proper, and the subsequent chapters will provide a guide to specific aspects of it. There remains a considerable amount of information ancillary to the study of a subject, some of which can be difficult to locate. Knowledge of these sources is part of the training and experience of qualified librarians, who know their way about such compendia as *Whitaker's almanac* (annual) with its population figures, lists of addresses of societies and associations, members of both Houses of Parliament, facts about Commonwealth countries, and a vast amount of other information. Note that there are two editions, of which the 'Library' one is the fuller. An American equivalent is the *Information please almanac*, which even includes the text of the US Constitution. A short guide to sources of information is G. Chandler's *How to find out* (3rd ed., Pergamon, 1967). For an annotated bibliography see A. J. Walford's *Guide to reference material: Vol. 2—Social and historical sciences* ... (Library Association, 1968), which is useful for basic reference works but has little to offer specifically on criminology; there is also the American-orientated *Guide to reference works* (8th ed., American Library Association, 1967).

By exploring the reference section of the library one learns by degrees the more specialised sources: for example, that the postal addresses of prisons are given in the annual *Report of the work of the Prison Department* (HMSO), but that for their telephone numbers one must turn to the (oddly arranged) *Police and constabulary almanac* (R. Hazell, annual) or the *Probation and after-care directory* (HMSO, annual, with supplements), which, however, excludes Scottish ones; or that the official *Directory of approved schools* (HMSO, 1965) is updated by a section in *Charities digest* (Family Welfare Association and Butterworths, annual). The latter also lists probation hostels. Only a selection of such sources can be given here, but it may serve as a starting point. The most convenient listing of social services, probation, clerks to justices, penal establishments, police, etc., is in *Social services year book* (Councils and Education P., annual).

Criminologists may also need information about the voluntary services concerned with offenders. Many are included in the *Charities digest*, mentioned above. Two other guides cover both sectors: the Family Welfare Association's *Guide to the social services* ... *information regarding the statutory and voluntary services* (Macdonald and Evans, annual), which states the official aims of the organisations including prison after-care, and how to contact them—it also has summaries of relevant legislation; and Phyllis Willmott's *Consumer's guide to the British social services* (Penguin, 1967), arranged by classes of people in social need, with emphasis on how to gain access to available services. Mrs Willmott also edits *Public social services: handbook* (NCSS, 1973). Voluntary work in general is described, with names and addresses of relevant organisations, by D. Hobman in *A guide to voluntary service* (rev. ed., HMSO, 1969) and by the National Council of Social Service's *Voluntary social services: directory and handbook* (NCSS, 1973). The National Children's Bureau (then the National Bureau for Co-operation in Child Care) classifies organisations in its field by their function in its *Directory of voluntary organisations concerned with children* (Longmans, 1969). Information about youth work is given in various publications of the National Youth Bureau formerly YSIC, 37 Belvoir Street, Leicester, LE 1.6 SL); and on voluntary and community work in *Quest News Service* (now taken over by Capital Radio, Euston Tower, London NW1 3 DR, but available for enquiries.

Organisations helping ex-offenders, especially those which run hostels, are listed in the *NACRO manual and directory* (National Association for the Care and Resettlement of Offenders, annual), which specifies the category of need which each seeks to meet. NACRO's predecessor was the National Association of Discharged Prisoners' Aid Societies, whose *Handbook*, published in 1956, may be of historical interest. There are at least two international guides to this field of work: the *International directory of prisoners' aid agencies* (526 W. Wisconsin Ave, Milwaukee 3, Wis.: International Prisoners' Aid Association, 1968), which lists voluntary after-care organisations in many countries, with a summary of the state of after-care in each country; and the *Directory of community resources* (2709 Sequoia Way, Belmont, Calif. 94002: International Halfway House Association, 1968), mainly confined to the USA and Canada. A *Probation and parole directory: USA and Canada* is published at intervals by the National Council on Crime and Delinquency (above, p. 9) which should be able to provide information about any other local guides such as the *Directory of California services for juvenile and adult offenders* (PO Box 20191, Sacramento, Calif. 95820: State of California Documents Section, 1968). A similar guide for Canada also outlines the criminal justice and penal system: *Handbook of correctional services in Canada* (55 Parkdale Ave., Ottawa 3: Canadian Corrections Association, 1965).

Of the many other kinds of information which may be needed, two will be mentioned here as examples of the processes involved in locating it.

News items in newspapers are difficult—but not impossible—to trace, unless the individual library systematically keeps cuttings. The *British Humanities Index* is useful for feature articles in the 'quality' daily and Sunday newspapers and the weekly journals, but excludes news items. For these, a starting point can be the *Index* of *The Times*, although this appears every two months, so that a search covering several years can be laborious, and it is slow in appearing. For other newspapers, one must establish the date of the incident concerned, either from *The Times'* index or from

Keesing's contemporary archives, which are selective but very up-to-date, or by tracing editorial comment in weekly periodicals such as *New Society, Justice of the Peace, British Medical Journal* or *New Law Journal* through their indexes or by looking through the issues since the last index appeared. Local events are often indexed by local public libraries. Otherwise newspapers within the last few months are apparently not indexed anywhere; the only way of tracing items seems to be through the paper's own librarian.

The second example of information which can prove hard to find is the biography and writings of a person. In addition to *Who's who* and *Who was who*, the *Dictionary of national biography* (*DNB*) may be consulted. Before 1900, the *Concise DNB* can be used; it includes all the names but has abbreviated entries. The *Concise dictionary of American biography* (Oxford U.P., 1964) summarises in the same way the *Dictionary of American biography*, which includes subjects whose death took place up to 1940. Some of the lists of members of learned societies and professions give brief particulars. Some of the dictionaries and encyclopaedias of special subjects (see pp. 2–3) have biographical articles; and, of course, the library catalogue should be consulted both for an author's works and to see if a biography has been written (most libraries make an entry in the author catalogue for the subject of a biography or the recipient of a volume of presented essays (Festschrift)). The indexes and bibliographies of general textbooks of the subject should be consulted. The founding fathers of criminology are brought together in H. Mannheim's *Pioneers in criminology* (Stevens, 1960). If a person's writings have been collected, that edition of his works should contain biographical notes. Published catalogues such as those of the London Library and the British Museum may be checked for his books and pamphlets, and the *London bibliography of the social sciences*, which, however, had an author index only in its earliest years. For a person's periodical articles, there are the indexes such as those mentioned above (pp. 2–3); but the leading nineteenth century one, *Poole's index* (Boston, 1802–1906) has no author index, and one must guess the subjects about which the author may have written. Many people eminent in their fields gave evidence at some time to a Royal Commission or other governmental enquiry: for example, Maconochie to the Select Committee on Transportation, 1856; Du Cane to the Select Committee on Prisons and Prison Ministers' Acts, 1870 and the Penal Servitude Acts Commission, 1879; Du Cane and Ruggles-Brise to the Gladstone Committee on Prisons, 1895. In more recent times, one of the only places where prison governors and others have placed their views on record is in evidence to Expenditure Committees of the House of Commons. Finally, some publishers have the helpful habit of giving an author's *curriculum vitae* on the dust jackets of his books; but some librarians fail to preserve them. (See also Chapter 11, pp. 199–202.)

2

Sociological aspects of criminology

Paul Wiles and *V. C. Wiles*

INTRODUCTION: ON SOCIOLOGY AND CRIMINOLOGY

'Sociology' and 'criminology'

'Criminology' is a vague term, meaning simply the study of crime
and related phenomena. The title of 'criminologist' may therefore
be applied to anybody interested in such study: to the policeman
as much as to the doctor, or to the detective novelist as well as
the academic. Generally speaking, academics interested in criminology will think of themselves as belonging to one of the social
sciences, and the concern of the present chapter is with the approach
of one such discipline: namely, sociology.

To the person approaching criminology for the first time, the
distinction between a discipline and an area of study may seem
somewhat esoteric, but it is important that it be made clear at
the outset, since otherwise the sociological work in this area is
difficult to understand. To oversimplify, in order to make it clearer,
we may say that the distinction is that 'sociology' is a discipline
and 'criminology' is an area of study. Sociology is a discipline in
the sense that it asks particular kinds of questions about the world,
and as a result tries to develop a body of coherent theories and
methods to answer these. Criminology, on the other hand, is much
more catholic: any kind of question we may wish to ask about

crime comes within its scope and it draws upon several disciplines for its methodology and its theories. Broadly, then, the study of criminology in universities may be concerned with different kinds of questions about crime, which differ according to the kinds of questions which particular disciplines ask about the world. We could therefore say that, for example, questions about the physical make-up of criminals belong to biological criminology; those about the personality of criminals, to psychological criminology; those about social behaviour and crime, to sociological criminology; and so on. In spite of several attempts to develop 'inter-disciplinary' theories for criminology, they have not, up to the present, been very successful.

The main implication of this, for somebody wishing to discover something about the sociological study of crime, is that such a study only tries to answer certain kinds of questions about crime, using concepts and methods which have been developed in relation to a wider sociological attempt to explain the social world in general. The concern of this chapter will be with the sociological literature on crime and 'deviant behaviour' (of which more in a moment), but, as will have become apparent, this will by no means be the only literature which a sociologist concerned with explaining criminal behaviour will use in his day-to-day work. He will in addition be interested in other criminological literature, but, more importantly, he will be interested in sociological literature which is not specifically about crime at all. For example, if he is concerned with subcultural theories of delinquency, then he will also be interested in work on cultures or groups in general.

Sociology

Sociology is usually defined as the study of social life by the methods of science. In saying that it is scientific, various philosophical and methodological problems are raised: for example, whether sociologists, being part of the very thing they are trying to study, introduce value-judgements into their work; or, what exactly are the 'facts' of the social world.

What, then, is meant by saying that sociology is scientific? Broadly, what is meant is that the study is empirical in that its ideas should be capable in principle of being tested in relation to factual observation; that it is theoretical in that it attempts to develop abstract and logical propositions to explain causal relationships; that it is systematic since it tries to build on existing knowledge to move to higher-level theories; and that it is non-normative in that it does not try to say how the social world should be organised but rather how it is organised.

The social life which is studied by these methods is, broadly, the social interaction of human beings, groups and the social structure; the sociological study of crime will therefore be concerned not solely with the question of how certain social institutions or structures may constrain activity towards the criminal, but also with how and why such forms develop and, perhaps most important of all, how and why does the social category of 'criminal' itself come about.

Space does not permit us to explore fully the debate about the nature of sociology and its relationship to criminology. We have tried to give a very brief overview, but are only too aware that this has involved considerable simplification of the issues involved. Those who are interested enough to go into these problems in more detail should consult the companion volume in this series called *Use of Social Sciences Literature* (Butterworths, to be published).

The sociology of crime and the sociology of deviance

It is perhaps perplexing for those reading criminology to find that the words 'crime' and 'deviance' seem to be used interchangeably. Although the present book is about 'criminology', in fact few sociologists would now regard the term as the most useful way of categorising the area of study. Instead most would refer to 'the sociology of deviant behaviour'. At first sight, crime would seem to be a useful behavioural category, being apparently clearly defined by the criminal law. However, from a sociological point of view it has certain disadvantages. Both the relativity, and at times the unclear behavioural definitions, of the law mean that the subject matter of criminology would not be constant. For example, suicide would at one time have been properly included in criminology, but later excluded after it ceased to be a criminal offence. Such a situation for the purposes of study would obviously be rather silly; but, more important, if we use the law to delineate our field of study, we make it much more difficult to ask questions about the sociological nature of the law itself. We take as an independent variable what we ought to take as dependent. Finally, and perhaps most importantly, we would treat the criminal law, and crime, as if they were quite different in principle from other kinds of rule making, and rule breaking.

We all know from our everyday life that membership of any social group imposes upon us rules of behaviour and sanctions for breaking those rules. Sociologists have therefore increasingly preferred to organise their work around the notion of deviant behaviour: that is, behaviour which violates normative rules, or, even more generally, normative standards or expectations which have not been formulated into specific rules. The study of such behaviour may then include all cases of rule making, rule breaking and rule enforcement, of which criminal law will be one particular example. Sociologists do, of course, recognise that criminal rules have special, or even unique, characteristics, but argue that these may be better understood by comparison with the general category of normative rules, and that we may learn something about the nature of crime by comparatively studying other kinds of deviance. This means that sociologists of deviant behaviour study not only crime but many other kinds of deviance as well.

In order to maintain the unity of the present book, what follows in the rest of the chapter is a discussion of the sociological literature on crime and related problems. However, it ought to be borne in mind that much of the more recent sociological work is part of an attempt to develop theories, not just about crime but more generally about deviant behaviour.

Sociology is a comparatively new science and has not yet developed adequate higher-level theories; indeed, some sociologists would argue that in practical terms it is never likely to. For whatever reasons there is not *a* sociological theory even in a relatively limited area such as criminal behaviour; instead there are a number of alternative, and sometimes incompatible, theories. The present chapter discusses the literature on some of the more important of these theoretical perspectives. The approach has been deliberately chosen, since we believe that it is the most meaningful way of introducing the literature. However, sociologists have undertaken a vast number of studies on crime, and any discussion can only include a small proportion of the total. In particular, it ought to be borne in mind that our approach excludes a large number of studies of particular types of crime which have not been consciously aimed at testing particular theories. Studies of this kind can be found referenced and discussed in the various textbooks and books of readings listed at the end of the chapter.

SOCIOLOGICAL LITERATURE ON CRIME AND DEVIANCE

Class theories and crime

Modern sociology has been profoundly influenced by Marxist theories of social class, and therefore one might have expected to find a similar influence in criminology. However, there has, in fact, been little systematic use of Marxist theory in the English-language criminological literature, and even such an obvious candidate as the concept of 'alienation' has been largely ignored or else bastardised into a crude psychological measure. To some extent this is due to the heavy dependence in such literature on American work, and the political and intellectual history of Marxism in that country. For all that, however, the gap remains a surprising one.

The work most often referred to in discussions of Marxist criminology is W. A. Bonger's *Criminality and economic conditions* (Little, Brown, 1916), but it is a somewhat crude and unimaginative application of Marxism (see also W. A. Bonger, *Introduction to criminology*, Methuen, 1934). Perhaps the best piece is Engels's own discussion of crime in his *The condition of the working class in England in 1844* (Allen and Unwin, 1968; originally published in German in 1845).

However, this lack of a consistent body of Marxist criminological literature in English does not mean that researchers have not been interested in the relationship between crime and economic structure: indeed, the correspondence between a society's poor and its criminals is one of criminology's most consistent observations. Theories about the nature of that relationship have changed considerably and few sociologists would now accept a simple causal connection between poverty and crime, but nevertheless many of the more recent theories place great stress on the individual's place in the class structure. The possibility of a straightforward causal relationship was most clearly questioned when, during the depression of the 1930s, the expected dramatic increase in crime did not occur. The best summary of research on this problem is Thorsten Sellin's *Research memorandum on crime in the depression* (New York: Social Science Research Council Bulletin, No. 27, 1937), and a classic study of the effects of unemployment on crime in Britain is Hermann Mannheim's *Social aspects of crime between the wars* (Allen and Unwin, 1940). Everyone accepts that the working class are proportionally over-represented among those convicted of criminal offences, but what is disputed is whether this is the result of a class bias in the operation of the legal process or of a class differential in the commission of crimes. A popular way of testing these alternatives is to carry out self-report studies—that is, studies where we rely upon people admitting offences rather than upon figures of those convicted. These studies are discussed in detail in the chapter on criminal statistics, and a useful discussion of such work can be found in R. G. Hood and R. F. Sparks's book *Key issues in criminology* (Weidenfeld, 1970). In England the most extensive study of this kind so far carried out is that by the Survey Research Unit, of which some of the results have been reported by W. A. Belson in 'The extent of stealing by London boys' (*Advancement of Science*, **25** (124), 171–184, 1968).

The more general relationship between social class and known criminal behaviour has also been explored, and particularly useful is J. W. B. Douglas and others' 'Delinquency and social class' (*British J. Criminology*, **6** (3), 294–302, 1966); L. McDonald's *Social class and delinquency* (Faber, 1969); and W. R. Little and V. R. Ntsekhe's 'Social class backgrounds of young offenders from London' (*British J. Delinquency*, **10** (3), 130–135, 1959).

Functionalist theory and the concept of anomie

Writers of criminological textbooks have tended to discuss the concept of anomie and subcultural theories together. Such a policy certainly makes the literature easier to explain, since there are many overlaps between anomie and subcultural theories and the Chicago school's ideas of social disorganisation. Indeed, in part of the later subcultural writing, represented by Richard A. Cloward and Lloyd E. Ohlin's *Delinquency and opportunity* (Routledge, 1961) the ideas are fused together. For all that, however, they belong to separate sociological traditions.

The sociological concept of anomie is put forward in its classic form by Emile Durkheim. He used 'anomie' to describe the state of normlessness which arose when the potentially insatiable desires of men were no longer controlled by the external regulatory force of the collective order. As such, he saw it as a fairly abnormal state resulting from the relatively dramatic social change of industrialisation. His theory is most fully stated in his book *Suicide* (Routledge, 1952; originally published in French in 1897), but the part played by the division of labour in this process is more extensively explored in *The division of labour in society* (Free Press, 1964; originally published in French in 1893).

Durkheim applied his concept to suicide but did not extend it to crime or deviant behaviour in general. A more general application was carried out by Robert K. Merton, first in his article 'Social structure and anomie' (*American Sociological Review*, **3** (4), 672–682, 1938), and later in his book *Social theory and social structure* (rev. ed., Free Press, 1968). However, in making it of wider application Merton also considerably modified the Durkheimian concept. In particular, he saw anomie as endemic to contemporary American society; he placed a greater stress on specifically economic goals; and he worked out a typology of possible adaptations to anomie. It is this Mertonian modification which has been most widely influential in the sociological study of crime and deviancy.

Merton's work, together with its wider theoretical framework of functionalism, has been heavily criticised and out of such criticisms have developed many of the later theories of delinquency and deviant behaviour. Some of these criticisms can be found in an excellent book of readings, edited by Marshall B. Clinard, entitled *Anomie and deviant behaviour* (Free Press, 1964). Two articles not included there and worth mentioning are Albert K. Cohen's 'The sociology of the deviant act: anomie theory and beyond' (*American Sociological Review*, **30** (1), 5–14, 1965), and G. Rose's 'Anomie and deprivation—a conceptual framework for empirical studies' (*British J. Sociology*, **17** (2), 29–45, 1966). Anomie has been widely used in sociological studies, and a very full annotated bibliography of discussions and research using the concept can be found in Clinard's reader. Research particularly relating anomie to crime or delinquency is reported in Bernard Lander's *Toward an understanding of juvenile delinquency* (Columbia U.P., 1954). See also the replication study by David J. Bordua, 'Juvenile delinquency and "anomie": an attempt at replication' (*Social Problems*, **6** (3), 230–238, 1958). A statistical critique of Lander's can be found in R. A. Gordon's 'Issues in the ecological study of delinquency' (*American Sociological Review*, **32** (6), 927–944, 1967). Other sources are Richard A. Cloward's 'remarks' in H. L. Witmer and R. Kotinsky (eds.), *New perspectives for research in juvenile delinquency* (US GPO, 1956); Daniel Glaser and Kent Rice's 'Crime, age and employment' (*American Sociological Review*, **24** (4), 679–686, 1959); the various articles of Albert J. Reiss and Albert L. Rhodes, *A socio-psychological study of adolescent conformity and deviation* (US GPO, 1959, OE33020), 'The distribution of juvenile delinquency in the social class structure'

(*American Sociological Review*, **26** (4), 720–732, 1961), 'Status deprivation and delinquent behaviour' (*Sociological Quarterly*, **4** (2), 135–149, 1963); and Arthur Stinchcombe's *Rebellion in a high school* (Free Press, 1967).

The concept of anomie has not only changed within sociology but has also been adopted in psychological studies. In such an adopted use its meaning is changed significantly, and instead of being a social structural property it becomes a state of mind. This psychological use of the word 'anomie' (or sometimes 'anomia') is outside the scope of the present chapter, but in reading the literature it is important to be clear in what sense the word is being used.

The wider sociological framework for anomie is that of functionalist theory: that is, that general body of sociological theory which conceives of society as an integrated whole, and studies the purpose of social activities in tending to maintain that whole. As stated above, many later theorists developed their ideas out of a general critique of this theory, and a good critique of the general theory of functionalism in relation to explanations of crime and deviancy can be found in David Matza's *Becoming deviant* (Prentice-Hall, 1969). Within the more general functionalist framework, a great many studies of crime and deviance were carried out. Particularly worth examining are: Kingsley Davis's essay on 'Sexual behaviour', in R. K. Merton and R. Nisbet (eds.), *Contemporary social problems* (3rd ed., Harcourt Brace, 1971); the essays of Daniel Bell in his book *The end of ideology* (Free Press, 1960); Kai Erickson's *Wayward Puritans* (Wiley, 1966); R. A. Dentler and K. T. Erickson's 'Functions of deviance in groups' (*Social Problems*, **7** (2), 98–107, 1959); and the work of Louis Coser (see, in particular, *The functions of social conflict*, Routledge, 1956).

The Chicago school and differential association

The development of sociology as a discipline was coincidental with the processes of urbanisation and industrialisation. It is hardly surprising, therefore, that nineteenth-century England spawned a host of reports and inquiries into the condition of people in the new towns and factories. Although their methodology was often crude by modern standards, such writers as Mayhew, Booth and Rowntree were pioneers in the use of sociological survey investigations. Much of this work belongs to the early history of sociology in Britain, rather than to sociological criminology specifically, and is discussed at greater length in P. Abrams's *The origins of British sociology* (U. of Chicago P., 1968). However, the work of Mayhew is particularly interesting, since it explored the relationship between crime and the new urban conditions, and Henry Mayhew's *London labour and the London poor* (4 vols., Charles Griffin, 1894) is a massive and detailed account of urban social life. Mayhew's work is undoubtedly a forerunner of the later ecological tradition as L. Lindesmith and Y. Levin point out ('English ecology and criminology of the past century', *J. Criminal Law, Criminology and Police Science*, **27** (6), 801–816, 1937), and his work gave due recognition to the relationship between social factors and the aetiology of crime. However, for all that, the work of the early English ecologists did not continue towards the development of macro-sociological theories; instead the pragmatic interests of the English investigators led them towards the needs of social reform.

It was left to the great school of sociology which flourished at the University of Chicago in the 1930s and 1940s to develop ecological studies into a coherent body of sociological theory. The Chicago school maintained that with the natural development of modern cities, slum areas were created near the city centre which were socially disorganised and lacked social cohesion. They did not propose any necessary connection between physical conditions and social behaviour, but rather asserted that such slum areas (or, as they called them, 'interstitial areas') were ones of migrant population in which a sense of community cohesion failed to develop. The result was an environment in which normal social controls were lacking, and delinquent and criminal behaviour could flourish.

For the general thesis of the development of urban patterns of growth the most accessible work is that edited by W. E. Park and E. W. Burgess, called *The city* (U. of Chicago P., 1967; originally published in 1924). For the more specifically criminological the *magnum opus* of the school is C. R. Shaw and H. D. McKay's *Juvenile delinquency and urban areas* (U. of Chicago P., 1942; republished 1969). Other works of the school should not be forgotten, such as Nils Anderson's *The hobo—the sociology of the homeless man* (U. of Chicago P., 1923; re-issued Phoenix, 1961); P. G. Cressey's *The taxi-dance hall—a sociological study in commercial recreation and city life* (U. of Chicago P., 1932); H. W. Zorbaugh's *The Gold Coast and the slum* (U. of Chicago P., 1929); C. R. Shaw's *The jackroller—a delinquent boy's own story* (U. of Chicago P., 1931); and Frederick Thrasher's classic gang study, called *The gang* (U. of Chicago P., 1927; abridged version re-issued 1963).

The ecological school's idea, of the relationship between social disorganisation and crime, has also been used in a number of English studies: in particular, Terence P. Morris's *The criminal area* (Routledge, 1958) and A. P. Jephcott, M. P. Carter and W. J. Sprott's *The social background of delinquency* (mimeog., U. of Nottingham, 1954). There is also a paper on delinquent areas in London by C. P. Wallis and R. Maliphant, 'Delinquent areas in the County of London—ecological factors' (*British J. Criminology*, 7 (2), 250–284, 1967), which contains a useful list of other English ecological studies.

The ecological theorists have been criticised on a number of grounds: in particular, for using figures of reported crimes, the fact of which may itself be influenced by the very poverty they were describing (see C. T. Jonassen, 'A revaluation and critique of the logic and some of the methods of Shaw and McKay', *American Sociological Review*, 14 (4), 608–617, 1949), and, perhaps more important, because they failed to distinguish between disorganisation and differential organisation (see for example, D. C. Gibbons's *Society, crime and criminal careers*, Prentice-Hall, 1968). For all that, they made a uniquely important contribution to the history of the sociological study of crime; in particular, their careful research work, which involved participating in, and understanding, social action before trying to explain it, stands as a model for later work. Very good critical summaries of the ecological tradition may be found either in Terence P. Morris (see above) or Judith A. Wilks, 'Ecological correlates of crime and delinquency', appendix A in President's Commission on Law Enforcement and Administration of Justice, *Task Force Report: Crime and its impact—an assessment* (US GPO, 1967), and a general critique of the ecological school in T. Hirschi and H. Selvin's *Delinquency research: an analytical appraisal* (Free Press, 1967). Of course, interest in the relationship between urban conditions and crime has continued, and some of the later work on the problem can be found in a book of readings edited by D. Glaser, called *Crime in the city* (Harper and Row, 1970).

However, it would be a mistake to associate the Chicago school just with the ideas of social disorganisation and ecology. Their main tenet was that delinquent behaviour can be subject to a process of cultural transmission: that is, it can be learnt as a mode of life. This idea was later developed by E. H. Sutherland in his famous theory of 'differential association'. Sutherland maintained that criminal behaviour is learnt in a process of interaction in society, which includes definitions both favourable and unfavourable to criminal behaviour. His theory was first put forward in his textbook, *Principles of criminology*, and later extended with his collaborator, Donald R. Cressey (see the various editions of E. H. Sutherland and D. R. Cressey, discussed later). For the other major writing by Sutherland on differential association, *The Sutherland papers*, edited by A. Cohen, A. Lindesmith and K. Schuessler (Indiana U.P., 1965) should be consulted; and also his studies *White-collar crime* (Holt, Rinehart, 1949) and *The professional thief* (U. of Chicago P., 1956). Two major works by Donald R. Cressey, in this area, are his book *Delinquency, crime and differential association* (Martinus Nijhoff, 1964) and his study *Other people's money* (Free Press, 1953). There is a great deal of literature about the theory of differential association, much of which is noted and discussed in Sutherland and Cressey's own textbook. However, especially worth mentioning are M. De Fleur and R. Quinney's article, 'A reformulation of Sutherland's differential association theory' (*J. Research in Crime and Delinquency*, 3 (1), 1–22, 1953); the article by D. Glaser called 'Differential association and criminal prediction' (*Social Problems*, 8 (1), 14–25, 1960); A. E. Liska's 'Interpreting the causal structure of differential association theory' (*Social Problems*, 16 (4), 485–492, 1969); A. J. Reiss and A. L. Rhodes's 'An empirical test of the differential association theory' (*J. Research in Crime and Delinquency*, 1 (1), 5–18, 1964); Edwin Lemert's chapter, 'An isolation and closure theory of naive cheque forgery', in E. Lemert's *Human deviance, social problems and social control* (Prentice-Hall, 1967; originally published in *J. Criminal Law, Criminology and Police Science*, 44 (3), 293–307, 1953); James Short's 'Differential association as a hypothesis: problems of empirical testing' (*Social Problems*, 8 (1), 14–25, 1960); and Daniel Glaser's 'Criminality theories and behavioral images' (*American J. Sociology*, 61 (5), 433–444, 1956).

Subcultural theories

The Chicago school, and the theory of differential association, stress the possibility that criminal behaviour may be socally learnt. This has meant that sociologists have been interested in values, norms and beliefs which may find expression in socially deviant behaviour. To be deviant they obviously could not be a part of the dominant culture (although, as we shall see later, the notion of a 'dominant' conforming culture has itself been challenged), but instead must be what sociologists have called a 'subculture'. This is a culture which is identifiable with a particular segment of society but differs from the larger culture in certain respects—in this case its normative prescriptions for action which is illegal or deviant. There is some ambiguity about the term 'subculture', and J. M. Yinger ('Contraculture and subculture', *American Sociological Review*, **25** (4), 625–635, 1960) has suggested that groups whose culture is oppositional to the dominant culture are more properly described as a 'contraculture'. In this sense the archetypal subculture would be a newly arrived immigrant group whose traditional culture was different from the host culture; while a delinquent group, having a culture which encourages behaviour known to be banned by the dominant culture, would be a contraculture. However, since the term 'subculture' is more generally used in the literature, we shall continue to use it.

The link with earlier theories has been pointed out above, but fully developed subcultural theories of delinquency are usually associated with writers of the mid-1950s onwards. Perhaps the classic work in this tradition is Albert K. Cohen's *Delinquent boys: the culture of the gang* (Free Press, 1955), with its central idea that delinquency is a shared 'reaction formation', developed in a process of interaction by those with the common problem of their inability to achieve socially accepted status. Richard A. Cloward and Lloyd E. Ohlin's *Delinquency and opportunity* (Routledge, 1961) is a modification of this position, with its emphasis on an ability to reach economic success goals by legitimate means and the style of the subcultural solution chosen being dependent upon the availability of alternative illegitimate means. This modification is the result of linking the idea of a subculture with those of Merton's 'anomie' (see p. 28), and Sutherland's 'differential association' (see p. 29). Yet another different version of a subcultural theory is that put forward by Walter B. Miller ('Lower class culture as a generating milieu of gang delinquency', *J. Social Issues*, **14** (1), 5–19, 1958), who sees delinquency as a variant of traditional lower-class culture.

The general idea of delinquency subcultures has been attacked, particularly in David Matza's *Delinquency and drift* (Wiley, 1964), and in his articles with Gresham M. Sykes ('Techniques of neutralization: a theory of delinquency', *American Sociological Review*, **22** (4), 664–670, 1957); 'Juvenile delinquency and subterranean values', *American Sociological Review*, **26** (4), 712–719, 1961). Matza sees the subcultural theories as having been conceived as over-solidaristic, and therefore over-predictive of delinquency. He argues that the idea of the relationship between the subculture and the dominant culture is an over-simplification, and that instead boys drift into delinquency due to 'shared misunderstandings'. However, it should be noted that in a later paper with J. F. Short, Cohen did not see Matza's ideas as being incompatible with his own (A. K. Cohen and J. F. Short, 'Research in delinquent subcultures', *J. Social Issues*, **14** (1), 20–37, 1958).

A great deal of empirical research into delinquent subcultures has been done, particularly in the USA. L. Yablonsky in his *Violent gang* (Macmillan, 1962) suggested that the structure of such groups was much more fluid than the theorists had suggested. This relative lack of permanence, and the relatively small size of the real core of such groups, is also stressed in J. F. Short and F. L. Strodtbeck's *Group process and gang delinquency* (U. of Chicago P., 1965) and in M. W. Klein and L. Y. Crawford's 'Groups, gangs and cohesiveness' (*J. Research in Crime and Delinquency*, **4** (2), 63–75, 1967). Most studies have not found the different types of subculture suggested by Cloward and Ohlin: one exception is the small-scale study by Irving Spergel, called *Racketville, Slumtown, Haulberg* (U. of Chicago P., 1964). The major English study in this area is David M. Downes's *The delinquent solution* (Routledge, 1966), which casts doubt on the central subcultural thesis of 'status frustration' in the English context. Downes suggests that lack of educational and occupational success leads to a process of opting out and an overemphasis of leisure goals. In another English study, Peter Willmott's *Adolescent boys of East London* (Routledge, 1966), a pattern of behaviour somewhat similar to Cohen's idea of 'reaction formation' was observed. A particularly careful study which discusses the relationship between the school and subculture is David Hargreaves's *Social relations in a secondary school* (Routledge, 1967). (See also his later paper, 'The delinquent subculture and the school', in W. G. Carson and P. Wiles (eds.), *Crime and delinquency in Britain: sociological readings*, M. Robertson, 1971.) The theory has been critically applied to bohemian culture by Jock Young in *The drugtakers* (Paladin, 1971) and to working-class youth culture in Stanley Cohen's *Folk devils and moral panics: the creation of the Mods and Rockers* (MacGibbon and Kee, 1972). Other British papers worth noting are Ian Taylor's 'Soccer consciousness and soccer hooliganism', in S. Cohen (ed.), *Images of deviance* (Penguin, 1971); P. Cohen's 'Subcultural conflict and working class community' and P. Willis's 'The motorbike within a subculture group', both in *Working papers in cultural studies* (2), University of Birmingham (1972).

Excellent discussions of subcultural theories of delinquency can be found in the works by D. M. Downes (see p. 32) and R. G. Hood and R. F. Sparks (see p. 25). Two useful critical articles are David J. Bordua's 'Delinquent subcultures: sociological interpretations of gang delinquency' (*Annals of the American Academy of Social and Political Science*, **338**, 120–136, 1961) and J. I. Kitsuse and D. C. Dietrick's 'Delinquent boys: a critique' (*American Sociological Review*, **24** (2), 208–215, 1959). There are also several good readers in this area. Particularly useful, because they focus specifically on subcultural theories, are David O. Arnold (ed.), *The sociology of subcultures* (Glendessary, 1970); James F. Short (ed.), *Gang delinquency and delinquent subcultures* (Harper and Row, 1968); and Malcolm W. Klein, *Juvenile gangs in context* (Prentice-Hall, 1967). For those who are interested in how subcultural theories relate to middle-class delinquency, the collection edited by Edmund W. Vaz, entitled *Middle-class juvenile delinquency* (Harper and Row, 1967), is useful. More general readers on juvenile delinquency also usually contain quite a lot of material on subcultures, and those by Ruth S. Cavan (*Readings in juvenile delinquency*, 2nd ed., Lippincott, 1969), Rose Giallombardo (*Juvenile delinquency: a book of readings*, Wiley, 1966) and James E. Teele (*Juvenile delinquency: a reader*, Peacock, 1970) have fairly extensive sections devoted to this topic.

Interactionist theory

One of the major theoretical focuses for sociological research on deviant behaviour over the last decade has been what has become known as the 'interactionist', 'labelling' or 'societal reactions' perspective. The main concern of this perspective, as Edwin Lemert points out in his *Social pathology* (McGraw-Hill, 1951), is an insistence that deviance cannot be explained as a static condition but must instead be seen as part of a dynamic social process. This process, by which an action becomes defined as deviant, consists of a series of actions and reactions: in other words, it is a process of social interaction. Howard Becker, in *Outsiders* (Free Press, 1964), stresses that whether an act will be defined as deviant depends on the reaction of others to the commission of the act. Within such a perspective the social control of deviant behaviour becomes of central importance, and the interactionist writers have greatly enriched our understanding of the complex interplay between the controllers and the controlled. Indeed, Edwin Lemert in *Human deviance, social problems and social control*

(Prentice-Hall, 1967) has suggested that the act of having been defined as deviant crucially sets the individual apart from those who have committed deviant acts but have not been so labelled.

Much of the general interactionist framework has been developed from the work of George Herbert Mead, which can be most conveniently found in his book, *Mind, self and society* (U. of Chicago P., 1934). One of the results of this influence of Meadian social psychology has been an interest in the effect of defining an individual as deviant upon his conception of himself, and by extension his later action. The idea that labelling a person as deviant may actually increase his deviance can be found in the early work of Frank Tannenbaum, with his notion of the 'dramatisation of evil' (*Crime and the community*, Ginn, 1938); and the same theme has been extended by all the interactionists, as, for example, in John Lofland's *Deviance and identity* (Prentice-Hall, 1969). The effects of labelling have been explored most fully by Erving Goffman, especially in his book *Stigma: notes on the management of spoilt identity* (Prentice-Hall, 1963), and have been put into a quasi-mathematical form in Leslie Wilkins's notion of 'deviance amplification' in *Social Deviance* (Tavistock, 1964). The most recent statement of the interactionist position is to be found in Edwin Schur's *Labelling deviant behavior: its sociological implications* (Random House, 1971).

The best discussion of the general interactionist approach to the study of social behaviour can be found in a series of papers edited by Arnold Rose, under the title of *Human behaviour and social process* (Routledge, 1962). Two good books of readings of interactionist studies are E. Rubington and M. Weinberg's *Deviance: the interactionist perspective* (Macmillan, 1968) and S. Dinitz and others' *Deviance: studies in the process of stigmatization and societal reactions* (Oxford U.P., 1969). A collection of papers by English sociologists studying deviance within the interactionist perspective, edited by Stanley Cohen, is *Images of deviance* (Penguin, 1971), and perhaps the most important collection of interactionist essays on deviance is that edited by Howard Becker and called *The other side* (Free Press, 1967). There have been many discursive and critical articles about interactionism in the journals, and perhaps the best of them are R. Akers's 'Problems in the sociology of deviance' (*Social Forces*, **46** (4), 455–465, 1968); Jack Gibbs's 'Conceptions of deviance' (*Pacific Sociological Review*, Spring, 9–14, 1966); E. M. Schur's 'Reactions to Deviance' (*American J. Sociology*, **75** (3), 309–322, 1969); T. P. Wilson's 'Conceptions of interaction' (*American Sociological Review*, **35**

(4), 697–710, 1970); and M. Mankoff's 'Societal reactions and career deviance' (*Sociological Quarterly*, **12** (1), 204–218, 1971).

Phenomenological theories

In many ways phenomenological theories are often difficult to distinguish from interactionist theories, since they both place great stress on the way the deviant himself sees the situation. However, phenomenology goes much further in insisting that the social world is itself socially constructed, and therefore presents a much more fundamental challenge to the basically positivist methodologies which dominate other sociological theories of deviance. The main focus for this tradition is therefore the way in which moral meaning is constructed within social action. Its intellectual origins are to be found in mainly European phenomenological philosophy, but it has also to some extent been influenced by existentialism. The key work which links this philosophical tradition to sociology is that of Alfred Schutz, which has been published in three volumes under the title *Collected papers* (3rd ed., Martinus Nijhoff, 1971. Vol. 1—The problem of social reality; Vol. 2—Studies in social theory; Vol. 3—Studies in phenomenological philosophy).

More recent sociological attempts to spell out a phenomenological sociology are Peter Berger and Thomas Luckman's *The social construction of reality* (Allen Lane, 1967) and H. Garfinkel's *Studies in ethnomethodology* (Prentice-Hall, 1967). Garfinkel has added to the terminological confusion by introducing the word 'ethnomethodology', but all he means by it is the methodology necessary for a phenomenological sociology. Aaron V. Cicourel has also explored the methodological implications in his book *Method and measurement in sociology* (Free Press, 1964).

In the more specific area of deviance there are an increasing number of studies using a phenomenological approach. Aaron V. Cicourel has studied the way in which social meaning is constructed within the organisational framework for dealing with juvenile delinquency in his book *The social organization of juvenile justice* (Wiley, 1968) and Jack D. Douglas has carried out a similar analysis for suicide in *The social meanings of suicide* (Princeton U.P., 1969). David Matza, in *Becoming deviant* (Prentice-Hall, 1969), has explored some of the issues involved for deviance in general, as has M. Phillipson in *Sociological aspects of crime and delinquency* (Routledge, 1971). For the study of mental illness Thomas Szasz's *The myth of mental illness* (Delta, 1967), R. D.

Laing's *The divided self* (Tavistock, 1959) and T. J. Scheff's *Being mentally ill* (Weidenfeld, 1966) are particularly worth noting. Many of the most recent studies in the phenomenology of deviance have been published in the various books of essays edited by Jack D. Douglas, and perhaps the best of these to date are *Deviance and respectability* (Basic Books, 1970), *The American social order* (Free Press, 1971) and *Understanding everyday life* (Wiley, 1968). Two articles particularly worth noting are D. Sudnow's 'Normal crimes: sociological features of the penal code in a Public Defender's office' (*Social Problems*, **12** (2), 98–112, 1965) and E. Bittner's 'The police on Skid Row: a study of peacekeeping' (*American Sociological Review*, **32** (5), 699–715, 1965).

Social control and the law

This section differs from the previous section in that a generally accepted theoretical perspective has not yet been developed in the area of social control. There have been many attempts, ranging from E. A. Ross's massive *Social control: a survey of the foundations of order* (Case Western Reserve University, 1969; originally published in 1901) to the more limited article by A. L. Clark and J. P. Gibbs, 'Social control: a reformulation' (*Social Problems*, **12** (4), 398–414, 1965). The difficulty lies in the fact that social order is a central problem for any sociology, and therefore nearly all sociologists in some sense are concerned with social control. At the more precise level of control by the criminal law, the relationship to the concept of power still remains to be adequately explained. For all that, the sociological study of crime cannot ignore the operation of law and the agencies for its enforcement, and, as we have seen, the more recent theories are beginning to try and explain crime as the result of a complex interaction between deviant and controller. Some of the literature in this area is, of course, discussed in the chapter on the treatment of offenders, but there is also a considerable body of work on the law itself and the work of the police.

Historically, the most significant work in terms of later writing has been E. H. Sutherland's discussions of 'white-collar' crime in was attempting to explore the relationship between social his book *White-collar crime* (Holt, Rinehart, 1949). Sutherland control by the criminal law and the structural distribution of power and prestige in society. While his writing indicated the need to develop systematic explanations of the law and the nature of its enforcement, he in fact never fully did so. Indeed, in many ways his so-called 'theory of white-collar crime' is not really a fully developed theory at all. One of the consequences of this has been a large and rather futile literature debating terminological points of his work. However, V. Aubert, in an article called 'White-collar crime and social structure' (*American J. Sociology*, **58** (2), 263–271, 1952), suggests more fruitful extensions of Sutherland's ideas, as also does Richard Quinney in his article 'The study of white-collar crime: towards a re-orientation in theory and research' (*J. Criminal Law, Criminology and Police Science*, **55** (2), 208–214, 1964). Clarence Ray Jeffrey's 'The structure of American criminological thought' (*J. Criminal Law, Criminology and Police Science*, **46** (4), 658–672, 1956) explains some of the reasons why Sutherland's theory was not developed in a more systematic way; and for the other literature, and empirical research, about white-collar crime there is an excellent book of readings edited by G. Geis, called *White collar crime* (Atherton P., 1968).

One direction in which Sutherland's work might have been developed was towards a sociology of law. Developments in that area have, however, only recently begun to take place as the international report edited by R. Treves and J. F. Glastra van Loon shows (*Norms in action: national reports on the sociology of law*, Martinus Nijhoff, 1968). Much of the most interesting work on the origins and nature of law has been done in America. Examples are Troy Duster's study of drugs legislation, *The legislation of morality* (Free Press, 1970); Gabriel Kolko's study of anti-trust legislation, *The triumph of conservatism* (Quadrangle, 1967); J. R. Gusfield's study of prohibition. *Symbolic crusade* (U. of Illinois P., 1968); and Jerome Hall's work on the law of theft, *Theft, law and society* (Bobbs-Merrill, 1952). Various studies have also been carried out focusing on the work of the courts, such as A. Blumberg's *The scales of justice* (Aldine, 1970); R. Emerson's *Judging delinquents* (Aldine, 1969); Roger Hood's *Sentencing in magistrates' courts* (Tavistock, 1962); and Edwin Lemert's *Social action and legal change* (Aldine, 1970). An excellent collection of essays on social control, edited by Stanton Wheeler, is *Controlling delinquents* (Wiley, 1968).

More general theories about the nature of criminal law still remain to be fully developed, but useful books at present available are Austin Turk's *Criminality and legal process* (Rand McNally, 1969); W. J. Chambliss and R. Seidman's *Law, order and power* (Addison-Wesley, 1971); R. Quinney's *The social reality of crime* (Little, Brown, 1970); and E. Schur's *Law and society*

(Random House, 1968). The resurgence of interest, among sociologists, in Marxist theories of law has meant that Karl Renner's
The institutions of private law and their social functions, ed. and
transl. by O. Kahn-Freund (Routledge, 1954), is of increasing
importance in this developing field.

Particularly useful books of readings are those edited by R. D.
Schwartz and J. H. Skolnick, *Society and the legal order* (Basic
Books, 1970); V. Aubert, *Sociology of law* (Penguin, 1969); and
W. R. Chambliss, *Crime and the legal process* (McGraw-Hill,
1969). These books of readings, together with the national reports
edited by R. Treves and J. F. Glastra van Loon (see p. 37), also
provide details of the international range of work at present being
done in this field.

The study of the police has always been an area of interest,
but compared with some other criminological problems it has produced fewer major pieces of sociological research. Several of the
earliest studies focused on examining the role of the policeman;
good examples are Michael Banton's *The policeman and the community* (Tavistock, 1964) and H. J. Ehrlich's *An examination of
role theory: the case of the State Police* (Nebraska U.P., 1966).
In many ways the most influential early work was W. A. Westley's
study of the police and violence, published in full as *Violence and
the Police* (M.I.T. Press, 1970). The question of how the police
actually go about their job has been examined by a number of
researchers, and perhaps the best reports of this kind of research
are J. H. Skolnick's *Justice without trial* (Wiley, 1966), W. R.
LaFave's *Arrest: the decision to take a suspect into custody*
(Little, Brown, 1965) and I. Piliavin and S. Briar's 'Police
encounters with juveniles' (*American J. Sociology*, **70** (2), 1, 206–
214, 1964). This kind of research is best represented in England
by J. R. Lambert's *Crime, police and race relations* (Oxford U.P.,
1970). More recent research has explored the relationship between
the organisation of the police and their behaviour—for example,
James Q. Wilson's *Varieties of police behavior* (Harvard U.P.,
1968). Albert J. Reiss, in *The police and the public* (Yale U.P.,
1971), provides the most detailed study yet of the relationship
between the police and the public, and brings together and expands
much of his earlier work done together with Donald Black for
*The United States President's Commission on Law Enforcement
and the Administration of Justice* (US GPO, 1967). Finally, a very
good collection of essays about the police, edited by David J.
Bordua, is *The police: six sociological essays* (Wiley, 1967).

TEXTBOOKS

The sociological study of crime is not an area which lends itself easily to the production of textbooks. Indeed, because the various sociological theories about crime, or deviant behaviour, are not necessarily compatible, some sociologists would regard the task as impossible in any meaningful sense. Books which are written as texts tend to attempt to cover the various disciplinary aspects of both criminology and penology, or else to be organised around a particular theoretical concern.

Of the latter more will be said below, but for those who would like to begin their reading with a general criminological introduction, with a sociological slant, then undoubtedly the best textbook available is E. H. Sutherland and D. R. Cressey's *Criminology* (8th ed., Lippincott, 1970; earlier editions published as *Principles of criminology*). This is a remarkably comprehensive over-view originally published in 1924, but its regular updating by new editions sets it apart from other textbooks. The footnotes and references which it includes provide a good guide to further reading in the field, although English readers may find its American focus a disadvantage, particularly in the sections on the courts and the penal system. The most comprehensive English textbook, with the whole of the second volume devoted to the sociology of crime, is Hermann Mannheim's *Comparative criminology* (2 vols., Routledge, 1965). While it is written within the context of crime in Britain, it is much more international in the scope of the materials used than any other general work, and discusses continental European work often neglected by American writers. It also contains a useful appendix, of similarly international scope, listing societies, institutes, journals, bibliographies, textbooks and encyclopaedias. The only drawback with the work is that recent sociological developments in the study of deviant behaviour have rapidly outdated it; nevertheless Mannheim's scholarship is so monumental as to make the book an outstanding and lasting reference store.

For the more recent sociological interest in deviant behaviour perhaps the best textbook is Marshall B. Clinard's *Sociology of deviant behaviour* (3rd ed., Holt, Rinehart, 1957), although, again, it does not include the most recent work. Other general works deserve to be noted because of their particular approaches. Don C. Gibbon's *Society, crime and criminal careers* (Prentice-Hall, 1968) is a textbook from, as the title suggests, the point of view of the development of crime as a career structure. H. A. Bloch and G. Geis's book *Man, crime and society* (Random House, 1962) focuses on behavioural systems in crime such as 'organised' and 'professional' crime. One older book still worth consideration, because of its unusual use of the notion of social conflict as an organising concept for examining crime, is George V. Vold's *Theoretical criminology* (Oxford U.P., 1958). Although not strictly a textbook, Roger Hood and Richard Sparks's *Key issues in criminology* (Weidenfeld, 1970) can be usefully mentioned here, since it contains good discussions of research in areas such as criminal statistics, hidden delinquency, juvenile gangs, classification, sentencing and various aspects of penological treatment. Two recent English textbooks are L. Taylor's *Deviance and society* (M. Joseph, 1971) and S. Box's *Deviance, reality and society* (Holt, Rinehart, 1971). The former is particularly useful for its attempt to discuss both sociological and psychological research within an integrated framework.

BOOKS OF READINGS

A recent phenomenon of the publishing world has been the production of books of readings: that is, a collection of papers, usually previously published as articles or as sections of earlier books, brought together around some common theme. The sociological study of crime, with its various perspectives, is particularly suited to such treatment, and in many ways books of readings have superseded textbooks in criminology teaching. They offer a variety of advantages to those who either do not have access to a large research library or do not wish to undertake extensive reading, since they include material often difficult to obtain and if well edited bring together widely scattered work on a common area.

Of the general criminological books of readings, the two most comprehensive are M. E. Wolfgang and others' *The sociology of crime and delinquency* (2nd ed., Wiley, 1970) and Leon Radzinowicz and Marvin E. Wolfgang's *Crime and justice* (3 vols., Basic Books, 1971). Other general books of readings are Simon Dinitz and Walter C. Reckless's *Critical issues in the study of crime* (Little, Brown, 1968) and W. A. Rushings's *Deviant behavior and social process* (Rand McNally, 1969). Gresham M. Sykes and Thomas E. Drabek's *Law and the lawless* (Random House, 1969) is, again, a general reader, but includes more political and philosophical material than most others. A reader with a more over-all sociological orientation is M. Lefton, J. K. Skipper and C. M. McCaghy's *Approaches to deviance* (Appleton, 1968), and a book of sociological readings which treats crime as one of a number of social problems is M. S. Minnis and W. J. Cartwright's *Sociological perspectives: readings in deviant behavior and social problems* (Wm. C. Brown, 1968). Marshall B. Clinard and Richard Quinney's *Criminal behavior systems* (Holt, Rinehart, 1967) could usefully be used in conjunction with Bloch and Geis's textbook (see p. 40). An alternative to American books is W. G. Carson and P. Wiles's *Crime and delinquency in Britain: sociological readings* (M. Robertson, 1971), a book of sociological readings about crime in Britain, some of which have not been published elsewhere.

In the more specific area of juvenile delinquency there are several good books of reading, such as Rose Giallombardo's; R. S. Cavan's; and J. E. Teele's (see p. 33 for all three).

For the more general area of the sociology of deviance there is almost an embarrassment of riches. Perhaps the best reader, organised around an interactionist approach to deviance, is E. Rubington and M. S. Weinberg's *Deviance—the interactionist perspective* (Macmillan, 1968). Two other books which set out a more general sociological approach but focus on the processes of interaction are Donald R. Cressey and David A. Ward's *Delinquency, crime and social process* (Harper and Row, 1969) and Carl A. Bersani's *Crime and delinquency* (Macmillan, 1970). S. Dinitz and others' *Deviance: studies in the process of stigmatization and societal reaction* (Oxford U.P., 1969) also contains useful articles, but has been editorially spoilt by the removal of all footnotes. Concentrating on the recent sociological interest in the phenomenology of deviance—in particular, the way in which social action is given moral meaning—there is an excellent reader edited by Jack D. Douglas entitled *Deviance and respectability: the social construction of moral meanings* (Basic Books, 1970). See also the more recent J. D. Douglas and R. Scott (eds.), *Theoretical perspectives on deviance* (Random House, 1972). These latter books are also indicative of a recent trend for books of readings increasingly to include original material, rather than just reprint articles. For those without access to the academic journals, such a trend, if continued, would mean that readers may become the easiest way to keep up to date in the field.

PERIODICALS

Before we go on to discuss specific periodicals, it may be helpful
to mention some of their general features as an information source.
They are the most useful means of keeping up with developments
in the field, article length often being more suitable to the working
out, and testing, of new ideas. They also provide the most convenient way of keeping abreast of new publications, via the book
reviews and lists of books received which most academic journals
include. The value of these is, of course, dependent upon the
quality and length of the reviews, and the arrangement of the
lists of books received, and how up to date these are.

The vast number of sociological and criminological journals now
being published means that some limits must be placed on what
is included here. We have tried to select those sociology journals
which are important in the field and continually include some
articles on crime or deviance, and those more general criminological journals which cover sociological aspects with some
regularity. Our selection has also been limited to periodicals published in the English language. For a comprehensive list of
periodicals in criminology, sociology and all the social sciences see
Ulrich's international periodicals directory (2 vols., 13th ed.,
Bowker, 1969–70).

Sociological journals

What follows is a selection of the major sociological journals,
several of which are published by, or for, the organisations and
societies in the field. All of these include a wide range of sociological articles of theoretical and empirical concern. How much
material they include on crime or deviance varies over time, and
obviously depends on the contemporary interests of sociologists
and of the editors.

British Journal of Sociology (1950–   , Routledge, quarterly). Book
reviews, comments pages. Sponsored and edited by the Sociology
Department of the London School of Economics and Political
Science.

New Society (1962–   , New Science Publications, weekly). Book
reviews, research findings and general news about the field. A

journal aimed to appeal to a less specialist audience, and often covering topical issues. Its magazine format limits the length of its articles and reviews, but the latter have the advantage of being more up to date than those in the more academic journals.

Sociological Review (1908– , new series 1953– , Staffordshire, U. of Keele, quarterly). One extensive book review, plus a number of shorter reviews.

Sociology (1967– , Oxford U.P., three issues a year). A few fairly lengthy reviews, plus several shorter reviews, list of books received, abstracts of articles. The journal of the British Sociological Association, set up comparatively recently to increase the number of academic sociology journals in Britain. The news and notes section gives information about appointments, and courses in the field, in the UK. Has to date only rarely carried articles of specific relevance to crime and deviancy.

American Behavioral Scientist (1957– , Beverly Hills, Sage Publications, monthly). Annotated guide to recent publications, and research notes. Whole issues are often focused on a particular theme.

American Journal of Sociology (1895– , U. of Chicago P., bi-monthly). Book reviews, lists of books received. Book reviews are extensive, and the journal regularly features a short commentary and debate section which acts as a forum for discussion of both its articles and book reviews.

American Sociological Review (1936– , Washington D.C., American Sociological Association, bi-monthly). Book reviews, publications received and articles abstracted. From 1972 onwards the American Sociological Association will publish a separate journal, solely of book reviews, called *Contemporary Sociology*; and continue to publish the *American Sociological Review* but without the review section. This change should make the review journal one of the most comprehensive in the field.

Annals of the American Academy of Political and Social Science (1890– , Pennsylvania, American Academy of Political and Social Science, bi-monthly). Book reviews organised by subject, list of other publications received, articles abstracted. Each issue is devoted to a particular topic.

Law and Society Review (1967–   , Beverly Hills, Law and Society Association, Sage Publications). Book reviews, interdisciplinary bibliographies. A recent journal created '... to explore the relationships between law and society in such a way as to contribute to the understanding of law as a social and political phenomenon and to expedite the utilization of law as a more effective instrument of public policy.' It contains articles on the relationship between law and the social sciences, and social science research focusing on law. As such it is a useful source of articles on an area which is increasingly interesting sociologists of deviance and crime.

Social Forces (1922–   , Chapel Hill, U. of North Carolina P., quarterly). Book reviews grouped according to subject, but the groups used change with each issue, depending on the books to be reviewed. All articles are abstracted.

Social Problems (1953–   , Indiana, Society for the Study of Social Problems, quarterly). List of publications received. It is not easy to make choices between the major academic journals, but for those interested in the sociological study of crime and deviant behaviour this is probably the single most important periodical. The articles it carries are more frequently specifically relevant to such study than in any other journal.

Society (formerly *Trans-action*, 1963–   , New Brunswick, Rutgers U., monthly). Book reviews, and suggested reading for each article. Again, a more topical approach, and its articles and the results of research are presented to make them easily intelligible to the non-specialist. It has often carried early, or shortened, versions of papers in the field of the sociological study of crime and deviance.

Other social science journals which occasionally carry articles of relevance are:

Journal of Social Issues (1945–   , Ann Arbor, Society for the Psychological Study of Social Issues, quarterly). *Acta Sociologica*: *Scandinavian Review of Sociology* (1956–   , Copenhagen, Acta Sociologica, quarterly). *International Social Science Journal* (1949–   , UNESCO, quarterly, published in English and French). As well as articles, the journal also sometimes features a bibliography on a special topic. It is particularly useful for its information on current research, international research and training centres, and the activities of associations in the field.

Criminological journals

Criminology journals, of course, cover the whole field of criminology and many of them are more concerned with corrections and treatment. The journals listed below, therefore, are only those which include articles of sociological interest.

British Journal of Criminology (1950– [formerly *British Journal of Delinquency*], Institute for the Study and Treatment of Delinquency, quarterly). Book reviews, research and methodology section, and a list of criminological articles which have appeared in other journals, broadly arranged by discipline. Sometimes includes articles of sociological interest.

Howard Journal of Penology and Crime Prevention (1921– , Howard League for Penal Reform, annual). Book reviews. Tends to be more concerned with corrections, or aspects of penal reform or social work. Sometimes includes articles of sociological interest.

Criminology (1963– , Talahassee, American Society for Criminology, Sage Publications, quarterly). Research notes and a news column. Covers criminology in general but gives some preference to empirical research and scientific methodology.

Federal Probation (1936– , Washington, D.C., United States Courts Administrative Office, quarterly). Book reviews, and abstracts and comments on articles appearing in other journals arranged by journal. Has a correctional orientation, but occasionally includes articles of sociological interest.

Issues in Criminology (1965– , Berkeley, U. of California, bi-annually). Book reviews, books received and occasional bibliographies. Published by the graduate students of the School of Criminology at Berkeley, and reflects their current interests in the field.

Journal of Criminal Law, Criminology and Police Science (1910– , Baltimore, North Western School of Law, bi-monthly). Book reviews. The number of sociological articles in the journal seems to have been declining recently. Divided in 1973 into *Journal of Criminal Law and Criminology* and *Journal of Police Science and Administration*.

Journal of Research in Crime and Delinquency (1964–   , New York, National Council on Crime and Delinquency, bi-annually). All articles are abstracted.

3

Psychiatric aspects of crime

T. G. Tennent

INTRODUCTION

The term 'forensic psychiatry' implies that aspect of psychiatry that is concerned with the legal process, both criminal and non-criminal. Indeed, for a long time this was the main area of involvement. Legal issues such as sanity, responsibility, fitness to plead and testimony preoccupied the minds of early forensic psychiatrists. In the early part of this century court clinics for juveniles were set up and attempts were made to understand, from a psychological viewpoint, offences and offenders; more recently still, psychiatrists have become increasingly interested in the treatment of offenders. This chapter will concern itself, then, with these three areas of involvement: (1) the legal aspects of psychiatry; (2) psychiatric views and theories regarding the aetiology of criminal behaviour, offences and offender groups; and (3) treatment programmes. Much of the literature is to be found in journals rather than books, and where these are quoted the main aim has been to provide introductory or review material which will serve as a starting point for other references. In general, only literature in English has been referred to and greater attention has been given to new or developing areas rather than those which are already well documented. It will be assumed also that the reader has at least some minor acquaintance with psychiatry, from such books as *Psychiatry for students*, by D. Stafford Clark (Allen and Unwin,

1970), or *New horizons in psychiatry*, by P. Hays (Penguin, 1964). For more detailed commentaries basic texts in psychiatry (*Clinical psychiatry*, by W. Mayer-Gross, Cassell, 1969; *Modern clinical psychiatry*, by A. P. Noyes and L. C. Kolb, Saunders, 1963) are available in most libraries, as also are psychiatric dictionaries, of which a useful example is L. E. Hinsie and R. J. Campbell's *Psychiatric dictionary* (4th ed., Oxford U.P., 1970). There are really no specifically forensic psychiatric libraries in the UK. The Institute of Criminology at Cambridge has a considerable number of books dealing with forensic psychiatry as well as some helpful bibliographies. The Royal College of Psychiatry and the Institute for the Study and Treatment of Delinquency have some of the older books, now largely of historical interest, which are not available from other sources.

One of the problems with this area is that the literature is distributed through an ever-increasing range of psychiatric and psychological journals. Where appropriate, specific journals are mentioned in the text of this chapter; a fuller list is available on pp. 60–61. Because of this wide scatter, the abstracting journals are invaluable (*Excerpta Medica: s. 32—Psychiatry, Abstracts on Criminology and Penology*, and *Crime and Delinquency Abstracts*), although they are always six months to a year out of date. The *Journal of Specialist Medicine* publishes reviews of clinical papers in Psychiatry and Neurology which are more extensive and up to date than those available in the *Excerpta Medica*, but covering a small number of journals. *Psychiatric Briefs* contain selected articles from *Excerpta Medica* and can be quite useful. Finally, MEDLARS (see p. 12) provides an extracting service for all journals abstracted in *Index Medicus* and, if sufficient care is taken in defining one's subject matter, this can be an invaluable system. Yet another problem is the increasing use of cyclostyled pamphlets or special series reports in which research results are being published. This undoubtedly reflects the difficulties experienced in getting results published. Notable in this group are the Research Reports from the California Department of Corrections and California Youth Authority. There are a number of different series of reports, such as the Home Office Research Unit Reports, Psychological Monographs from the Office of the Chief Psychologist of the Prison Department, publications of the Institute for the Study and Treatment of Delinquency, and Special Hospitals Research Reports, issued by the Special Hospitals Research Unit, Broadmoor Hospital. There are also many doctoral theses up and down the country, for which the reader must rely on the Aslib

Index to Theses, Dissertation Abstracts International and the other reference works listed on p. 14.

LEGAL

There are a number of textbooks concerned with the legal aspects of psychiatry. *Forensic psychiatry*, by H. A. Davidson (Ronald P., 1965), is concerned largely with the legal problems faced by a psychiatrist: the examination of forensic patients, testimony and responsibility. H. J. Wily and K. R. Stallworthy in *Mental abnormality and the law* (Christchurch: Peryer, 1962) are concerned with forensic aspects of psychiatric disorders (they are both New Zealanders but the book is very relevant to British practice). From a historical viewpoint, *An introduction to forensic psychiatry in the criminal courts*, by W. Norwood East (Churchill, 1927), is of interest. M. S. Guttmacher and H. Weihofen in *Psychiatry and the law* (Norton, 1952) try to cover both aspects. J. M. Macdonald's *Psychiatry and the criminal* (C. C. Thomas, 1969) contains a particularly good chapter on the 'Assessment of dangerousness'. The Isaac Ray Award series of lectures devoted to the relationship between the law and psychiatry contains interesting contributions from both psychiatrists and lawyers and reveals how entangled both sides become, particularly over the issue of responsibility. If psychiatrists do not agree among themselves, neither apparently do lawyers, as has been shown by H. L. A. Hart, in *Law, liberty and morality* (Oxford U.P., 1963), and Lord (Patrick) Devlin's *The enforcement of morals* (Oxford U.P., 1959; reprinted 1965). The historical origins of insanity as a defence in England have been traced in Nigel Walker's *Crime and insanity in England* (Edinburgh U.P., 1968); see also F. A. Whitlock's *Mental illness and criminal responsibility* (Butterworths, 1963). Walker's book recounts the legal position regarding automatism, and G. W. Fenton, in a recent review article, 'Epilepsy and automatism' (*British J. Hospital Medicine*, **7** (1), 57–64, 1972), discusses it from a medical viewpoint. Amnesia, another perennial legal issue, is comprehensively discussed from a general viewpoint in *Amnesia*, ed. O. L. Zangwill (Butterworths, 1966), and from a forensic one by J. S. Hopwood in *J. Mental Science*, **79** (Jan.), 27–41 (1933) and B. A. O'Connell in *British J. Delinquency*, **10** (April), 262 (1959). Ganser's original paper has been translated into English by C. E. Schorer (*British J. Criminology*, **5**, 120, 1965) and the syndrome further analysed. The role of the psychiatrist as expert witness (cf. P. D. Scott, *British J. Criminology*, **1**, 116, 1960), the development of court clinics and the format and use of psychiatric reports to the court (B. W. Murphy, *J. Nervous and Mental Diseases*, **126**, 554, 1958) are all fairly extensively documented. Of recent interest, particularly in the USA, have been the legal rights of offenders detained under treatment orders. *A right to treatment*, ed. Donald S. Burris (New York: Springer, 1969), contains a collection of papers on this subject. *A Bibliography of medico-legal works in English* (Sweet and Maxwell, 1962) has been prepared by R. Brittain, its usefulness limited by being arranged alphabetically by author, instead of subject, and by the lack of an adequate subject index.

AETIOLOGY, OFFENDERS, OFFENCES AND TYPOLOGIES

A physical basis for criminality has long been sought and this is markedly reflected in medical writing. It has taken many different forms, including somatotypes, described by W. H. Sheldon in *The atlas of men* (Harper, 1954) and by S. Glueck and E. Glueck in *Physique and delinquency* (Harper, 1956). Continua of reproductive morbidity are studied by E. Pasamanick in *American J. Psychiatry*, **112**, 653 (1956), and infective agencies predominantly relating to the post encephalitis lethargica syndrome by G. Onuaguluchi in *Brain*, **84**, 395 (1961), but recently this has been reactivated to include other viral infections (cf. J. Cleobury and others, *British Medical J.*, **1**, 438–439, 1971), mental subnormality *per se* (D. J. Power, *Medicine, Science and Law*, **9**, 83 and 162, 1969) or the role of low intelligence in criminality (M. Woodward, *Low intelligence and delinquency*, I.S.T.D., 1963). All these reflect the same fundamental interest, as does the interest in epilepsy and criminal behaviour. Epilepsy in general has been surveyed by W. G. Lennox and M. A. Lennox in *Epilepsy and related disorders* (2 vols., Little, Brown, 1960), and in criminals by J. Gunn in *Epilepsy in prisoners* (Birmingham, M.D. thesis, 1969). More recently, interest has focused on temporal lobe epilepsy, reviewed in *J. Psychosomatic Research*, **13**, 229 (1969) by D. Taylor. Genetic determinants of criminal behaviour have also been postulated—for example, by J. Lange in *Crime as destiny: a study of criminal twins* (Allen and Unwin, 1931)—but more specific interest has been in sex chromosome anomalies, as in *Criminological implications of chromosome abnormalities*, a 'Cropwood conference' ed. D. J.

West (Cambridge Institute of Criminology, 1969), and S. Kessler and R. H. Moos, *J. Psychiatric Research*, **7**, 153 (1970). For continuing developments in this field the *Annals of Human Genetics* and *Nature* should be included in any literature survey.

Application of theoretical psychiatric concepts has been mainly based on Freudian or neo-Freudian concepts; for a simple introduction to these see J. A. C. Brown's *Freud and the post-Freudians* (Penguin, 1964). O. Fenichel's *The psycho-analytic theory of neurosis* (Routledge, 1946) remains the standard classical analytical reference book for many of these concepts. The whole basis of this school of thought is critically discussed by A. Kardiner (*J. Nervous and Mental Diseases*, **129**, 11–19, 1959). E. Glover's *Roots of crime*, reprinted in *Selected Papers in Psychoanalysis*, Vol. 2 (Imago, 1960), was a pioneering British contribution. A. Aichhorn's *Wayward youth* (Viking, 1935), and K. Friedlander's *The psycho-analytical approach to juvenile delinquency* (Routledge, 1947) are two other notable contributions. G. Zilborg in *International J. Psychoanalysis*, **37**, 318–324 (1956) discusses the contribution of psychoanalysis to forensic psychiatry. In *The criminal, the judge and the public* (Collier-Macmillan, 1939) F. Alexander and H. Staub present an offender typology based on psychoanalytical concepts. *Psychoanalytical Quarterly* and the *International Journal of Psychoanalysis* are the journals most likely to contain references in this area. The *International Journal of Offender Therapy* has also a heavy analytical bias.

Theoretical models based on the ideas of Erikson and Sullivan are currently of great interest—in particular, the concept of Interpersonal Maturity Scales. Offender typologies in the light of experience with this system are reviewed by M. Warren in *Canadian J. Corrections*, **12**, 451 (1970). Much of the original work is only available in mimeographed reports entitled *Community Treatment Project* and issued by the California Youth Authority. The earlier ones are now out of print and obtainable only through libraries. Other typologies are those of P. D. Scott in *Penal practice in a changing society* (I.S.T.D., 1960), based on a modified learning approach; those based on motive, such as W. Healy and A. F. Bronner's *New light on delinquency* (Yale U.P., 1950); and that of J. Rich in *Lancet*, **1**, 496 (1956). D. H. Stott in *Delinquency and human nature* (Carnegie UK Trust, 1950) uses a combination of motives and reaction patterns. These contrast with the approach of A. L. Baldwin (*Psychological Monographs*, **58**, 1, 1945), who based a typology on the parental patterns of behaviour, and of L. E. Hewitt and R. L. Jenkins in *Fundamental patterns of* *maladjustment* (Springfield, Ill.: State Printer, 1946), whose more elaborate typology attempted to relate specific patterns of child behaviour with particular parental pathology. An attempt to replicate this by E. Field, *A validation study of Hewitt and Jenkins' hypothesis*, Home Office Research Unit Report, No. 10 (HMSO, 1967) points to many of the problems inherent in this approach. M. Argyle in *Psychology and social problems* (Methuen, 1964) attempts to bring together several of these apparently different approaches.

The developmental approach

Considerable interest has focused on developmental aspects, and this has increasingly involved the need of reference to normal populations. Retrospective studies such as L. N. Robbins's *Deviant children grown up* (Williams and Wilkins, 1966) and prospective studies involving total national (J. W. B. Douglas and J. M. Blomfield, *Children under five*, Allen and Unwin, 1958), or local population studies that are now available cause increased doubt with regard to theories that stress any one particular aspect of child development as being of primary significance (W. McCord and J. McCord, *Origins of crime*, Columbia U.P., 1959). Most interest has focused on parental roles (for example, R. G. Andry, *Delinquency and parental pathology*, Methuen, 1960)—in particular, that of the mother. Following J. Bowlby's classical papers *Forty-four juvenile thieves* (Balliere, Tindall and Cox, 1946) and *Maternal care and mental health* (Geneva: WHO, 1952), there is now an extensive literature on this subject. *Early experience and behaviour*, edited by G. Newton and S. Levine (C. C. Thomas, 1968), contains a series of first-class review articles on all aspects of this field and underlines for any reader the problems of controlling independent variables in such research design.

Psychopathy

Equally voluminous, though often lacking the same scientific rigour of approach, is the literature on psychopathy. M. J. Craft's *Ten studies in psychopathy* (J. Wright, 1965) contains both a review of past literature and important original work. Earlier writing by D. K. Henderson and R. D. Gillespie in their *Texbook of psychiatry* (Oxford U.P., 1956) remains an important contribution, at least in practical terms, to a typology of psychopaths. K. Schneider's idea of a continuum from neurosis to personality disorder and subdivision within this is also of some clinical interest; see his *Psychopathic personalities* (Cassell, 1958). H. Cleckley's *Mask of sanity* (Mosby, 1956) is much quoted by American writers and serves as the basis of many research projects—his descriptions, though accurate, are difficult to apply prospectively and much research has been hampered by this approach. The tendency in more recent studies has been to limit investigation to psychopaths as defined by scores on certain questionnaires, as described by H. C. Quay in *Child Development*, **35**, 479 (1964), and emphasis is being placed on functioning of the autonomic nervous system in this group by authors such as R. D. Hare (*Psychopathy*, Wiley, 1969). H. Burn's *The autonomic nervous system* (4th ed., Blackwell, 1971) remains an excellent primer for those wishing to understand something of the autonomic nervous system.

Offences and offenders

Particular offences or offender groups have come to be associated with psychiatric interest: in particular, violent offences against the person (including murder, the battered child syndrome and infanticide) or against property (arson and vandalism), and sexual offences.

There are a number of theories on the origin of aggression and each of these finds expression in turn in theories put forward to explain crimes of violence. There are, therefore, many hundreds of references in this area. A good reader containing a cross-sectional sample of the literature is *Dynamics of aggression*, edited by E. Megargee and J. E. Hokanson (Harper and Row, 1970). Most psychiatric literature has been concerned with homicide: cf. W. L. Neustatter (*Lancet*, **1**, 861, 1965); J. Gould (*Recent Progress in Psychiatry*, **3**, 303, 1959); E. Tanay (*American J. Psychiatry*, **125**, 146, 1969); and many others who have contributed to this literature. D. J. West's *Murder followed by suicide* (Heinemann, 1965) and M. E. Wolfgang's *Patterns in criminal homicide* (Wiley, 1966) are also of relevance, as is R. Blackburn's more recent classification in *British J. Criminology*, **11**, 14 (1971). A typescript bibliography of homicide and psychosis is available at the Institute of Criminology, Cambridge. President Johnson's National Commission on the Causes and Prevention of Violence produced a number of excellent Staff Reports, of which Vol. 9, *Mass media and* *violence*, and Vols. 11, 12 and 13, *Crimes of violence*, provide both useful reviews of the literature and fruitful source of references. On battered babies, R. E. Helfer and C. H. Kempe's *The battered child* (U. of Chicago P., 1969) remains the standard text. The ongoing reports by the N.S.P.C.C., of which the first is *78 battered children*, by A. Skinner and R. L. Castle (1969), may well provide interesting data as the projects come to fruition. P. J. Resnick, in 'A psychiatric review of neonaticide' (*American J. Psychiatry*, **126**, 1970), reviews neontacide on p. 1415 and filicide on p. 73. Another special aspect of homicide is examined by R. R. Mowat in *Morbid jealousy and murder* (Tavistock, 1966). The role of mental illness in aggressive and dangerous behaviour has been the subject of a number of studies, the over-all results being open to varied interpretations. Dangerousness, its prediction and control, are topics of current interest. For discussion, see N. Morris and G. Hawkins, *The honest politician's guide to crime control* (U. of Chicago P., 1970) and recent review articles by T. G. Tennent (*British J. Hospital Medicine*, **6**, 269, 1971) and C. Greenland (*Seminars in Psychiatry*, **3** (3), 1971).

Arson has long been a subject of interest to the psychiatrist. Early papers such as W. Stekel's *Peculiarities of behaviour*, Vol. 2 (Boni and Liveright, 1924) tend to stress an underlying sexual component; more recent ones tend towards a displaced aggression hypothesis, as in D. W. McKerracher and A. J. I. Dacre's 'A study of arsonists in a special security hospital' (*British J. Psychiatry*, **112**, 1151–1154, 1966). The most comprehensive English-language study is by N. D. C. Lewis and H. Yarnell (*Nervous and mental diseases*, Monograph No. 82, New York, 1951). J. G. Frazer's *Myths of the origin of fire* (Macmillan, 1930) is an interesting cross-cultural study.

Sexual offences

Some of the most important contributions in the last 20 years have been advances in knowledge of normal sexual practices across societies (for example, C. S. Ford and F. A. Beach's *Patterns of sexual behaviour*, Methuen, 1965), and within a given society, as in the pioneering studies of A. C. Kinsey and others (*Sexual behaviour in the human male*, Saunders, 1948, and *Sexual behaviour in the human female*, Saunders, 1953). W. H. Masters and V. E. Johnston have pointed to differences in individual responsiveness in *Human sexual response* (Little, Brown, 1966). The same thoroughness of technique has been applied to the study of sex offenders by P. H. Gebhart in *The sex offenders* (Harper and Row, 1965), although this is limited to institutionalised offenders. M. Schofield, in *Sociological aspects of homosexuality* (Longmans, 1965), studying homosexuals inside and outside prison, questions how far we can draw conclusions from such populations. A simple introduction to homosexuality, as seen from different approaches, is provided by D. J. West's *Homosexuality* (3rd ed., Duckworth, 1965). C. Allens's *Textbook of psychosexual disorders* (2nd ed., Oxford U.P., 1969) is based primarily on clinical experience and has a strong analytical slant. I. Rosen's *The pathology and treatment of sexual disorders* (Oxford U.P., 1964) is a collection of papers representing different theoretical approaches to the subject. J. W. Mohr and others base their *Pedophilia and exhibitionism* (Toronto U.P., 1964) on out-patient clinic material. A discussion of the classification of rapists can be found in M. L. Cohen and others' 'The psychology of rapists' (*Seminars in Psychiatry*, **3** (3), August, 1971). *Transsexualism and sex reassignment*, ed. R. Green and J. Money (Johns Hopkins P., 1969), provides a comprehensive coverage of transsexualism. L. V. Frisbie's 15-year follow-up study of sex offenders treated in California, 'Another look at sex offenders in California' (California Mental Health Monograph No. 12, 1969), is of some interest. Of more specifically psychiatric orientation is the chapter by R. Brittain in R. B. H. Gradwohl's *Legal medicine* (J. Wright, 1968) on the sexual asphyxias. In *Child victims of sex offences*, an I.S.T.D. publication (1963), T. C. N. Gibbens and J. Prince correct some popular myths about sex offences, and L. Burton's *Vulnerable children* (Routledge, 1968) is a good follow-up study of children so involved. The Cambridge series publication *Sexual offences*, by F. J. Odgers and F. H. McClintock, ed. L. Radzinowicz (Macmillan, 1957), provides an over-all picture, although now somewhat dated.

Pornography arouses considerable current interest. The majority of President Nixon's Commission on Obscenity and Pornography, in its *Report* (US GPO, 1970, reprinted by Random House and in paperback by Bantam Books), came out in favour of liberalisation of laws, and some of the Technical Reports prepared for this Commission have now been released—for example, Vol. 7, *Erotica and antisocial behavior*, and Vol. 8, *Erotica and social behavior*. Abstracts from some of these have appeared in a new journal, *Archives of Sexual behaviour*. The Danish experience, and some associated research, can be found in B. Kutschinsky's contributions to Vols. 4, 7 and 8, and his *Studies on pornography and sex crimes in Denmark* (Copenhagen: *New Social Science Monographs*, 1970).

Female offenders

In general, although fewer in number, female offenders seem to show a higher rate of psychiatric disturbance or maladjustment than males. The literature, particularly for the younger age group, is well reviewed by J. Cowie and others in *Delinquency in girls* (Heinemann, 1968). T. C. N. Gibbens has reviewed female offenders in *British J. Hospital Medicine*, **6**, 279 (1971), and currently a number of papers are being produced in connection with the Holloway project (S. Dell and T. C. N. Gibbens, *Medicine, Science and Law*, 117, 1971; P. T. d'Orban, ibid., 104). Prostitution now attracts more sociological than psychological interest but E. Glover's *The psychopathology of prostitution* (I.S.T.D., 1957) remains an important contribution, as does T. C. N. Gibbens and J. Prince's *Shoplifting*, also published by the I.S.T.D. (1962). A more recent report on this study is provided by Gibbens and others in *British Medical J.*, **3**, 612 (1971).

Vandalism

Juvenile vandalism, by J. M. Martin (C. C. Thomas, 1961), remains one of the few major texts, but based on North American material. H. Mannheim wrote on the UK problem in *Federal Probation*, **18** (1), 14–15 (1954), and S. Cohen from a sociological viewpoint in *Howard Journal*, **12**, 121 (1967); but there is more interest now in football hooliganism (cf. Ian Taylor's contribution to *Images of Deviance*, ed. S. Cohen, Penguin, 1971).

TREATMENT

The role of psychiatry in the treatment of offenders is still subject to debate. Criticisms by psychiatrists of past attempts to reform prisoners, such as K. Menninger's *The crime of punishment* (Viking, 1969), have, in turn, been criticised for overselling psychiatry (cf. *International J. Psychiatry*, **9**, 558, 1970). The distribution of psychiatric disorders among various offender groups has been studied: for out-patients, by M. Grünhut in *Probation* *and mental treatment* (Tavistock, 1963), which also reports on the results of out-patient psychiatric treatment in less pessimistic terms than those of the evaluating psychiatrists; for prison remands, by J. Bearcroft and others (*British Medical J.*, **2**, 1519, 1965); for prisons, by W. Norwood East and W. H. de B. Hubert in *Report on the psychological treatment of crime* (HMSO, 1939); for borstals, by T. C. N. Gibbens in *Psychiatric studies of borstal lads* (Oxford U.P., 1963); for approved schools, by P. D. Scott (*British J. Criminology*, **4**, 525, 1964) and by P. Mason in *The residential treatment of disturbed and delinquent boys* (2nd 'Cropwood conference', ed. R. F. Sparks and R. G. Hood, Cambridge Institute of Criminology, 1968); for hospitalised offenders, by H. R. Rollin in *The mentally abnormal offender and the law* (Pergamon, 1969). Conflict centres around where they should be treated, be it prison or hospital: the Royal Commission on the Law Relating to Mental Illness and Mental Deficiency (HMSO, 1954–57, Cmnd. 169) considers this. From a practical viewpoint this is discussed by H. R. Rollin (see above); by P. D. Scott in *British Medical J.*, **2**, 167–169 (1970); and by J. A. Whitehead and others in *Lancet*, **1**, 135 (1970). On the role of psychiatrists in such treatment, particularly in relation to behaviour disorders, relevant discussions are those by Aubrey Lewis in *British J. Sociology*, **4**, 109 (1953), W. G. Albee in *American J. Psychiatry*, **125**, 870 (1969) and R. Leifer in *International J. Psychiatry*, **9**, 13 (1971), together with the discussants' papers.

Psychiatric treatment of offenders has largely been on an institutional basis, and out-patient or within-community facilities have received less attention. The Cambridge–Somerville experiment, described by E. Powers and H. Witmer in *An experiment in the prevention of delinquency* (Columbia U.P., 1951), provided an example of individualised counselling approach. Forensic psychiatric clinics which provide a treatment service as well as a diagnostic facility are few and of relatively recent development. The Clarke Institute of Toronto is one such clinic. Publications have mainly been concerned with the treatment of sex offenders (cf. A. Gigeroff and others in *Federal Probation*, **32** (3), 18 and **32** (4), 17, 1968). A more general philosophy is outlined by P. D. Scott in *British Medical J.*, **1**, 424–426 (1969), and the working of the Douglas Inch Clinic for Forensic Psychiatry by K. Wardrop in the *Report 1969 and 1970* (Glasgow: Western Regional Hospital Board, 1970). Portman Clinic material has been collated by W. Litauer in *Juvenile delinquents in a psychiatric clinic*, an I.S.T.D. publication (1957). The last applies psychoanalytical principles to the treatment of offenders. In the same vein are R. W. Shields's *A cure of delinquents* (2nd ed., Heinemann, 1971) and D. Miller's *Growth to freedom* (Tavistock, 1964)—one relating to residential treatment, the other based on experience of a borstal boys' after-care hostel.

California has been the centre for a number of studies attempting to evaluate different treatment regimes—notably *Youthful offenders at Highfields*, by H. A. Weeks (U. of Michigan P., 1958) and S. Adams's evaluation of the PICO project, 'Interaction between individual interview therapy and treatment amenability in older Youth Authority wards', in *Inquiries concerning kinds of treatment for kinds of delinquents* (Sacramento: California Board of Corrections, 1961). The most important of these has been the Community Treatment Project (already mentioned, p. 51). Some of the early work by J. D. and M. Q. Grant on naval detainees is of interest, especially their important paper 'A group dynamics approach to the treatment of non-conformists in the Navy' (*Annals of the American Academy of Political and Social Science*, **332**, 126–135, 1959).

The greatest impact on this area has been the application of group therapy, milieu therapy and therapeutic community approaches to the treatment of offenders. Group therapy has been conducted at all levels from group counselling (for example, N. Fenton's *An introduction to group counselling in the correctional service*, American Correctional Association, 1957) to group psychoanalysis (discussed in *Group psychoanalysis*, by N. Locke, New York U.P., 1961). Some problems of conducting groups in closed institutions have been discussed by R. Morrison in *Howard Journal*, **10**, 279 (1961) and by H. V. R. Jones and J. Williams, with particular reference to staff, in *Medicine, Science and Law*, **13** (1), 61–73 (1973). More important have been attempts not just to run groups within institutions but to run whole institutions as therapeutic communities, the pioneer in this field being Maxwell Jones, who has described his own experiences, both in the UK and in the USA, in *Social psychiatry in practice* (Penguin, 1968) and *Beyond the therapeutic community* (Yale U.P., 1968). Some attempts have been made to evaluate such treatment—for example, B. R. Philip and H. E. Peirotto (*Canadian J. Psychology*, **13**, 273, 1959) and J. S. Whiteley, 'The response of psychopaths to a therapeutic community' (*British J. Psychiatry*, **116**, 517–529, 1970). Further descriptive papers of variable quality can be found in *Interaction*, ed. P. de Berker (Cassirer, 1969).

Specific institutions for chronic or dangerous offenders and the regimes and treatment philosophies applied have been described:

the English Special Hospitals by P. McGrath in *Howard Journal*, **10**, 38 (1958), D. Street in *Lancet*, **2**, 143 (1960), and, more recently, C. Greenland in *Medicine, Science and Law*, **9**, 253–265 (1969), **10**, 93–103, 180–188 (1970); the Danish experience at Herstedvester by G. Stürup in *Treating the untreatable: chronic criminals at Herstedvester* (Johns Hopkins U.P., 1968); and the Van der Hoeven Clinic, Utrecht by A. M. Roosenburg in *The unwilling patient* (I.S.T.D., 1966). In the USA there are many other such institutions; reports on these tend to be in mimeographed form. One area of interest there has been the fate of patients discharged by the Baxstrom decision considered by Steadman and others in *Seminars in Psychiatry*, **3** (3), 376 (1971).

In general, psychotic offenders apart, physical methods of treatment have been of little use in the treatment of offenders. The exception to this has been in the treatment of sex offenders with female sex hormones, particularly depot slow release preparations, reported by L. H. Field and M. Williams in *Medicine, Science and Law*, **10**, 27–34 (1970). Other drugs are also being developed, including anti-androgens—cf. cyproterone acetate, recently reviewed by M. Briggs in *Medical J. of Zambia*, **1**, 125 (1971), and a butyrophenone, Benperidol, reported by P. Sterkmans and F. Geerts in *Acta Neurologica et Psychiatrica Belgica*, **66**, 1030 (1966). Surgery, similarly, has played but a small role in the treatment of offenders. Castration of sex offenders has now been abandoned (although J. Bremmer, in *Asexualisation*, Oslo U.P., 1958, and G. Stürup, in *Acta Psychiatrica Scandinavica*, Suppl. 204, claim that it is effective under certain conditions), as has leucotomy for behaviour disorders (G. W. Mackay, *Lancet*, **94**, 834, 1948). Recently, interest has developed in amygdalotomy for aggressive behaviour: see H. Narabayashi and others (*Confinia Neurologica*, **27**, 168, 1966) and R. F. Heimburger and others (*J. American Medical Association*, **198** (7), 741, 1966). Brain surgery for sexual disorders has also been tried (cf. review leader, *British Medical J.*, **4**, 250, 1969). Cosmetic surgery as an adjunct to other treatment has also been used with some success, and D. A. Ogden summarises 5 years' experience in 'Use of surgical rehabilitation in young delinquents' (*British Medical J.*, **1**, 432–434, 1959).

Increasingly, attention is being directed towards behavioural techniques for the modification of behaviour. *Behaviour therapy in clinical psychiatry*, by V. Meyer and E. S. Cheeser (Penguin, 1970), serves as a good introduction to the techniques which have been particularly used with sexual deviants. The token economy is another approach applied to some disordered offenders. *Token economy,* by T. Ayllon and N. Azrin (Appleton, 1968), provides a useful introduction and *The development and legal regulation of coercive behaviour modification techniques with offenders,* by R. K. Schwitzgebel (NIMH Public Health Service Publication No. 2067, 1971), points to some of the ethical problems raised by this approach. The application of a token economy at the Robert F. Kennedy Youth Center, Morgantown, W. Virginia, is described by L. Karacki and R. B. Levinson in *Howard J.,* **13** (1), 20–30 (1970).

BIBLIOGRAPHIES

There are no good bibliographies specifically related to forensic psychiatry. At the Institute of Criminology in Cambridge a mimeographed bibliography on forensic psychiatry covering the years 1930–1965 has been prepared but even this only covers some aspects of the subject. Other more specialised bibliographies have been referred to in the text. The bibliography on *Psychoanalysis, psychology and literature,* ed. N. Kiell (U. of Wisconsin P., 1963), covers the period 1900–1961 and includes references to crime and punishment; and *Research in infant behaviour,* by Y. Brackbill (Williams and Wilkins, 1964), is also worth noting, as are publications from the US Children's Bureau which appear from time to time.

ABSTRACTING JOURNALS

Some of these (*Excerpta Medica, Abstracts on Criminology and Penology, Crime and Delinquency Abstracts*) have already been referred to. *Mental Retardation Abstracts* (published, like *Crime and Delinquency Abstracts,* by the US Department of Health, Education and Welfare) contains some relevant sections. Consult also the section on Clinical psychology in *Psychological Abstracts.* More limited but more up to date references can be found from time to time in the *British Journal of Criminology;* unfortunately they are arranged only by broad subject headings, and there is no author or subject index.

PERIODICALS

There are a large number of psychiatric journals, any of which from time to time may carry an article of some criminological interest. The *British Journal of Psychiatry* (formerly *Journal of Mental Science*, 1853–) and *Psychological Medicine* (1970–) are the premier British journals likely to carry original articles in this field; although they may be found less frequently in the *British Medical Journal* (1832–), the *Lancet* (1823–) and the *Proceedings of the Royal Society of Medicine* (1907–). *Medicine, Science and the Law* (1960–) is the official organ of the British Academy of Forensic Sciences and papers reflect psychiatry's involvement with other branches of forensic medicine; the *Medico-Legal Journal* (quarterly), its involvement with the law; and the *British Journal of Criminology* (formerly *of Delinquency,* 1950–), its contacts with other disciplines involved in the study of deviance. The *Howard Journal* (1921–), published by the Howard League for Penal Reform should also perhaps be mentioned. The *Journal of Child Psychology and Psychiatry* (1960–), as its name suggests, is concerned entirely with juveniles and occasionally carries articles of forensic interest. The *British Journal of Hospital Medicine* (1966–) presents review articles covering the whole of medicine and surgery but, although there is on average only about one article a month on psychiatry, these are generally of a very high standard. From the USA the *American Journal of Psychiatry* (1844–), *Archives of General Psychiatry* (1959–) and the *Journal of Criminal Law, Criminology and Police Science* (1910–) should be consulted. Other journals of importance are *Psychoanalytic Quarterly* (1932–), *Acta Psychiatrica Scandinavica* (1961–), the *International Journal of Offender Therapy* (1957–) and the *International Journal of Group Psychotherapy* (1951–). The *International Journal of Psychiatry* (1965–) is an interesting journal published annually and containing papers and discussions of these papers.

This list should not be regarded as in any way exhaustive, but search of these journals should provide the reader with the majority of forensic texts.

4

Criminological aspects of psychology

David P. Farrington

INTRODUCTION

Psychology is usually defined as the scientific study of the behaviour of living organisms. This definition may seem a little surprising to the proverbial 'educated layman' but should be borne in mind in what follows. Psychology is also concerned with processes such as learning and perception, and with factors such as motivation and personality, which are supposed to underlie behaviour. Since all processes and factors are likely to be operating simultaneously, it is difficult, if not impossible, to study one in isolation from another. However, this is usually attempted. Psychology overlaps with many other fields, particularly physiology, psychiatry, sociology and education. Because of this overlapping, the psychological literature is scattered over a variety of sources.

There are many points of contact between psychology and criminology. Criminologists are particularly interested in kinds of behaviour which contravene the current criminal law or are otherwise regarded as deviant, such as stealing and aggressive actions. They are also interested in the behaviour of classes of individuals concerned directly or indirectly with the law, such as policemen, prison officers, magistrates, judges and court witnesses. Any area of criminology which involves the study of behaviour might be considered also to be an area of psychology.

This chapter contains an outline of the fields of psychology and of the application of psychological theories, methods and results in criminology. Of course, the aspects of psychology which have proved the most fruitful for criminology in the past may not also prove the most significant in the future. This is one of the reasons why all fields of psychology are briefly surveyed here. A review of sources of psychological information is also included. Special attention is paid to journals, as psychologists seem to be more dependent on journal articles than most other social scientists. The date given after each journal is the year in which its first volume was published, whether or not at that time the journal had its present name. No attempt is made to survey literature in languages other than English, and publications which have appeared during the last 20 years or so have been preferred.

FIELDS OF PSYCHOLOGY

Any division of psychology into fields is bound to be open to some objections, since it is as difficult to identify rigid boundaries within the subject as it is to identify them between psychology and other subjects. In the present chapter, five fields are delineated, as follows:

(1) General psychology, history, theories and methods.
(2) Experimental, physiological and animal psychology.
(3) Personality and clinical psychology.
(4) Developmental and social psychology.
(5) Educational and industrial psychology.

These headings should be interpreted rather widely.

GENERAL PSYCHOLOGY, HISTORY, THEORIES AND METHODS

Perhaps the best and most comprehensive general introduction to psychology is provided by C. T. Morgan and R. A. King's *Introduction to psychology* (4th ed., McGraw-Hill, 1971), together with the accompanying *Readings for an introduction to psychology*, ed. R. A. King (3rd ed., McGraw-Hill, 1971). The most wide-ranging general introduction to criminological aspects of psychology is probably *Legal and criminal psychology*, ed. H. Toch (Holt, Rinehart, 1961), while G. J. Dudycha's *Psychology for law enforcement officers* (C. C. Thomas, 1955) can also be recommended. Some general introductions to criminological topics also contain psychological material: for example, N. D. Walker's *Crime and punishment in Britain* (2nd ed., Edinburgh U.P., 1968), D. J. West's *The young offender* (Penguin, 1967) and *Juvenile delinquency*, ed. H. C. Quay (Van Nostrand, 1965).

Psychological journals covering the whole field include the *American Journal of Psychology* (1887–), the *British Journal of Psychology* (1904–), the *Canadian Journal of Psychology* (1947–), the *Australian Journal of Psychology* (1949–) and the European journal *Acta Psychologica* (1936–). However, these journals rarely carry articles of direct relevance to criminology. The *Journal of Psychology* (1935–), the *Journal of General Psychology* (1928–), *Psychological Reports* (1955–) and *Psychonomic Science* (1964–), which in the main contain brief research reports, are somewhat more fruitful in this respect.

There is a great need for an academic journal specialising in the borderland between criminology and psychology. Two professional journals which do this to some extent are the *Correctional Psychologist* (1967–) and the *Journal of Correctional Education* (1949–). Of the criminological journals, the *British Journal of Criminology* (1960–) is the most fertile source of psychological articles. The *American Journal of Correction* (1939–), the *Canadian Journal of Criminology and Corrections* (1958–), the *Australian and New Zealand Journal of Criminology* (1968–), *Crime and Delinquency* (1955–), the *Journal of Criminal Law and Criminology* (1910–) and the *Journal of Research in Crime and Delinquency* (1964–) occasionally contain such papers.

The history of psychology is well documented by E. G. Boring in *A history of experimental psychology* (2nd ed., Appleton, 1950), and in the more recent *The Pelican history of psychology*, by R. Thomson (Penguin, 1968). The most important historical journal is the *Journal of the History of the Behavioral Sciences* (1965–).

A general review of psychological theories can be found in *Systems and theories in psychology*, by M. H. Marx and W. A. Hillix (McGraw-Hill, 1963), and in the collection of articles edited by M. H. Marx entitled *Theories in contemporary psychology* (Macmillan, 1963). The most influential theoretical journal is the *Psychological Review* (1894–). Mathematical model-building, in some quarters regarded as the new armchair psychology, has been the fastest-growing theoretical fashion during the last decade. F. Restle and J. G. Greeno's *Introduction to mathematical psychology* (Addison-Wesley, 1970) is a most promising elementary text, while models mushroom in the *Journal of Mathematical Psychology* (1964–). It cannot be long before such models appear in profusion in criminology. B. P. Cohen's *Conflict and conformity* (M.I.T. Press, 1963) is in this tradition, as is the recent *Delinquency in a birth cohort* by M. E. Wolfgang and others (U. of Chicago P., 1972).

The experimental method is widely used in fundamental psychological research, and is clearly described by F. J. McGuigan in *Experimental psychology: a methodological approach* (2nd ed., Prentice-Hall, 1968). One of the most important methodological artefacts is discussed in R. Rosenthal's *Experimenter effects in behavioral research* (Appleton, 1966). Truly experimental methods are comparatively rare in criminology, perhaps because of the incompatibility of experimentation and justice. The most common criminological experiments are those designed to compare the effects of different treatment techniques, and as an example the famous Cambridge–Somerville study may be cited. This is described in *An experiment in the prevention of delinquency* by E. Powers and H. L. Witmer (Columbia U.P., 1951). The method of systematic observation is popular in certain fields of psychology, and is explained in *Research methods in the behavioral sciences*, ed. L. Festinger and D. Katz (Dryden, 1953). This technique is perhaps dominant in criminology, and D. J. West's *Present conduct and future delinquency* (Heinemann, 1969) may be mentioned as an example. Finally, clinical methods are also used in both psychology and criminology, involving intensive case studies and the application of psychological tests. These tests will be specified in more detail below (pp. 70–71). The most prestigious methodological journal is the *Psychological Bulletin* (1904–), and the 1967 issue (**68**, 178–220) contains an index to publications appearing in this journal in the years 1940–1966.

Both parametric and non-parametric statistics are utilised in the analysis of psychological and criminological data. *Psychological statistics*, by Q. McNemar (4th ed., Wiley, 1969) covers most of these, although it is as well to study also *Non-parametric statistics for the behavioral sciences*, by S. Siegel (McGraw-Hill, 1956). Computers are also used widely in both subjects, and an elementary manual such as D. J. Veldman's *Fortran programming for the behavioral sciences* (Holt, Rinehart, 1967) is thus particularly valuable. Factor analysis and information theory are two statistical methods which are especially popular in psychology. The former is described in H. H. Harman's *Modern factor analysis* (2nd ed., U. of Chicago P., 1967), and has also been extensively employed in criminology—for example, in R. G. Andry's *The short-term prisoner* (Stevens, 1963). Information theory is expounded in W. R. Garner's *Uncertainty and structure as psychological concepts* (Wiley, 1962), but has had very little impact on criminology. An interesting recent development is M. A. P. Willmer's *Crime and information theory* (Edinburgh U.P., 1970). The *British Journal of Mathematical and Statistical Psychology* (1947–) contains papers on many aspects of mathematical modelling and statistics.

EXPERIMENTAL, PHYSIOLOGICAL AND ANIMAL PSYCHOLOGY

B. J. Underwood's *Experimental psychology* (2nd ed., Appleton, 1966) is a useful introductory textbook, while P. L. Broadhurst's *The science of animal behaviour* (Penguin, 1963) is eminently readable. *The machinery of the brain*, by D. E. Wooldridge (McGraw-Hill, 1963), is popularly written for the beginner in physiological psychology, whereas R. F. Thompson's *Foundations of physiological psychology* (Harper and Row, 1970) is more advanced. The major journals are the *Journal of Experimental Psychology* (1916–), the *Quarterly Journal of Experimental Psychology* (1948–), and the *Journal of Comparative and Physiological Psychology* (1921–). The most important topics investigated are (1) human learning and thinking, (2) animal learning, motivation and emotion, and (3) sensation and perception.

Human learning and thinking

Human learning is treated with commendable detail and amazing clarity in W. Kintsch's *Learning, memory and conceptual processes* (Wiley, 1970), while the most significant specialist journal is the *Journal of Verbal Learning and Verbal Behavior* (1962–). Little of this body of knowledge has been applied in criminology, although some experiments which are potentially of great relevance are surveyed in *Reward and punishment in human learning*, by J. Nuttin and A. Greenwald (Academic P., 1968). There have been sporadic attempts extending over the last 60 years to use known facts about remembering to secure a greater awareness of the fallibility of eye-witness testimony. J. Marshall's provocatively titled *Law and psychology in conflict* (Bobbs-Merrill, 1966) represents one such endeavour, while perhaps the most recent is D. S. Greer's article in *British J. Criminology*, **11**, 131–154 (1971) entitled

'Anything but the truth? The reliability of testimony in criminal trials'.

The psychological study of thinking is well represented in the set of readings entitled *Thinking and reasoning*, ed. P. C. Wason and P. N. Johnson-Laird (Penguin, 1968). However, this field has had little direct relevance to criminology, although *Straight and crooked thinking*, by R. H. Thouless (rev. and enl. ed., 8th pr., Pan, 1964) exposes the many dishonest tricks of argument favoured by trial lawyers. *Cognitive Psychology* (1970–) is an important journal covering thinking, learning and perception. The related topic of decision-making is more obviously significant, although the many criminological investigations on this subject appear to have been carried out in almost complete ignorance of this voluminous literature. *Decision-making: selected readings*, ed. W. Edwards and A. Tversky (Penguin, 1967), and W. Lee's *Decision theory and human behavior* (Wiley, 1971) outline the psychological research. Finally, *Risk taking*, by N. Kogan and M. A. Wallach (Holt, Rinehart, 1964), is an illuminating text on an associated topic with obvious criminological implications, some of which are outlined in J. Cohen's *Psychological probability* (Allen and Unwin, 1972).

Animal learning, motivation and emotion

Both human and animal learning experiments are described in *The psychology of learning*, by J. Deese and S. H. Hulse (3rd ed., McGraw-Hill, 1967), while animal learning is also covered in E. R. Hilgard and D. G. Marquis's classic *Conditioning and learning* (rev. by G. A. Kimble; Appleton, 1961). D. Bindra's *Motivation: a systematic reinterpretation* (Ronald, 1958) represents an important contribution to this field, and a comprehensive collection of readings can be found in *Current research in motivation*, ed. R. N. Haber (Holt, Rinehart, 1966). P. T. Young's *Motivation and emotion* (Wiley, 1961) is especially strong on the emotional aspects, while *The nature of emotion*, ed. M. B. Arnold (Penguin, 1968), comprises a varied selection of readings. S. Schachter's *Emotion, obesity and crime* (Academic P., 1971) contains two chapters which should be of interest to criminologists. Animal journals include *Behaviour* (1947–), *Animal Behaviour* (1953–), *Learning and Motivation* (1970–) and the *Journal of the Experimental Analysis of Behavior* (1958–), while the more physiological journals include *Neuropsychologia* (1963–), *Cortex* 1964–), *Brain,*

Behavior and Evolution (1968–) and *Experimental Brain Research* (1966–). The annual *Nebraska Symposium on Motivation* (1953–) contains some papers which are particularly relevant to criminology. Finally, the *Journal of Applied Behavior Analysis* (1968–) deserves special mention, as it carries many articles concerned with the application to human problems of concepts derived from animal experimentation.

The animal experiments have given rise to a 'learning theory', although a glance at E. R. Hilgard and G. H. Bower's *Theories of learning* (3rd ed., Appleton, 1966) reveals that in actual fact many different learning theories exist. These theories have been extensively applied in other areas of psychology (e.g. socialisation: see p. 75), and have inspired a number of explanations of criminal behaviour. G. B. Trasler's *The explanation of criminality* (Routledge, 1962) and H. J. Eysenck's *Crime and personality* (rev. ed., Paladin, 1970) are impressive examples. Animal experiments have often examined the effect of reward or punishment on learning, and this topic is explored in detail in F. A. Logan and A. P. Wagner's *Reward and punishment* (Allyn and Bacon, 1965). Criminologists interested in the question of punishment would do well to consult *Punishment: issues and experiments*, ed. E. E. Boe and R. M. Church (Appleton, 1968) or *Punishment and aversive behavior*, ed. B. A. Campbell and R. M. Church (Appleton, 1969).

One area of psychology which might possibly be included within the field of motivation and emotion is adjustment, exemplified by I. F. Tucker's textbook *Adjustment: models and mechanisms* (Academic P., 1970). The frustration–aggression hypothesis is a momentous aspect of adjustment, and is of considerable interest to criminologists. L. Berkowitz's two books *Aggression: a social psychological analysis* (McGraw-Hill, 1962) and *Roots of aggression: a re-examination of the frustration–aggression hypothesis* (Atherton, 1969) are extremely relevant at this point. A. J. Yates's *Frustration and conflict* (Methuen, 1962) contains a great deal of experimental evidence, while a variety of viewpoints emerge in *The dynamics of aggression*, ed. E. I. Megargee and J. E. Hokanson (Harper and Row, 1970). A. H. Buss's *The psychology of aggression* (Wiley, 1961) is the most notable and comprehensive textbook on aggression.

The more physiological approach to aggression can be seen in the concise *Violence and the brain*, by V. H. Mark and F. R. Ervin (Harper and Row, 1970), and in two collections of conference papers. One is entitled *Aggression and defense* and is edited by C. D. Clemente and D. B. Lindsley (U.C.L.A. Press, 1967), while the other is entitled *Aggressive behaviour* and is edited by S. Garattini and E. B. Sigg (Excerpta Medica Foundation, 1969). The physiological psychology of emotion has had an important application in criminology, namely the lie-detector technique. This is described in J. E. Reid and F. E. Inbau's *Truth and deception: the polygraph ('lie detector') technique* (Williams and Wilkins, 1966).

Sensation and perception

Excellent introductions to these topics can be found in *Sensory processes*, by M. Alpern and others (Brooks/Cole, 1967) and in *Perception*, by J. E. Hochberg (Prentice-Hall, 1964). U. Neisser's *Cognitive psychology* (Appleton, 1967) also has considerable merit, although it is rather wider in scope. *Perception and Psychophysics* (1966–), *Vision Research* (1961–) and the *Journal of Auditory Research* (1960–) are reputable specialist journals. This field of psychology has as yet made little contribution to criminology, although *The measurement of delinquency*, by T. Sellin and M. E. Wolfgang (Wiley, 1964), contains a sophisticated application of psychophysical scaling procedures. Social psychological studies of the perception and definition of persons and situations—for example, *The perception of people and events*, by P. B. Warr and C. Knapper (Wiley, 1968)—are more likely to be relevant. Time perception constitutes one of the major parts of P. Fraisse's *The psychology of time* (Eyre and Spottiswoode, 1964). It is an important consideration in imprisonment, as can be seen in *Psychological survival*, by S. Cohen and L. Taylor (Penguin, 1972).

PERSONALITY AND CLINICAL PSYCHOLOGY

There is little doubt that these areas of psychology have in the past made a more profound impact on criminology than any other. One problem in considering them is to distinguish between clinical psychology and psychiatry. It should be stated at the outset that some readers may feel that psychiatric subjects have been included here, and others may feel that clinical psychology ones have been excluded. J. B. Rotter's *Clinical psychology* (2nd ed., Prentice-Hall, 1971) is a standard textbook, while *Readings in clinical psychology*, ed. R. D. Savage (Pergamon, 1966), also deserves perusal. The *Journal of Clinical Psychology* (1945–), the *Journal of Consulting and Clinical Psychology* (1937–), the

Journal of Abnormal Psychology (1906–) and the *British Journal of Social and Clinical Psychology* (1962–) all contain articles of direct relevance to criminology. *The psychology of personality*, by R. Stagner (3rd ed., McGraw-Hill, 1961), is a creditable introductory work, while the major personality journals are the *Journal of Personality* (1932–), the *Journal of Personality and Social Psychology* (1965–) and the *Journal of Experimental Research in Personality* (1965–). These periodicals are also criminologically relevant. Finally, it should be pointed out that psychiatric journals, such as the *American Journal of Psychiatry* (1921–), the *British Journal of Psychiatry* (1853–) and the *American Journal of Orthopsychiatry* (1930–), regularly contain papers on personality and clinical psychology. This section will be divided into four parts, for convenience entitled psychological tests, personality theories, behaviour disorders and therapeutic methods.

Psychological tests

L. J. Cronbach's *Essentials of psychological testing* (3rd ed., Harper and Row, 1970) and A. Anastasi's *Psychological testing* (3rd ed., Macmillan, 1968) are indispensable elementary volumes. The *Seventh mental measurements yearbook*, ed. O. K. Buros (Gryphon, 1971) is an encyclopaedic source of information about tests, and the same author's *Personality tests and reviews* (Gryphon, 1970) is also an essential reference work. For light relief from these weighty tomes, an appendix entitled 'How to cheat on personality tests' in W. H. Whyte's *The organization man* (Cape, 1957) is good value. The tests themselves can be obtained by qualified persons from the N.F.E.R. Publishing Co., 2, Jennings Buildings, Thames Avenue, Windsor, Berks., SL4 1QS. The most important journals are *Educational and Psychological Measurement* (1941–), *Psychometrika* (1936–) and the *Journal of Projective Techniques and Personality Assessment* (1936–). The third of these is the most likely to carry criminological articles.

P. E. Vernon's *Intelligence and attainment tests* (U. of London P., 1960) is a standard textbook on intelligence tests. These have been extensively utilised in criminology, and a critical appraisal of the literature can be found in M. Woodward's *Low intelligence and delinquency* (I.S.T.D., 1963). F. Ferracuti's *Intelligence and criminality: a bibliography* (Milan: Giuffré, 1966) is a valuable source of references. Psychomotor tests have also been employed, and the most popular of these is the Porteus Maze. A first-hand account of this is presented in *Porteus Maze Test: fifty years' application*, by S. D. Porteus (Pacific Books, 1965), while T. C. N. Gibbens's *Psychiatric studies of borstal lads* (Oxford U.P., 1963) can be cited as an example of its use in criminology.

The most conspicuous personality inventory is undoubtedly the Minnesota Multiphasic Personality Inventory (MMPI). S. R. Hathaway and E. D. Monachesi's two books *Analyzing and predicting juvenile delinquency with the MMPI* (U. of Minnesota P., 1953) and *Adolescent personality and behavior* (U. of Minnesota P., 1963) provide outstanding instances of its criminological significance. J. C. Ball's *Social deviancy and adolescent personality* (U. of Kentucky P., 1962) is another example. The Jesness Inventory was more criminologically orientated from the start, and two recent Home Office Research Unit reports (Nos. 12 and 13) reveal its versatility. These are M. Davies's *The use of the Jesness Inventory on a sample of British probationers* (HMSO, 1967) and J. Mott's *The Jesness Inventory: application to approved school boys* (HMSO, 1969). Many projective personality tests have also found criminological application. The Rorschach is incorporated in S. and E. Glueck's *Unraveling juvenile delinquency* (Harvard U.P., 1950), while T. Grygier's *Oppression: a study in social and criminal psychology* (Routledge, 1954) discusses the Thematic Apperception and Picture Frustration tests. H. Walder's *Drive structure and criminality* (C. C. Thomas, 1959) leans heavily on the Szondi, and a promising, comparatively recent test is described in *The hand test: a new projective test with special reference to the prediction of overt aggressive behavior*, by B. Bricklin and others (2nd pr., C. C. Thomas, 1970). Controversial estimates of the value of personality tests in criminology have been provided by K. F. Schuessler and D. R. Cressey ('Personality characteristics of criminals' in *American J. Sociology*, **55**, 476–484, 1950) and by G. P. Waldo and S. Dinitz ('Personality attributes of the criminal' in *J. Research in Crime and Delinquency*, **4**, 185–201, 1967).

The use of rating scales, particularly those completed by teachers, in detecting symptoms of delinquent behaviour should also be mentioned. This method can be seen in D. H. Stott's *Studies of troublesome children* (Tavistock, 1966) and in *Anxious youth: dynamics of delinquency*, by W. C. Kvaraceus (Merrill, 1966).

Personality theories

C. S. Hall and G. Lindzey's *Theories of personality* (2nd ed., Wiley,

1970) is an excellent textbook, while good supplementary reading is contained in *Theories of personality: primary sources and research*, ed. G. Lindzey and C. S. Hall (Wiley, 1965). Psychoanalysis is a profoundly influential theory and can be studied at first hand with the aid of S. Freud's *Introductory lectures on psychoanalysis* (2nd ed., 11th imp., Allen and Unwin, 1968). Psychoanalytic journals include *The Psychoanalytic Study of the Child* (1945–   ), the *Psychoanalytic Quarterly* (1932–   ) and the *International Journal of Psycho-analysis* (1920–   ). The *Index of Psychoanalytical Writings*, ed. A. Grinstein (9 vols., International Universities P., 1956–1966), is an essential reference work. This theory has been widely drawn upon in explaining criminal behaviour, and D. Abrahamsen's *The psychology of crime* (Columbia U.P., 1960) and E. Glover's *The roots of crime* (Imago, 1960) can be referred to as examples. *Delinquent and neurotic children*, by I. V. Bennett (Tavistock, 1960), represents a significant attempt to test empirically the ramifications of this theory. Impulsiveness is an aspect of personality which is known to be related to criminality, and it is described in *Character structure and impulsiveness*, by D. Kipnis (Academic P., 1971).

Typological explanations of personality have also achieved some prominence, and one of the most popular of these relates personality to physique. R. W. Parnell's *Behaviour and physique* (Arnold, 1958) is admirably detailed, while W. H. Sheldon's *Varieties of delinquent youth* (Harper, 1949) and S. and E. Glueck's *Physique and delinquency* (Harper, 1956) comprise substantial criminological applications. Another well-known typology is the theme of *Readings in extraversion–introversion*, ed. H. J. Eysenck (3 vols., Staples Press, 1970–71). The second of these volumes, in particular, contains some criminologically relevant readings. Specifically criminological typologies are discussed in the classical *Fundamental patterns of maladjustment*, by L. E. Hewitt and R. L. Jenkins (Springfield, Ill.: State Printer, 1946), and in S. and E. Glueck's *Towards a typology of juvenile offenders* (Grune and Stratton, 1970). The usefulness of such typologies is critically evaluated in T. N. Ferdinand's *Typologies of delinquency* (Random House, 1966). Finally, the learning theory approach to personality and socialisation, as exemplified by *Social learning and personality development*, by A. Bandura and R. H. Walters (Holt, Rinehart, 1963), will be discussed below (p. 75) as a developmental psychology topic.

Behaviour disorders

Behaviour disorders are set out in L. P. Ullman and L. Krasner's *A psychological approach to abnormal behavior* (Prentice-Hall, 1969) and in the informative *Reviews of research in behavior pathology*, ed. D. S. Holmes (Wiley, 1968). The *Handbook of abnormal psychology*, ed. H. J. Eysenck (2nd ed., Pitman, 1973) can also be confidently recommended. The overlapping between psychology and psychiatry is particularly extensive in this field. Since psychiatry is discussed elsewhere in this book, only two topics—psychopathy and sexual deviation—have been chosen for examination here. Other topics which could be considered include neuroses, psychoses, addiction and mental deficiency.

Psychopathy: theory and research, by R. D. Hare (Wiley, 1970), provides a splendid coverage of this subject, while W. and J. McCord's *The psychopath: an essay on the criminal mind* (Grune and Stratton, 1964) is also worth mentioning. M. Craft's *Ten studies into psychopathic personality* (J. Wright, 1965) contains detailed empirical information, and R. D. and A. S. Hare's 'Psychopathic behavior: a bibliography' (*Excerpta Criminologica*, **7**, 365–386, 1967) is an excellent source of references. Regarding sexual deviance, *The pathology and treatment of sexual deviation*, ed. I. Rosen (Oxford U.P., 1964), and *Dynamics of deviant sexuality*, ed. J. H. Masserman (Grune and Stratton, 1969), are both valuable. Classic expositions of different types of deviation can be found in D. J. West's *Homosexuality* (3rd ed., Duckworth, 1968) and in *Pedophilia and exhibitionism*, by J. W. Mohr, R. E. Turner and M. B. Jerry (Toronto U.P., 1964). *Sex offenders*, by P. H. Gebhard and others (Harper and Row, 1965), is particularly relevant to criminology, and A. Ellis and R. Brancale's *The psychology of sex offenders* (C. C. Thomas, 1956) reports a useful piece of empirical research.

Therapeutic methods

Psychotherapy is comprehensively discussed in D. H. Ford and H. B. Urban's *Systems of psychotherapy* (Wiley, 1963), while *Group psychotherapy*, by S. H. Foulkes and E. J. Anthony (2nd ed., Penguin, 1965), also deserves attention. J. Wolpe's *The practice of behavior therapy* (Pergamon, 1969) is perhaps the clearest exposition of this technique, while a (not wholly unbiased) point-by-point comparison of psychotherapy and behaviour therapy can be found in *The causes and cures of neurosis*, by H. J. Eysenck and S. Rachman (Routledge, 1965). One type of behaviour therapy is described in *Aversion therapy and behaviour disorders*, by S. Rachman and J. Teasdale (Routledge, 1969), and another is outlined in *The token economy*, by T. Ayllon and N. Azrin (Appleton, 1968). The most important therapeutic journals are the *American Journal of Psychotherapy* (1947–   ), *Psychotherapy* (1963–   ), *Group Psychotherapy* (1947–   ), the *International Journal of Group Psychotherapy* (1951–   ), *Behaviour Research and Therapy* (1963–   ) and the *Journal of Behavior Therapy and Experimental Psychiatry* (1970–   ).

Criminological applications of therapeutic techniques are critically surveyed in *Changing the lawbreaker*, by D. C. Gibbons (Prentice-Hall, 1965), while an impressive bibliography of the literature on group treatment in correctional institutions is contained in *J. Criminal Law, Criminology and Police Science*, **59**, 41–56 (1968). The *International Journal of Offender Therapy and Comparative Criminology* (1957–   ) and *Corrective Psychiatry and Journal of Social Therapy* (1955–   ) are especially pertinent treatment journals. As far as individual contributions are concerned, *A cure of delinquents*, by R. W. Shields (2nd ed., Heinemann, 1971), and *No water in my cup*, by R-R. M. Jurjevich (Libra, 1968), report on the use of psychotherapy with delinquent boys and girls, respectively. H. Jones's *Reluctant rebels* (Tavistock, 1960) and *The Highfields story*, by L. W. McCorkle and others (Holt, 1958), both record the employment of group therapy with young offenders. Group counselling is elucidated in N. Fenton's two works *An introduction to group counseling in the State Correctional Service* (American Correctional Association, 1958) and *Explorations in the use of group counseling in the County Correctional Program* (Pacific Books, 1962). Finally, *Behaviour therapy*, by A. J. Yates (Wiley, 1970), includes an examination of this technique as applied to delinquents and criminals.

DEVELOPMENTAL AND SOCIAL PSYCHOLOGY

Child development and personality, by P. H. Mussen and others (3rd ed., Harper and Row, 1969), is an excellent developmental psychology text, while the associated *Readings in child development and personality*, edited by the same authors (2nd ed., Harper and Row, 1970) has considerable merit. A. L. Baldwin's *Theories of child development* (Wiley, 1967) also deserves careful study. The most influential journals, sometimes containing criminologically relevant articles, are *Child Development* (1930–), the *Journal of Genetic Psychology* (1891–), *Developmental Psychology* (1969–), *Adolescence* (1966–), the *Journal of Experimental Child Psychology* (1964–) and the *Journal of Child Psychology and Psychiatry* (1960–). *Child Development Abstracts and Bibliography* (1927–) is an invaluable reference source.

R. Brown's *Social psychology* (Free Press, 1965) is a useful introductory work in this field, while *The individual in society*, by D. Krech and others (McGraw-Hill, 1962), can also be recommended. Perhaps the most extensive collection of readings can be found in the *Handbook of social psychology*, ed. G. Lindzey and E. Aronson (2nd ed., 5 vols., Addison-Wesley, 1968–1969). The major journals are *Sociometry* (1937–), the *Journal of Social Psychology* (1930–), the *Journal of Experimental Social Psychology* (1965–), the *Journal of Personality and Social Psychology* (1965–) and the *British Journal of Social and Clinical Psychology* (1962–). These all include some criminologically relevant papers, but the *Journal of Applied Social Psychology* (1971–) may prove to be particularly fruitful in this respect. Just as it was difficult to disentangle clinical psychology from psychiatry, it is hard to separate social psychology and sociology. In view of this, it will come as no surprise to discover that several more or less sociologically orientated journals, such as *Human Relations* (1947–), the *Journal of Social Issues* (1945–) and the *American Sociological Review* (1936–), regularly carry contributions to social psychology. From the viewpoint of criminology, the subject of socialisation, which belongs to both developmental and social psychology, demands special attention. Consequently, this subject will be treated first, followed initially by other developmental topics and then by other social topics.

Socialisation

Human socialization, by E. B. McNeill (Brooks/Cole, 1969), is an elementary textbook notable for its illustrations. The *Handbook of socialization theory and research*, ed. D. A. Goslin (Rand McNally, 1969) and *Early experiences and the processes of socialization*, ed. R. A. Hoppe and others (Academic P., 1970), both comprise reputable collections of readings. R. E. Grinder's *Studies in adolescence* (2nd ed., Macmillan, 1969) is also in the main concerned with socialisation. H. J. Eysenck's *Crime and personality* (rev. ed., Paladin, 1970) and G. B. Trasler's *The explanation of criminality* (Routledge, 1962), which have both been referred to in connection with 'learning theory', are two of the most explicit statements of the relationship between social learning and crime.

Socialisation is in many ways associated with moral development, and both of these topics are discussed in J. Aronfreed's *Conduct and conscience* (Academic P., 1968). *The psychology of moral behaviour*, by D. Wright (Penguin, 1971), is an excellent and quite wide-ranging review of experimental studies in moral development, and includes much of relevance to criminology. W. Kay's *Moral development* (Allen and Unwin, 1968) is a more orthodox developmental psychology text. *The psychology of character development*, by R. F. Peck and R. J. Havighurst (Wiley, 1960), and N. J. Bull's *Moral judgement from childhood to adolescence* (Routledge, 1969) describe extremely interesting empirical studies, while *The Development of conscience*, by G. M. Stevenson (Routledge, 1966), is also worthy of note.

Other developmental psychology topics

One segment of developmental psychology which has attracted a great deal of criminological interest is child-rearing. Research in this area is critically evaluated in *Child-rearing: an inquiry into research and methods*, by M. R. Yarrow and others (Jossey-Bass, 1968), while *Patterns of child rearing*, by R. R. Sears and others (Row, Peterson, 1957), summarises an outstanding research project. A. Bandura and R. H. Walters's *Adolescent aggression* (Ronald, 1959) is of particular criminological interest, as it constitutes an investigation into the different child-rearing practices which precede aggressive adolescent behaviour.

There has also been a great deal of research into the importance of certain aspects of the parent–child relationship as precursors of delinquency. This idea is embodied in the famous (S. and E.) Glueck Social Prediction Table, as expounded in their *Predicting delinquency and crime* (Harvard U.P., 1959). It can also be seen in R. G. Andry's *Delinquency and parental pathology* (rev. ed., Staples, 1971) and in *Delinquency and child neglect*, by H. C. Wilson (Allen and Unwin, 1962). *Readings in the psychology of parent–child relations*, ed. G. R. Medinnus (Wiley, 1967), contains much of value. One of the most famous criminological hypotheses points to the role of maternal deprivation in the genesis of delinquency. Some evidence pertinent to this question is reviewed in

B. Wootton's *Social science and social pathology* (Allen and Unwin, 1959). J. Bowlby's *Child care and the growth of love* (2nd ed., Penguin, 1965) is a classical source of information, while *Deprivation of maternal care*, by M. D. Ainsworth, R. G. Andry and others (WHO, 1962), contains a variety of viewpoints. R. S. Stearne's *Delinquent conduct and broken homes* (College and University P., 1964) describes a creditable empirical study, while *Brief separations*, by C. M. Heinicke and I. J. Westheimer (Longmans, 1965), includes some promising material.

One cannot leave the topic of developmental psychology without referring to the problem of the relative importance of heredity and environment in the development of criminal and other behaviours. In general, the crucial studies have been investigations of twins, and these are splendidly reviewed in P. Mittler's *The study of twins* (Penguin, 1971). They are also mentioned in *Genetic theory and abnormal behavior*, by D. Rosenthal (McGraw-Hill, 1970). Finally, the significance of 'critical periods' in the early stages of life should be touched on, and an admirable collection of readings relevant to this subject can be found in *Early experience and behaviour*, ed. G. Newton and S. Levine (C. C. Thomas, 1968).

Other social psychology topics

Two important topics are attitudes and group dynamics. An impressive selection of articles entitled *Attitudes* is edited by M. Jahoda and N. Warren (Penguin, 1966). Attitude change is of some concern to criminologists, since many rehabilitative programmes are designed to change the attitudes of delinquents or criminals. *Attitude change*, by C. A. Keisler and others (Wiley, 1969), covers much ground, while *Youthful offenders at Highfields*, by H. A. Weeks (U. of Michigan P., 1958), outlines changes in the attitudes of delinquent boys occurring as a result of group therapy. J. C. Glidewell's *Parental attitudes and child behavior* (C. C. Thomas, 1961) is relevant both to attitudes and to parent–child relationships (mentioned on p. 76). The existence of authoritarian attitudes has many criminological implications, and the classic in this field is *The authoritarian personality*, by T. W. Adorno and others (Harper, 1950). In order to obtain a balanced picture, this book should be consulted with *Studies in the scope and method of the authoritarian personality*, ed. M. Jahoda and R. Christie (Free Press, 1954).

Group dynamics, ed. D. Cartwright and A. Zander (3rd ed., Tavistock, 1968), is a standard reference work. The phenomena of conformity and deviance in small groups, as seen in, for instance, J. L. Freedman and A. N. Doob's *Deviancy: the psychology of being different* (Academic P., 1968) and *Conformity and deviation*, ed. I. A. Berg and B. M. Bass (Harper, 1961), is of particular interest to criminologists. Some of the most famous 'sociological' theories of delinquency seem to be based on hypotheses about interaction processes in small groups. This is certainly true of 'differential association', as expounded in the latest version of E. H. Sutherland and D. R. Cressey's textbook *Criminology* (8th ed., Lippincott, 1970). It also applies to some extent to the 'delinquent subculture' theories—for example, that described in *Delinquency and opportunity*, by R. A. Cloward and L. E. Ohlin (Free Press, 1960). These theories have been more fully discussed elsewhere in this book (Chapter 2). It should also be pointed out that many of the methods of group therapy (mentioned on p. 74) take cognisance of research in group dynamics. Finally, aspects of social psychology with obvious implications for the situational determinants of crime are described in *Social interaction*, by M. Argyle (Methuen, 1969). Another relevant volume is *The unresponsive bystander: Why doesn't he help?*, by B. Latané and J. M. Darley (Appleton, 1970).

EDUCATIONAL AND INDUSTRIAL PSYCHOLOGY

All aspects of industrial psychology are specified in A. Anastasi's admirably detailed *Fields of applied psychology* (Macmillan, 1966) and in *Applied psychology*, by J. M. Brown and others (McGraw-Hill, 1964). These two books are especially significant, because they both contain sections in which crime is treated as a problem in applied psychology. The major journals are the *Journal of Applied Psychology* (1917–), *Occupational Psychology* (1922–), *Personnel Psychology* (1948–), *Ergonomics* (1957–), the *Journal of Industrial Psychology* (1963–) and the *Journal of Engineering Psychology* (1962–). The first of these is the most likely to carry criminological articles. L. J. Cronbach's *Educational psychology* (2nd ed., 2nd imp., Hart-Davis, 1970) is a reputable textbook. The *Journal of Educational Psychology* (1910–) and the *British Journal of Educational Psychology* (1931–) both include papers of interest to criminologists, but *The Journal of Moral Education* (1971–) will perhaps prove even more fertile.

Although there are a number of criminology books which discuss industrial or educational psychology topics, it is very difficult positively to identify a work which is genuinely dependent on either field. *Social deviance*, by L. T. Wilkins (Tavistock, 1964), outlines some general concepts derived from operational research, while P. B. Weston's *Supervision in the administration of justice* (C. C. Thomas, 1965) is also concerned with industrial psychology topics such as supervision, training, management and work appraisal. Educational psychology can be glimpsed when problems of educating institutionalised delinquents and criminals are discussed, and when deviant behaviour in schools is considered. E. Stratta's *The education of borstal boys* (Routledge, 1970) and *Teach them to live: a study of education in English prisons*, by F. Banks (Parrish, 1958), fall into the former category, and G. J. Blackham's *The deviant child in the classroom* (Wadsworth, 1967) and R. H. Woody's *Behavioral problem children in the schools* (Appleton, 1969) in the latter.

SOURCES OF PSYCHOLOGICAL INFORMATION

Guides to the literature

Undoubtedly the finest post-war guide to the psychological literature can be found in *Professional problems in psychology*, by R. S. Daniel and C. M. Louttit (Prentice-Hall, 1953). *A Guide to the documentation of psychology*, by C. K. Elliott (Bingley, 1971), and *The student psychologist's handbook*, by T. R. Sarbin and W. C. Coe (Schenkman, 1969), are more limited in scope, but more up to date.

A moderately comprehensive guide is contained in *Sources of information in the social sciences*, ed. C. M. White (Bedminster P., 1964), while a rather less comprehensive but more critical guide is included in *A reader's guide to the social sciences*, ed. B. F. Hoselitz (rev. ed., Free Press, 1970).

Encyclopaedias

A new *Encyclopaedia of psychology*, ed. H. J. Eysenck and others (3 vols., Search P., 1972) has recently appeared. The entries vary greatly, from dictionary definitions to academic treatises. The six volumes edited by S. Koch entitled *Psychology: a study of a science* (McGraw-Hill, 1959-1963) are encyclopaedic in quality and of a uniformly high standard. However, the beginning student would probably be better advised to consult the psychological entries in the excellent *International encyclopaedia of the social sciences*, ed. D. L. Sills (Macmillan and Free Press, 1968).

Dictionaries

The best dictionary of psychology is in all probability that by H. B. and A. C. English entitled *A comprehensive dictionary of psychological and psychoanalytical terms* (Longmans, Green, 1958), although *A dictionary of psychology*, by J. Drever (rev. H. Wallerstein, Penguin, 1964) also has much to recommend it.

Bibliographies, book reviews, abstracts

The major bibliographical source in psychology is *Psychological Abstracts* (1927–   ), which contains non-evaluative summaries of the world's psychological literature. Recently G. K. Hall has published a *Cumulative author index to Psychological Index, 1894–1935, and Psychological Abstracts, 1927–1958* (5 vols.), together with 3 supplementary volumes covering the period 1959–1968, and a *Cumulative subject index to Psychological Abstracts, 1927–1960* (2 vols.), together with 1 supplementary volume covering the period 1961–1965. Between them, these 11 massive volumes cover virtually all the psychological literature ever published. Useful reviews of areas of psychology, together with large bibliographies, can be found in the *Annual Review of Psychology* (1950–   ). In addition, of course, all the books mentioned in the main part of this chapter contain bibliographies which can be used to direct further reading. Regrettably, the last separate 'Bibliography of bibliographies on psychology' seems to be C. M. Louttit's famous 1928 work (*Bulletin, National Research Council, National Academy of Sciences*, No. 65). However, bibliographies on psychology are indexed in *Psychological Abstracts*, as are reviews of the psychological literature.

The *Quarterly Checklist of Psychology* (1961–   ) is an ongoing bibliography of psychological books published. These are also listed in *Perceptual and Motor Skills* (1949–   ), and are indexed, but not normally abstracted, in *Psychological Abstracts*. The best annotated bibliography of psychological books is probably the *Harvard list of books in psychology*, ed. S. S. Stevens and G. Stevens (4th ed., Harvard U.P., 1971), although the *Reader's guide to books on psychology* (Library Association, 1962) is also useful. Psychological books are reviewed in many psychological journals, and *Contemporary Psychology* (1956–), noted for its witty and memorable headlines, is entirely devoted to this function. Psychological book reviews are indexed in the *Mental Health Book Review Index* (1956–); in 1969, the *Cumulative author-title index* for volumes 1–12 of this journal appeared (New York U. Council for Research on Bibliography). *A checklist of serials in psychology and allied fields*, by M. Tompkins and N. Shirley (Whitston, 1969), gives valuable information about virtually all psychological journals.

Dissertations

There appears to be no separate bibliography of psychological dissertations. *Dissertation Abstracts International* (1938–) contains long abstracts from most American dissertations, and all psychological entries in this publication are indexed in *Psychological Abstracts*. British dissertations are indexed in the *Index of Theses Accepted for Higher Degrees by the Universities of Great Britain and Ireland and the Council for National Academic Awards* (1950–).

Science Citation Index

Whereas most bibliographical methods permit searches backward in time from a particular article, the *Science Citation Index* (1961–) and, from 1973, *Social Sciences Citation Index* permit a search forward as well. For all articles published in the past, all articles published in the present which cite the past article in their bibliography are cited. Hence, it is possible to follow up any past article. Many psychological journals are covered.

Computer searches

The best method of searching the psychological literature in England is to use MEDLARS (see p. 12). A search using MEDLARS is based on a set of key words from MeSH (Medical Subject Headings). It is equivalent to searching *Index Medicus* (1960–), which covers many psychological journals. In the USA it is possible to search and retrieve, by computer, information contained in *Psychological Abstracts*.

Current research in progress

Psychological Abstracts tends to be a few months behind the published literature. *Current Contents* comes out almost simultaneously with the published literature, and consists of copies of the contents pages of journals. It appears in several parts, and those of interest to psychologists cover *Behavioral, Social and Educational Sciences* (1969–) and *Life Sciences* (1967–). However, the current published literature is itself some years behind the current research being carried out. In order to disseminate information about research in progress, a new journal entitled *Behavioral Science in Progress* started in 1971. Another way to find out about current research is to study the reports of conference proceedings in such professional journals as the *American Psychologist* (1946–) or the *Bulletin of the British Psychological Society* (1948–). Conference proceedings are sometimes published (e.g. *Proceedings of the 80th annual convention of the American Psychological Association,* 1972).

5

Alcoholism and crime—an introductory bibliography

Timothy Cook and *Celia Hensman*

HISTORICAL

For centuries there has been a commonly-held view that drinking and drunkenness are at the root of a substantial amount of law-breaking. Henry Fielding in his work *An enquiry into the causes of the late increase of robbers* (1751) commented on this view. Hogarth portrayed it. Dickens fictionalised it. Nineteenth-century social historians give us some authoritative comment on it. And two Government Reports of that period contain extensive impressionistic evidence on the possible link between drunkenness and the committing of crimes: the *Report from the Select Committee on Enquiry into Drunkenness* (1834) and *Report from the Select Committee on Habitual Drunkards* (1872), both reprinted by the Irish U.P. in 1968.

Discussion of the relationship between alcohol and crime figured frequently in nineteenth-century professional journals. For example, in 1866 W. S. Chipley wrote an article on 'Homicide and drunkenness' (*American J. Insanity*, **1** (21), 1–45). In 1900 W. E. Sullivan looked at 'Alcoholic homicide' (*Lancet*, **2**, 1821–1822). An invaluable bibliography of the very early alcoholism literature, reproduced by the (Canadian) Addiction Research Foundation in Toronto and only obtainable with difficulty in the UK, is E. Abderhalden's *Bibliographie ... über den Alkohol und Alkoholismus* (1904), originally published by Urban and Schwarzenberg, Berlin. This volume contains a wealth of world-wide references that help to provide a full historical perspective. Glancing through its pages, it is possible to see how soon academics as well as clinicians had begun to look at questions of drink and crime, often in relation to criminal responsibility and insanity. A brief but useful look at the relationship between drinking and crime in England is contained in J. J. Tobias's *Crime and industrial society in the 19th century* (Batsford, 1967). References of value, placed in a wider context, can be found in a recent edition of *The unknown Mayhew*, ed. E. Thompson and E. Yeo (Merlin P., 1971) and in B. Harrison's *Drink and the Victorians* (Faber, 1971). Four important and historically interesting books published during the eighteenth century are available to those with a good knowledge of German. These are J. H. B. Justi's *Grundsätze der Polizeiwissenschaft*, published in Göttingen in 1756; Jozef Sonnenfels's *Grundsätze der Polizhandlung und Finanz*, published in Vienna in 1765; Jan Peter Frank's *System einer vollständigen medizinischen Polizei*, the work of the first physician known to have shown an interest in medical police work, published towards the end of the eighteenth century; and Z. T. Hasztyho's *Diskum über die medizinische Polizei*, published in Bratislava–Lipsko in 1766.

DEFINITIONS

Already it is clear that various terms such as 'drinking', 'alcohol', 'drunkenness' and 'alcoholism' are frequently used very loosely. Early literature was rarely precise, and scientific definitions of what is really meant by the term 'drunkenness', for example, were rare indeed. Any attempt to establish a link between alcoholism and crime needs to include an attempt at the definition of alcoholism, otherwise the widely different concepts and definitions used in different studies make it difficult to compare the differing results. To understand some of the general problems relating to definitions of alcoholism, reference should be made to M. Keller's article 'Alcoholism: nature and extent of problem' (*Annals of American Academy of Political and Social Science*, 315, 1958), and a more recent work by D. L. Davies, 'Alcoholism: defining the problem' (*Update*, **3**, 885, 1971). For an overview of alcoholism in all its aspects, essential introductory reading is contained in N. Kessel and H. Walton's *Alcoholism* (Penguin, 1965). Wider aspects still are covered in D. Pittman and C. R. Snyder's *Society, culture* *and drinking patterns* (Wiley, 1962). See also H. Jones's *Alcohol addiction* (Tavistock, 1963).

CRIMINAL RESPONSIBILITY

An important issue in the relationship between alcoholism and crime is the extent to which criminal responsibility has been regarded by the Courts as being affected by intoxication. Most criminal law textbooks cover the subject, though often inadequately. Glanville Williams, in *Criminal law: the general part* (2nd ed., Stevens, 1961), provides a good review of cases in which drunkenness has been pleaded as a defence to crime in this country. The *Criminal Law Review* irregularly contains reference to current cases, as do the medico-legal notes in the *Quarterly Journal of Studies on Alcohol* (*Q.J.S.A.*) for other countries. Additional studies of importance are E. M. Scott's 'Alcoholism in criminal behaviour', in *Mental abnormality and crime*, ed. L. Radzinowicz and J. W. C. Turner (Macmillan, 1949); G. N. Thompson's 'Legal aspects of pathological intoxication' (*J. Social Theory*, **2**, 182–187, 1956); W. N. East's 'Medico-legal aspects of alcoholism' (*British J. Addiction*, **45**, 93–111, 1948); and F. A. Whitlock's *Criminal responsibility and mental illness* (Butterworths, 1963). Also note 'Some observations on the relation of alcohol to criminal insanity', by J. S. Hopwood and K. O. Milner (*British J. Inebriety*, **38**, 51–70, 1940). R. A. Moore's article 'Legal responsibility and chronic alcoholism' (*American J. Psychiatry*, **122**, 748–756, 1966) is a masterly review of US legal opinion and court decisions in which alcohol intoxication as a form of mental illness has been at issue, and includes an extensive bibliography. S. A. Kirbens's 'Chronic alcohol addiction and criminal responsibility' (*American Bar Association J.*, **54**, 877–883, 1968) has an equally extensive bibliography including historical references. The situation with regard to diminished responsibility in England and Scotland is fully illustrated in J. L. Edwards's chapter on 'Diminished responsibility' in E. W. Mueller's *Essays in Criminal Science* (Sweet and Maxwell, 1961). Still further back, the question of whether or not 'drunkenness' constitutes a form of insanity had dominated the literature, and the relevant parts of Isaac Ray's now classic *Treatise on the medical jurisprudence of insanity* (1838) have recently been put in their modern context in the USA in J. R. Quen's 'Isaac Ray on drunkenness' (*Bulletin Historical Medicine*, **41**, 342–348, 1967). An outline of intoxication as dealt with by the criminal law in Canada is given, along with a description of the modern courts' dealing with the intoxicated offender and the effects of alcohol on the individual offender, by S. M. Beck and G. E. Parker in 'The intoxicated offender: a problem of responsibility' (*Canadian Bar Review*, **45**, 563–609, 1966); see also G. G. Baird's 'Science and the legal responsibility of the drunkard' (*Q.J.S.A.*, **5**, 628–646, 1948).

STUDIES OF ALCOHOLIC OFFENDERS

Countless studies of alcoholics have been published which have elicited information about the criminal history, if any, of the groups under study. General investigations of samples of alcoholics frequently reveal some marginally relevant data. Usually, however, such studies in no way establish a relationship between offences admitted and alcohol intake, and often there is little evidence to show whether offences occurred before, during or after the onset of alcohol dependence. Indeed, repeated offences of drunkenness may be the only ones which we can safely assume are related to alcoholism itself. Studies of alcoholic populations reported in the volumes of the *Quarterly Journal of Studies on Alcohol* and in the *Classified Alcohol Archives* would therefore repay close attention. One European study of particular importance is C. Amark's 'A study in alcoholism' (*Acta Neurologia et Psychiatria Scandinavica*, Supplement 70, 1951).

General studies of offender populations have frequently investigated, among other things, the offender's drinking history. Often, however, findings are couched in rather general terms with reference to 'heavy drinking' and 'excessive drinking'. This means that, while an indication is certainly given about the probable proportion of alcoholic offenders, such studies cannot be relied on to indicate a definite causal link between alcoholism and crime. Works of importance which refer to this aspect include T. Michael and M. J. Adler's *Crime, law and social science* (Routledge, 1933); N. Morris's *The habitual criminal* (Longmans, 1951); D. J. West's *The habitual prisoner* (Macmillan, 1963) and his *The young offender* (Penguin, 1967); and K. Tornquist's *Persistent criminals* (Stockholm: Norstedt, 1966). Consideration of these studies suggests that about 30–40% of the *recidivist* population have a serious drinking problem. R. F. Sparks's study *Local prisons: the crisis in the English penal system* (Heinemann, 1971) is the most thorough in its investigation although, again, limited by being placed in a much wider context. F. E. Norris's 'The delinquent's attitude towards alcohol' (*British J. Inebriety*, **38**, 112–117, 1941) and L. B. Robinson and others' 'Psychiatric assessment of criminal offenders' (*Medicine, Science and Law*, **5**, 140–146, 1965) should also be mentioned. See also R. Walmsley's report *Steps from prison* (Inner London Probation and After-Care Service, 1972).

Turning now to studies of specific types of offenders, we again find references to drinking habits but not too much reliance can be placed on them, as terminology is often uncertain—'drinking at the time of the offence', for instance—and descriptions of drinking habits only form a small part of such studies. Many of the specific offender studies of the Institute of Criminology, Cambridge, fall into this category. Particularly worth noting are F. H. McClintock's *Crimes of violence* (Macmillan, 1964) and F. J. Odgers and F. H. McClintock's *Sexual offences*, ed. L. Radzinowicz (Macmillan, 1957). Another general study is *Criminal on the road*, by T. C. Willett (Tavistock, 1965), which examines six types of driving offences, one of which was driving under the influence of drink or drugs. It is probably true to say that most general studies of specific groups of offenders or inmates of specific institutions refer at some point directly or indirectly to drinking patterns.

ALCOHOLISM AND HOMELESSNESS

Another general area of research which often reveals links between drinking and criminal behaviour is the study of homeless men, on skid row or in various forms of destitution. American studies are the most prolific in this field. Once more they are for the most part general studies which report separately on drinking and criminal activity without necessarily correlating the two. The most comprehensive American study is *Skid Row in American cities* (Chicago: Community and Family Study Center, 1963), in which D. J. Bogue gives a wealth of detail and gives other references also. British studies have looked at homeless men in a variety of settings and should be included. Of particular importance are the National Assistance Board's Report on *Homeless single persons* (HMSO, 1966); G. Edwards and others' 'Census of a reception centre' (*British J. Psychiatry*, **114**, 1031–1039, 1968); G. Edwards and others' 'London's Skid Row' (*Lancet*, **1**, 249–252, 1966); I. C. Lodge Patch's 'Homeless men in London: demographic findings in a lodging house sample' (*British J. Psychiatry*, **118**, 313–317, 1971); R. J. Priest's 'Homeless men: a United States/United

Kingdom comparison' (*Proc. Royal Society of Medicine*, **63**, 441, 1970); and S. I. A. Laidlaw's *Glasgow common lodging houses and the people living in them* (Glasgow Corporation, 1956). A key American study of more specific content is R. Straus's 'Alcohol and the homeless man' (*Q.J.S.A.*, **7**, 360–404, 1946).

CRIMINALITY

Many attempts have been made to *review* the total problem of alcoholism and crime and the relationship between them. While these are not usually studies in themselves, they raise problems of concern to anyone attempting a specific investigation in this area. One of the most recent as well as the most thorough attempts, which contains an excellent bibliography, is 'Alcoholism and crime', by A. A. Bartholomew, in *Australia and New Zealand J. Criminology*, **1**, 70–98 (1968). This is one of the few reports that seriously tries to validate the findings by obtaining independent accounts of the prisoners' drinking histories. The proportion is high—43·4% of all serious offenders in whom alcohol played 'some real importance in their criminal behaviour'. Among the central articles also dealing with the general link between the two phenomena is M. J. Rowe's 'Alcohol and crime' (*J. Delinquency*, **4**, 135–151, 1919). J. McGeorge, in 'Alcohol and crime' (*Medicine, Science and Law*, **3**, 27–48, 1963) shows how different offences apparently involve vastly different proportions of alcoholic offenders. M. M. Glatt's 'Crime, alcohol and alcoholism' (*Howard J.*, **11**, 274–284, 1965) attempts to distinguish 'alcoholic criminals' from 'criminal alcoholics' and points to the common precipitating factors and personality characteristics of the two groups, and Glatt considers the younger offender in 'Alcoholism, crime and juvenile delinquency' (*British J. Delinquency*, **9**, 84–93, 1959). The issue of *Crime and Delinquency* for January 1963 (**9** (1)) is given over to this problem, introduced by an article by S. D. Bacon on 'Alcohol, alcoholism and crime' (pp. 1–14). Other works include: *Alcohol, alcoholism and crime*, ed. D. W. Hangley and N. A. Neiberg (Proceedings of Chatham Conference, Mass., 1962); H. T. Blane's 'Drinking and crime' (*Federal Probation*, **29** (2), 25–29, 1965); R. V. Seliger's 'Alcohol and crime' (*J. Criminal Law, Criminology and Police Science*, **44**, 438–441, 1953); H. Jones's 'Alcohol and corrections' (*Canadian J. Corrections*, **1**, 29–33, 1959); D. J. Myerson and J. Mayer's 'The origin, treatment and destiny of Skid Row alcoholic men' (*New England J. Medicine*, **275**, 419–425,

1966). See also an interesting but dated study by R. S. Banaym, 'Alcoholism and crime' (*Q.J.S.A.*, **2**, 686–716, 1942). Two European studies that can be referred to in particular are D. Wiklund's 'Alcoholism and crime: Swedish methods' (*Howard J.*, **7**, 121–126, 1947) and H. J. Krauweel's 'Drinking and criminality in the Netherlands' (*Q.J.S.A.*, **16**, 290–294, 1955).

We now turn to reports on investigations that have sought to examine the relationship between alcoholism and crime in specific groups of offenders. These studies either examine the problem generally or investigate specific offences with relation to the disease of alcoholism in the offender. With regard to the first and more general enquiries, early studies reported include A. A. Bartholomew and M. T. Kelly's Australian study, 'The incidence of a criminal record in 1,000 consecutive alcoholics' (*British J. Criminology*, **5**, 143–149, 1965); and, in the UK, A. P. R. Lewis's 'Alcohol as an alleged cause of loss of memory in young delinquents' (*British J. Inebriety*, **42**, 21–43, 1944). More recently, T. C. N. Gibbens and M. Silberman have made a valuable study of 'Alcoholism among prisoners' (*Psychological Medicine*, **1**, 73–78, 1970) and G. Edwards and others, discussing 'Drinking problems amongst recidivist prisoners' in *Psychological Medicine*, **5**, 388–399 (1971), review literature of importance and list five main methodological problems involved in all such studies. They also attempt to establish a 'dependency score' and, with this rigorous approach, produce a lower percentage than usually reported of men in prison with severe drinking problems. There are three early studies of note by W. N. East: 'The problem of alcohol and drug addiction in relation to crime' (*British J. Inebriety*, **37**, 55–73, 1939); 'Alcoholism and crime in relation to manic depressive disorder' (*Lancet*, **230**, 161–163, 1936); and 'Psychopathic personality and crime' (*J. Mental Science*, **91**, 428–446, 1945). G. Slot's 'Medico-legal aspects of drunkenness' (*British J. Inebriety*, **33**, 114–123, 1936) contains a full review of this aspect. Men recently out of prison were studied by J. Cooper and H. G. Maule in 'Alcoholism and crime: a study of the drinking and criminal habits of 50 discharged prisoners' (*British J. Addiction*, **61**, 201–212, 1963). For an interesting reflection on alcoholics in prison see E. Rubington's 'The alcoholic and the jail' (*Federal Probation*, **29** (2), June, 30–33, 1965). L. G. Measey's 'Alcohol and the Royal Naval Officer' (*British J. Criminology*, **13**, 280–283, 1973) is also worthy of note.

Habitual drunken offenders

When it comes to reviewing the studies on specific offences, possibly no group has been more investigated than the habitual drunkenness offender. As this condition is in some countries, such as Sweden and certain American states, no longer an offence, such studies may become merely of historical value; at present, however, this is not the case. The most important American works are D. J. Pittman and C. W. Gordon's *The revolving door: a study of the chronic police court inebriate* (Free Press, 1958) and E. Rubington's 'The chronic drunkenness offender' (*Annals American Academy of Political and Social Science*, **315**, 65–72, 1966). J. Hall's 'Drunkenness as a criminal offence' in *Q.J.S.A.*, **1**, 751–766 (1941) and *J. Criminal Law and Criminology*, **39**, 297–309 (1941) provide a relatively complete review not only of the numbers of drunkenness offences recorded in a number of US states but also of the status of drunkenness as an offence since its inauguration as such in English law in 1606. G. Forbes gives a further particularly useful early review which includes a historical sketch of controls of intoxication both in the UK and the USA in 'Drunkenness and the criminal law' (*Medical Press*, **223**, 74–77, 1950). In Scotland an important recent paper is one by R. A. W. Ratcliffe: 'Characteristics of those imprisoned in Scotland in 1965 on conviction for primarily alcoholic offences' (*Health Bulletin* (*Edinburgh*), **24**, 68–70, 1966). In England the subject has recently been exhaustively reviewed in the Home Office Working Party Report, *Habitual drunken offenders* (HMSO, 1971). The Proceedings of an international conference on the subject which contained a useful selection of papers were edited in 1969 by T. Cook, D. Gath and C. Hensman as *The drunkenness offence* (Pergamon). There is also an as yet unpublished study by H. D. Willcock, *Drinking offences in Great Britain* (Office of Population Censuses and Surveys). An invaluable American report is the President's Commission on Law Enforcement and Administration of Justice, *Task Force Report—Drunkenness* (US GPO, 1967). Finally, it is worth drawing attention to the considerable legal problem in the USA and the volume of recent literature as to whether it is lawful to arrest an alcoholic for being drunk in public if he or she is thought to have the disease of alcoholism. This literature is usefully reviewed by R. J. Driver in 'The U.S. Supreme Court and the chronic drunkenness offender' (*Q.J.S.A.*, **30**, 165–172, 1969) and by R. Slovenko in 'Alcoholism and the criminal law: scope of the problem' (*Bulletin of the Menninger Clinic*, **31**, 105–116, 1967).

Alcohol on the road

An equal or even greater amount of attention in the literature has been given to the drunken driving traffic offence, with an increasing number of studies examining the contribution of alcohol to the total problem of road safety. A relatively early study of key importance is that provided by W. S. Schmidt and R. G. Smart in 'Alcoholics, drinking and traffic accidents' (*Q.J.S.A.*, **20**, 631–644, 1959). Since the contribution of alcohol to the problem of road traffic has been the subject of conferences, national and international, over the past half-century, it is natural that examination of the role of alcohol in the total situation, the contribution attributable to alcoholics, the rate of conviction or reconviction of alcoholics including treated patients for this offence and the relative effectiveness of specific controls should appear in conference proceedings and be subject to research investigations. Thus, a full analysis of 'Driving under the influence of alcohol: comparative legislation relating to Scandinavia, Western Europe and a number of U.S. States' was published in *J. Forensic Medicine*, **9–13** (1962–1966). A small-scale study conducted in England was reported by N. I. Spriggs in *Medical Practitioner*, (933), 965–970, 1968. Other useful articles are by S. Freeman, 'The drinking driver' (*British Medical J.*, **2**, 1634–1636, 1964); M. L. Selzer, 'Alcoholism, mental illness and the drunk driver' (*American J. Psychiatry*, **20**, 326–331, 1964); M. M. Glatt, 'Alcoholism in impaired and drunken driving' (*Lancet*, **1**, 161–163, 1964); J. D. J. Havard, 'Road accidents and the drinking driver' (*New Scientist*, **23**, 24–26, 1964); and R. E. Popham, 'Alcoholism and traffic accidents' (*Q.J.S.A.*, **17**, 225–232, 1956). Havard reviewed alcohol in relation to road traffic in R. B. H. Gradwohl's *Legal medicine*, 2nd ed. by F. E. Camps (J. Wright, 1968), pp. 566–583. The results of the British Medical Association's deliberations on the subject are contained in a summary of its report on the 'Relation of alcohol to road abuse' (*British Medical J.*, **1**, 269–272, 1960).

Other crimes and criminals

Study of the relationship between alcoholism and specific offences has tended, apart from the two categories above, to be confined to the more serious offences. The authors have not been able to discover, for example, investigations of alcoholism and housebreaking or of alcoholism and theft. An essential article concerning sexual offences is 'Alcohol and forcible rape' (*British J. Addiction*, **62**, 219–232, 1967), in which M. Amir looks usefully at the previous literature in this area and develops the notion of a situation being 'alcoholised', i.e. offenders and victims both being under the influence of alcohol. A valuable study on attempted suicide (which was a crime at the time of the study) is I. R. C. Batchelor's 'Alcoholism and attempted suicide' (*J. Mental Science*, **100**, 451–461, 1954). There have been several key studies on violent death, notably H. Gillies's 'Murder in the West of Scotland' (*British J. Psychiatry*, **111**, 1087–1094, 1965); D. M. Spain and others' 'Alcohol and violent death' (*J. American Medical Association*, **146**, 334–335, 1951); M. E. Wolfgang and R. B. Strohm's 'The relationship between alcohol and criminal homicide' (*Q.J.S.A.*, **17**, 411–425, 1956); and L. C. Le Roux and L. S. Smith's 'Violent deaths and alcoholic intoxication' (*J. Forensic Medicine*, **11**, 131–147, 1944). See also T. P. Morris and L. Blom-Cooper's *A calendar of murder* (M. Joseph, 1964) and their *Criminal homicide in England since 1957* (mimeog., Legal Research Unit, Dept. of Sociology, Bedford College, 1969). See also references to case histories of particular interest in 'Drink, epilepsy, murders and amnesia' (*British Medical J.*, **1**, 656, 1960). R. S. Banay's article on 'Alcohol and aggression', in *Alcohol, Science and Society* (*Q.J.S.A. Supplement*, 1945), is also of value, giving much tabulated material relating to a number of countries. With reference to child abuse and 'child molesting', alcoholism is still considered the greatest contributor to this offence and several references can be found by means of the Classified Alcohol Archive cards described at the end of this chapter.

There have been important psychiatric investigations of offender populations which have looked, among other things, at family histories of alcoholism in offenders, and which have obtained valuable general information relevant to our specific topic. Important studies include R. V. Seliger's 'Psychiatric orientation of the alcoholic criminal' (*J. American Medical Association*, **129**, 421–424, 1945); S. B. Guze and others' 'Psychiatric illness and crime with particular reference to alcoholism: a study of 233 criminals' (*J. Nervous and Mental Disorder*, **134** (16), 512–521, 1962); C. B. Robinson and others' 'The psychiatric assessment of criminal offenders' (*Medicine, Science and Law*, **5**, 140–146, 1965); and S. B. Guze and others' 'Psychiatric illness in families of convicted criminals: a study of 519 first degree relatives' (*J. Diseases of the Nervous System*, **28**, 651–659, 1967).

Certain sub-groups of offenders have been particularly investigated and deserve special mention, notably studies of women offenders who are also alcoholics. Although a minority group in the entire offender population, there is a growing literature on these, and in addition to East's classic article (1939, op. cit., see p. 89) the following reports should be noted: E. S. Lisansky's 'Alcoholism in women: social and psychological concomitants' (*Q.J.S.A.*, **18**, 588–591, 1957); D. J. Myerson's 'Clinical observations on a group of alcoholic prisoners with special reference to women' (*Q.J.S.A.*, **20**, 555–572, 1959); D. J. Myerson and others' 'A report of a rehabilitation programme for alcoholic women prisoners' (*Q.J.S.A.*, Supp. 1, 151–157, 1961); M. Woodside's 'Women drinkers committed to Holloway Prison in February 1960' (*British J. Criminology*, **1**, 221–235, 1961); M. J. Cramer and E. Blacker's 'Early and late problem drinkers among female prisoners' (*J. Health and Human Behaviour*, **4**, 283–290, 1963) and 'Social class and drinking experience of female drunkenness offenders' (*J. Health and Human Behaviour*, **7**, 276–283, 1966); and T. C. N. Gibbens and S. Dell's 'Remands of women offenders for medical reports' (*Medicine, Science and Law*, **11**, 117–127, 1971). A useful 'Study of teenagers arrested for drunkenness' has been made by W. W. Wattenberg and J. B. Moir in *Q.J.S.A.*, **7**, 426–436 (1956). See also N. Goodman's 'Manchester Senior Attendance Centre' (*British J. Criminology*, **5**, 288–295, 1965). Individual histories can also provide illuminating material. Supreme among these is Tony Parker's *The unknown citizen* (Penguin, 1966). See also J. Gunn's 'The recovered alcoholic—case presentation', in *The drunkenness offence* (see p. 90, op. cit., 67–75, 1969) and R. J. Blackburn's *I am an alcoholic* (Allan Wingate, 1959).

TREATMENT

The question of treatment for the alcoholic offender is a thorny one, and the literature on it, both descriptive and evaluative, is very extensive. Key articles relating to various situations in the penal spectrum are: M. Margolis and others' 'Psychotherapy with alcoholic offenders' (*Q.J.S.A.*, **25**, 88–99, 1964); A. A. McCormick's 'Penal and correctional aspects of the alcohol problem' (*Q.J.S.A.*, **2**, 241–259, 1941); D. M. Gallant and others' 'Enforced clinic treatment of paroled criminal alcoholics: a pilot evaluation' (*Q.J.S.A.*, **29**, 77–83, 1968); S. B. Guze and D. P. Cantwell's 'Alcoholism: parole observations and criminal recidivism' (*American J. Psychiatry*, **122**, 757–762, 1966); and L. N. Roth and others' 'Prison adjustment of alcoholic felons' (*Q.J.S.A.*, **32**, 382–392, 1971). D. J. Pittman's 'New approaches to the public drunkenness offender: an international over-view', from the *Proceedings of the 15th International Institute, Budapest, 1969* (Lausanne: Int. Council on Alcohol and the Addictions, 1970), is particularly valuable also. Some of these articles raise the complex issues of *compulsion*. Important English articles relating to this issue are that by P. D. Scott in *British Medical J.*, **1**, 291, with replies on pp. 358–359 and 480–481 (1966) and T. Bewley's 'Treatment of compulsorily detained alcoholics (*British J. Addiction*, **62**, 241–247, 1967). A useful editorial round-up on the historical evolution of answers to this problem is contained in 'The 19th century statutory provision for the treatment of alcoholism' (*British Medical J.*, **1**, 992–1052, 1966).

More recently, hostels or half-way houses have been used as one treatment method for homeless alcoholics often with a criminal record. See particularly articles by E. Rubington: 'The halfway house for the alcoholic' (*Mental Hygiene*, **51** (4), 1967); 'The future of the halfway house' (*Q.J.S.A.*, **31**, 350–361, 1970); and 'Referral past treatment contacts and length of stay in a halfway house' (*Q.J.S.A.*, **31**, 659–688, 1970). An English project, 'The Rathcoole experiment: the first years at a hostel for vagrant alcoholics', has been described by T. Cook and others in *British Medical J.*, **1**, 240–242 (1968) and in T. Cook and B. Pollack's *In place of Skid Row* (N.A.C.R.O., Reprint No. 4, 1971).

PERIODICALS

The references cited above will indicate most of the journals in which the problems of alcoholism and its relation to criminality are regularly discussed. The leading ones are the *British Journal of Addiction* (1903–); the *Quarterly Journal of Studies on Alcohol* (1940–), and the associated *Classified Archives of the Alcohol Literature*, a set of which is housed in the Medical Council on Alcoholism's library in London; and the *International Journal of the Addictions* (1966–). Articles also appear fairly frequently in many of the criminological journals listed at the end of Chapter 2 on sociological aspects, and the psychiatric periodicals mentioned in Chapter 3. Another regular publication is the Proceedings of the Annual Conferences organised by the International Council on Alcohol and the Addictions, P.O. Box 1400, Lausanne, Switzerland.

ABSTRACTS

There is no abstracting service specialising in alcoholism, but the leading criminological, medical and psychological abstracting journals provide, between them, a good coverage (see Chapters 1 (pp. 9–12), 3 (pp. 48–60) and 4 (pp. 80–81)).

BIBLIOGRAPHIES

The most substantial bibliographies are R. J. Gibbins's *Chronic alcoholism and alcohol addiction: a survey of current literature* (Toronto: Alcoholism Research Foundation, 1953) and the 31-language *International bibliography of studies on alcohol*, ed. M. Keller (New Brunswick, N.J.: Rutgers Center of Alcohol Studies, 1966), with a separate volume of indexes (1968). The bibliography is arranged chronologically, with an insufficiently detailed subject index and an author index. H. M. Bahr has compiled *Disaffiliated man: essays and bibliography on Skid Row, vagrancy and outsiders* (Toronto U.P., 1970), and some typescript lists of references are available from the Cambridge Institute of Criminology.

STATISTICS

The Home Office, and the Scottish Home and Health Department, publish yearly figures of drunkenness convictions (*Offences of drunkenness*) in which the total drunkenness offences are broken down by sex, age and geographical area. Their annual *Criminal statistics* include figures for offences by publicans and others against the liquor licensing laws, and the punishments imposed; and some of the figures for *Offences relating to motor vehicles* are also relevant. All are published by HMSO, in London and Edinburgh, respectively.

The Christian Economic and Social Research Foundation, London, publishes an annual interpretation of the previous year's drunkenness and drunken driving statistics, with comments relating them to those of previous years.

Reference should perhaps be made to J. Zacune and C. Hensman's *Drugs, alcohol and tobacco: the problem and the response* (Heinemann Medical, 1971). This includes an analysis of available data on the production, control, and normal and abnormal use of alcohol; and treatment, prevention and facilities for education and rehabilitation.

6

Introduction to the literature of drug dependence

J. H. Willis

INTRODUCTION

Drug addiction is a complex phenomenon which generates heat, invites speculation and at times appears to defy analysis as fast as it grows. The literature has expanded far beyond the limit of information saturation at a rate which may be compared with the growth rate of the literature on schizophrenia, where publications and clear understanding often seem to be in inverse proportion.

In writing about addiction, doctors stress its medical aspects, lawyers its legal aspects, and sociologists its social aspects; but while everyone pays lip service to the general desirability of multidisciplinary studies, there is yet no easy way through a maze of half-truths, repeated anecdote and biased or semi-biased observations.

Obviously, the criminology student has special needs—he or she needs a clear guide to the interrelations between drug usage and crime. But even this is not simple—for instance, a recent bibliography in *Contemporary Drug Problems*, (2) (1972) listed over 25 American legal journals in all of which important papers about drug abuse and crime have appeared in the last year. However, one has to start somewhere, so it may at this point be useful to clarify certain terms that are used—paraphrasing the definitions recommended by the World Health Organisation in the *16th Report* of its Expert Committee on Drug Dependence (WHO technical report series No. 407, 1969).

DEFINITIONS

A drug is defined as any substance which when taken into the living organism may modify one or more of its functions. In medical practice this covers a wide range of therapeutic substances: antibiotics as used in treating infections, antimetabolites in leukemia, insulin in diabetes, sedatives, hypnotics, tranquillisers, etc. In fact, as far as addiction is concerned, the drugs involved are those which may be broadly categorised as 'mind altering', i.e. they can affect the person's thinking, feeling and perception or behaviour—or indeed any combination of these.

Drug abuse is defined as sporadic intermittent drug use which may be excessive and is so regarded because it is inconsistent with use in acceptable medical practice. This includes such examples as people who become 'high' on sleeping pills, stimulants and hallucinogenic drugs.

Drug dependence (*addiction*) is defined as a state which may be either physically or psychologically determined—or both—in which a person's continued taking of the drug leads him to a state where he is unable to stop doing so either because he gets sick (withdrawal symptoms) or because he values the subjective effect of the drug and feels unable to go without it. States of dependence or addiction may be classified by naming the type of drug involved, e.g. morphine type, barbiturate type, etc. Other characteristics of dependence include craving, which is not always present and when it is may be variable. Also worthy of mention are the states of personal involvement with drug taking which may lead to crucial changes in life style—'subcultural' drug use, etc. The term 'dependence' is preferred to addiction, since people found it hard to agree on a definition of addiction but in practice the terms 'addiction' and 'dependence' are to be regarded as synonyms. Since the non-medical student will usually have little or no knowledge of the medical and pharmacological issues involved, it is necessary briefly to refer to definitions and guidelines that may aid him to arrive at the topic armed with some basic ideas about the 'drug-related' aspects of drug addiction.

Clearly drug addiction is not a purely medical phenomenon; rather it appears to be the end product of a variety of factors in which drug activity itself may appear at times almost to be irrelevant though remaining the final expression of a confluence of social, psychological and personal vectors.

In considering drug addiction it should be remembered that the crucial topical aspects of the problem are primarily concerned with a special variety of drug addiction, namely the increasing incidence and prevalence of hedonistic drug taking in Western society by an increasingly youthful population which is predominantly male. The 'therapeutic' addicts, the solitary neurotic drug takers and the middle-aged sleeping-pill and tranquilliser addicts, though numerous, are not involved, by and large, in criminal acts.

GENERAL

A good standard guide to drugs in general and their action is to be found in *A dictionary of drugs*, by R. B. Fisher and G. A. Christie (Paladin, 1971). This provides a useful glossary of contemporary pharmacology for the non-scientific reader. An excellent reference book for both scientific terms and current addicts' jargon is *Drugs from A to Z: a dictionary*, by Richard Lingeman (Allen Lane, 1970). Another interesting work is *Psychopharmacology: dimensions and perspectives*, ed. C. R. B. Joyce (Tavistock, 1971). Although highly technical in certain chapters, the section by Blum on 'The sociology of drug use' is a mine of varied information with the added bonus of an extensive bibliography (over 100 references). There is also an excellent chapter on the history of psychopharmacology by A. Horden. A simple guide to drug dependence in general is *Drug dependence*, by J. H. Willis (Faber, 1969). This attempts to give a bird's eye view of the topic in relatively non-technical language. An excellent over-all review of drug dependence is contained in the *Interim report* of the Canadian Government Commission of Inquiry into the Non-medical Uses of Drugs (Ottawa: Information Canada, 1970; published by Penguin as *The non-medical uses of drugs*, 1971); this is comprehensive, clear and a valuable source work. Other reliable straightforward introductions to the subject include *Drugs*, by Peter Laurie (Penguin, 1967); *Social problems of drug abuse*, by F. Dawtry (Butterworths, 1968); *Drug dependence*, by Antony Wood (Corporation of Bristol and Bristol Council of Social Services, 1969); *The Release report on drug offenders and the law*, by C. Coon and R. Harris (Sphere, 1970); *Drug addiction* (Office of Health Economics, 1967); *The pleasure-seekers: the drug crisis, youth and society*, by Joel Fort (Bobbs-Merrill, 1969); *Drug addiction*, by L. Kolb (C. C. Thomas, 1962); *The drug scene*, by D. B. Louria (McGraw-Hill, 1968); *Narcotics and narcotic addiction*, by D. W. Maurer and V. H. Vogel (3rd ed., C. C. Thomas, 1967); *Drugs and human behaviour*, by G. Claridge (Allen Lane, 1970); *Where on drugs*, ed. Beryl McAlhone (Cambridge: Advisory Centre for Education, 1970); and *Drugs, society and personal choice*, by H. and O. J. Kalant (Paperjacks, 1971).

HISTORICAL

Since Man has long shown a conspicuous tendency to self-medication, it is not surprising that his excessive zeal in this direction has for long been a subject for social and literary comment not only in scientific articles but also in plays, satire, etc. The problems of casual and directed self-medication have been reviewed by authors such as M. Mintz in *The therapeutic nightmare* (Houghton Mifflin, 1965) and G. Johnson in *The pill conspiracy* (Sherbourne, 1967). The pharmaceutical industry in Britain has been explored by William Breckon in *The drug makers* (Eyre Methuen, 1972) and the legal and medical aspects of the thalidomide tragedy by H. Sjöström and R. Nilsson in *Thalidomide and the power of the drug companies* (Penguin, 1972). Two excellent historical perspectives are given in *The pursuit of intoxication*, by Andrew Malcolm (Addiction Research Foundation Books, 1971) and *Unreason in an age of reason* by Griffith Edwards (Royal Society of Medicine, 1971). The short and provocative *Mystification and drug misuse*, by Henry Lennard and Associates (Harper and Row, 1972), is highly recommended.

Creative writers have for years recorded their drug-induced experiences—two classic examples being Thomas De Quincey's *Confessions of an English opium eater* (originally published in 1822) and Baudelaire's *Les paradis artificiels: opium et haschisch* (originally published in 1860; English translation by N. Cameron, Weidenfeld, 1960). More recent works include A. Huxley's observations on hallucinogenic drugs in *Doors of perception* (Chatto, 1954), and books such as *The naked lunch*, by William Burroughs (Corgi, 1968), and *Cain's book*, by Alexander Trocchi (Calder, 1963). An account of drug use and imprisonment for drug possession is given by Brian Barritt in *Whisper* (Whisper promotions, 1971). An excellent synthesis of the history of 'creative' drug use and opiate use in Britain is to be found in *Opium and the creative imagination*, by Althea Hayter (Faber, 1968). This work collates almost all the information presented in the works previously described and is an invaluable source of reference to classic historical works. The changing official attitude is reflected in the two *Reports* of the Interdepartmental Committee on Drug Addiction, under the chairmanship of Lord Brain (HMSO, 1961 and 1965).

EPIDEMIOLOGY

Epidemiology is an area of prime concern for the criminologist, since addiction is a topic frequently viewed in distorted perspective and commented on in emotional terms nourished by unverifiable assertion. There is an expanding literature on this from American sources. American experience cannot be ignored, although transcultural comparisons are notoriously difficult to make. *Narcotics*, ed. D. M. Wilner and G. G. Kassebaum (McGraw-Hill, 1965), provides a comprehensive coverage of the American situation and there is a good chapter by Winick dealing with the epidemiology of American drug use. Further information of this sort is clearly set out in *Narcotics and Drugs*—the Task Force Report of the President's Commission and Law Enforcement and Administration of Justice Commission (US GPO, 1967). The main part of this work—Appendices A1, A2 and A3, which cover mind-altering drugs, dangerous behaviour and social policy, by Richard Blum and colleagues—contains an extensive review of the topic, valuable commentary and a wide bibliography. There is also a clear account of the epidemiology of drug abuse. One of the most clear-headed accounts of the American drug scene is in the recent *Dealing with drug abuse: a report to the Ford Foundation* (Macmillan, 1972).

The epidemiology of drug abuse in the UK has been described in a widening range of scientific papers but the whole area has now been reviewed in a definitive fashion by J. Zacune and C. Hensman in *Drugs, alcohol and tobacco in Great Britain* (Heinemann Medical, 1971). This is absolutely basic reading and should be invaluable for criminologists and sociologists—indeed anyone with any serious interest in the topic. It is concise, clearly written and free from bias. Earlier attempts to review this topic in the UK have, in general, been sketchy and often inaccurate, although *The drug scene in Great Britain*, by M. M. Glatt and others (Arnold, 1967), provides a valuable starting point in this direction.

Although readers will no doubt be mindful of the warnings about statistical information given in Chapter 10, some information may be obtained from a document issued annually by the Drugs Branch of the Home Office: *Report to the United Nations by H.M. Government ... on the working of the international treaties on narcotic drugs.*

A recent excellent survey of the epidemiology of opiate dependence in the USA is that by J. C. Ball and C. D. Chambers, *The epidemiology of opiate addiction in the United States* (C. C. Thomas, 1970).

SOCIOLOGICAL ASPECTS

Again, there is an extensive literature dealing with US experience, but as yet little from the UK sources. A start in this direction has been made by Jock Young in *The drugtakers* (Paladin, 1971. Paperback: Panther). A valuable source book of sociological and demographic data from America is to be found in *Social and psychological factors in opiate addiction*, ed. A. S. Meyer (Columbia University: Bureau of Applied Social Research, 1952). This is a review of research findings and an annotated bibliography set out in the form of tabulated data and summary. Despite its age, it still provides a mass of hard data about American experience. There is as yet no recent successor to it.

A more recent review of the sociological aspects of drug addiction in the USA is *Narcotics, delinquency and social policy: the road to H*, by I. Chein and colleagues (Tavistock, 1964). This book describes the results of a research study into the epidemiology and sociology of adolescent drug use in New York and is particularly relevant in its findings and commentaries on the relationship of drugs and criminology.

One of the most influential writers on sociological aspects of drug addiction is undoubtedly Alfred Lindesmith, two of whose works are to be regarded as basic texts in addiction and its relationships to social psychology and the law. The first is *Opiate addiction* (Principia P., 1947; rev. as *Addiction and opiates*, Aldine, 1968); and the second, *The addict and the law* (Indiana U.P., 1965). In *Opiate addiction* he propounds a theory of addiction which provides a good hypothetical model, while the second work deals extensively and critically with the place of the addict vis-à-vis the law in America, the history of legal intervention and a provocative commentary on addiction and criminality.

Another important sociological contribution is made by R. A. Cloward and L. E. Ohlin in *Delinquency and opportunity: a theory of delinquent gangs* (Free Press, 1960). The authors relate drug addiction to the concepts of anomie, alienation and retreatism. A succinct review of this area is to be found in *Drug addiction: physiological, psychological and sociological aspects*, by D. P. Ausubel (Random House, 1958).

The most encyclopaedic works so far available are *Society and drugs: social and cultural observations*, by R. Blum and associates (Jossey-Bass, 1969), and the companion volume on *Students and drugs* (also 1969). These two works are extensive, authoritative and an absolute mine of information.

TREATMENT

The use of the word 'treatment' implies acceptance of a medical model of addiction, since by definition treatment is a procedure aimed at modifying the course of an illness. For a variety of reasons, some of them good, others not so good, the addictive states are regarded as being, if not illnesses, at least sick behaviour for the basic reason of their self-destructive nature.

However, even cursory examination of 'treatment' of addiction reveals that this is a process which strays far from a strictly medical or psychiatric model and may fairly be applied to any measure aimed at modifying the addictive state.

To be sure, there are strictly medical aspects of treatment, e.g. those involving the use of medication to allay withdrawal sickness, to block craving for drugs and to relieve abnormal mental states induced by drugs, but these are fairly clearly defined and to a certain extent limited. However, the basis of treatment as written about and commented on has to do with the application of sociological and psychological forces to the addictive state and the individual involved in it. Perhaps the term 'treatment' might be better reserved for the more strictly medical and psychiatric aspects and the term 'rehabilitation' applied to the process mentioned.

Modern trends in drug dependence and alcoholism, ed. R. Philipson (Butterworths, 1970), provides a definitive chapter on treatment by Philip H. Connell. There is also a very good chapter on New York experience by Henry Brill and others on legal control of drug abuse in the USA and the UK. *The tunnel back: Synanon*, by L. Yablonsky (Macmillan, 1965), gives a good account of the Synanon adaptation of therapeutic community techniques. There are also excellent chapters on treatment in *The scientific basis of drug dependence*, ed. Hannah Steinberg (Livingstone, 1969). Marie Nyswander's book *The drug addict as patient* (Grune and Stratton, 1956) is thoughtful and informative.

ADDICTION AND CRIME

Drug users tend to be crime-prone people. Usually the fact of addiction implies an illegal status, since society does not usually condone the free use of mind-altering drugs outside defined medical settings. Hence, unless an addict is so because of a medically induced addiction, he is at some stage or another obliged to obtain drugs illicitly; and, depending on which society he lives in, his illicit career will be either aggravated or diminished by the sanctions imposed by that society.

Oddly enough, in America, usually credited with a 'hard line' attitude towards addiction, the drug user is not automatically placed outside the law. Indeed an attempt to do so was revoked by the US Supreme Court in *Robinson v. California* (1962). Here the US Supreme Court argument was that it was unconstitutional to regard an addict as anything but a sick person—hence, it would be a 'cruel and unusual punishment' to imprison him, in the same way that it would be to imprison a man because he had pneumonia. Extracts from the judgement are given in F. J. Remington's *Cases and materials on criminal law and its procedure* (Mundelein, Ill.: Callaghan, 1969).

Although drugs are often credited with inducing people to behave in a criminal way, the back up evidence for this is nowhere as clear as in the case of alcohol, whose role in road and traffic accidents and in homicide has been clearly demonstrated in many studies.

Works dealing specifically with addiction and crime are thin on the ground. Most of this information has either to be extracted from sociological texts or found in certain papers. Happily the British situation has been remedied by the recent publication of *Drug abuse and personality in young offenders*, by R. Cockett (Butterworths, 1971). This book describes the findings of a large-scale survey of young male offenders on remand. It is to be regarded as required reading, particularly for criminologists, as it contains not only hard data but also sensible discussion about the possible relationships of drugs usage to crime in Britain. The text is clear and the bibliography extensive.

An international review of the problem, with bibliographical references, is given in the UN *Bulletin on Narcotics*, **24** (4) (1972) and **25** (1) (1973).

The English legal position, and the extent of implementation of the *Misuse of Drugs Act 1971*, is reviewed in *Criminal Law Rev.* (December 1972) by R. I. E. Card.

Much of the available literature is in the form of periodical articles—often from North America—so that while they have relevance on the British scene, they should be read with an awareness of the differences in drug legislation. These are indicated by R. Card in 'Aspects of British drug legislation' (*U. of Toronto Law J.*, **20**, 88, 1970). Much attention has been given in the USA to the possibility of combating addiction otherwise than through the criminal law enforcement process—for example, in 'Civil commitment of narcotic addicts' (*Yale Law J.*, **76**, 1160, 1967). General articles on crime and addiction include J. O'Donnell's 'Narcotic addiction and crime' (*Social Problems*, **13**, 374, 1966); R. Blum's 'Drugs, behaviour and crime' (*Annals of the American Academy of Political and Social Sciences*, **374**, 135, 1967); and C. Winick's 'Drug addiction and crime' (*Current History*, **52**, 349, 1967). A legal point of view is given in 'Heroin, marijuana and crime: a socio-legal analysis' (*St John's Law Review*, **45**, 119, 1970) and the more specific question of criminal responsibility is considered by G. Parker in 'Criminal law—police practices—the relevance of entrapment as a defence—public duty as negativing *mens rea*' (*Canadian Bar Review*, **48**, 178, 1970) and from a British standpoint by D. Napley in 'Drugs and criminal responsibility' (*British J. Addiction*, **63**, 83, 1968). Further aspects are dealt with by, for example, McMorrisse in 'Can we punish for acts of addiction?' (*American Bar Association J.*, **54**, 1081, 1968) and, with reference to the particular problems posed by homicide, in 'Drunkenness, drugs and manslaughter' (*Criminal Law Review*, **132**, 1970); and E. Ellwood's article on 'Assault and homicide associated with amphetamine abuse' (*American J. Psychiatry*, **127**, 1170, 1971). Another important factor is international narcotics control, the subject of an article by I. G. Waddell in *American J. International Law*, **64**, 310 (1970).

CANNABIS

In this country, as in the USA, the majority of drug-related offences involve the possession and sale of cannabis; therefore its possible relationships to criminality may be misleading, since cannabis occupies a special place in substance abuse. Although classified by international agreement as a narcotic drug, it is clearly not to be regarded under the same heading as opiates or central stimulants. The topic of cannabis use, which has aroused extremes of feeling one way or the other, is now more clearly understood, but debate continues over such aspects as its relationship to further drug use and its place in criminal behaviour.

Long-term cannabis effects are the subject of speculation and research, although the latter is hampered by the illegal status of the substance. To date, certainly the most monumental work on the subject is the Report of the Indian Hemp Drugs Commission (1894). This work, in several volumes, attempted to examine various supposed cannabis effects, including that which was supposed to relate to criminal behaviour. It is not an easy work to obtain—libraries such as that of the Royal Society of Medicine have it on their shelves. It is written in clear Victorian prose, which contrasts very well with present-day jargon. It has recently been republished in America (Mellifont, 1971).

A valuable recent summary of cannabis and its place in drug abuse and relations to criminality is to be found in *An interim guide to the cannabis (marihuana) literature*, by O. J. Kalant (1968), published by the Addiction Research Foundation, Toronto. This is a clear and comprehensive review of the literature and as such is highly recommended. Two American works of relevance are Helen Nowlis's book *Drugs on the college campus* (Doubleday, 1969), which provides a useful guide to campus cannabis use and is a good reflection of the change in attitude towards cannabis by young Americans, and *Marijuana in Latin America: the threat it constitutes*, by P. O. Wolff (Linacre P., 1949). This latter tends to be anecdotal and was for years regarded as an authoritative work. It is recommended for a negative reason in that its emotional title is a good guide to the prevalence of the climate of unreason that can surround any drug that has an illegal status.

Perhaps the most recent succinct and useful account of cannabis is a British Home Office publication—*Cannabis: report by the Advisory Committee on Drug Dependence*: Chairman, Sir E. Wayne; chairman of sub-committee, Baroness Wootton (HMSO, 1968). Appendix 1, by Sir Aubrey Lewis, is a model of informed good sense. Other useful works include The First Report of the National Commission on Marihuana and Drugs of Abuse—*Marihuana: a signal of misunderstanding* (US GPO, 1972), which is timely, informal and full of good sense, as is *Marijuana and health: a report to the Congress from the Secretary, Department of Health*

Education and Welfare (US GPO, 1971). Two articles about cannabis that are well worth reading are 'Man and marijuana', by G. S. Chopra (*International J. Addictions*, **4**, 215, 1969), and 'Marijuana and the assassins—an etymological investigation', by D. Castro (*International J. Addictions*, **5**, 747, 1970). Another good review of marijuana is *The marijuana papers*, ed. D. Solomon (Bobbs-Merrill, 1966). This contains among other things a slightly shortened version of Mayor La Guardia's Commission Report on Marijuana, 1938. Other recommended works include: F. Goode's *The marijuana smokers* (Basic Books, 1970); J. Kaplan's *Marijuana: the new prohibition* (World Publishing, 1970); P. R. Bloomquist's *Marijuana—the second trip* (Collier-Macmillan, 1972); D. E. Smith's *The new social drug: cultural, medical and legal perspectives on marijuana* (Prentice-Hall, 1970); Lester Grinspoon's *Marijuana reconsidered* (Bantam Books, 1971), probably the best of the lot; Charles Tart's *On being stoned: a psychological study of marijuana intoxication* (Science and Behavioural Books, 1971); and Michael Schofield's *The strange case of pot* (Penguin, 1971).

BIBLIOGRAPHIES AND ABSTRACTS

The extensive literature of addiction has not yet been well served by bibliographers, but the New York Public Library has compiled 'A commentary and annotated bibliography on the relationship between narcotics, addiction and crime' (*Municipal Library Reference Notes*, 1968 (1)). A new bibliography and its supplement are, however, now available as *Drugs of addiction and non-addiction, their use and abuse: a comprehensive bibliography 1960–69*, by Joseph Menditto (Whitston, 1970) and *Drug abuse bibliography for 1970*, by J. C. Advena (Whitston, 1971). There is also Kalant's bibliography referred to above in the section on cannabis.

Until *Drug Dependence* (1972–) provided a specialist abstracting service, it was necessary to depend on the criminological and medical services, and to some extent the psychological and sociological ones, which have been referred to in the chapters on sociological and psychiatric aspects.

PERIODICALS

The basic journals, providing a regular flow of information, are the *British Journal of Addiction* (1903–), *the Quarterly Journal of Studies on Alcohol* (1940–) and the *International Journal of the Addictions* (1966–). A newcomer is the quarterly legal journal *Contemporary Drug Problems* (1972–), published by Martin Greenberg–Federal Legal Publications Inc., 95 Merton Street, New York, N.Y. 10014. This is an interdisciplinary journal which should be of special interest to lawyers and criminologists. *Drugs and Society* (1971–) is aimed at a more general readership, but in-includes penological implications; it is published by Macmillans and edited by the Institute for the Study of Drug Dependence, London, which is building up a useful library.

Occasional articles on addiction appear in criminological, medical and psychiatric journals, especially in the late 1960s.

An international perspective is provided by the UN *Bulletin on Narcotics* (1949–).

7

The treatment of offenders

A. E. Bottoms and *A. F. Rutherford*

The way in which persons who are known to have committed criminal offences are dealt with by societal agencies forms a huge field of study. It ranges, for example, from basic philosophical and political issues about the nature and purpose of legal punishment, through complex intellectual problems such as how to assess the efficacy of penal measures, to intensely practical matters such as prison architecture. In this chapter we hope to offer a sampling of some of the relevant literature on these very diverse topics.

One initial problem is that of nationality, since the penal systems of various countries obviously differ considerably. We have mainly concentrated upon England, with occasional references to the sparse Scottish literature and with a short final section on foreign penal systems. On the more theoretical aspects of the subject, however, we have drawn freely upon the important and extensive American literature, which is for the most part fairly readily available in this country.

GENERAL PUBLICATIONS

Textbooks

There are three main English textbooks on the penal system, namely (in order of publication) Nigel Walker's *Crime and punishment in Britain* (rev. ed., Edinburgh U.P., 1968), J. D. McClean and J. C. Wood's *Criminal justice and the treatment of offenders*

(Sweet and Maxwell, 1969) and J. E. Hall Williams's *The English penal system in transition* (Butterworths, 1970). All three are very useful starting books: Walker is particularly good on evaluation of penal measures, but the other two give more rounded accounts of the actual content of the various measures, especially imprisonment. All three books are, however, relatively lacking in consideration of the more explicitly sociological aspects of penology. This gap is partially filled by the penological chapters of Roger Hood and Richard Sparks's *Key issues in criminology* (Weidenfeld, 1970), an excellent review of literature on various specific topics.

Some American theoretical textbooks and readers are of considerable value for the English reader. Perhaps the best-known is N. Johnston and others' *The sociology of punishment and correction* (rev. ed., Wiley, 1970), a massive tome containing 75 separate papers; a more recent reader is L. Radzinowicz and M. E. Wolfgang's *Crime and justice* (Harper and Row, 1971), of which Vols. 2 and 3 are concerned with social reaction to crime. A reader specifically on the sociology of imprisonment is L. Hazelrigg's *Prison within society* (Doubleday, 1966). Two other important books, both concerned only with the treatment of juveniles, are *Controlling delinquents*, ed. S. Wheeler (Wiley, 1966), and *Delinquency and social policy*, ed. P. Lerman (Praeger, 1970). These last are both of wider interest than their specific subject matter, since they reflect a recent shift in penological study away from a purely 'correctional' perspective (i.e. one concerned with providing programmes for the effective amelioration of delinquents and criminals) towards a more 'processual' approach, viewing penal measures as a continuing transactional process between the offender and societal agents, and exhibiting a considerable interest in the behaviour patterns of the latter. In particular, it is asked how the agents of social control set about defining and selecting persons for the criminal process, and what the implications of such definitions are upon the subsequent behaviour of the offender.

Periodicals

All the standard criminological periodicals referred to elsewhere in this volume naturally contain penological articles. Additionally, there are a number of journals, mostly aimed at practitioners, which are specifically of penological interest. In England the best of these are the *Prison Service Journal* and *Probation*, published by the National Association of Probation Officers (NAPO). Others include *The Magistrate, The Justice of the Peace,* the *Prison Officers' Magazine* and the *Community Schools Gazette* (formerly the *Approved Schools Gazette*). In a special category comes the very good 'annual periodical' produced by the Howard League for Penal Reform, the *Howard Journal.* Additionally, journals for social workers sometimes contain important articles relevant to the treatment of offenders: among these are the *British Journal of Social Work, Case Conference, Social Work Today* and *Applied Social Studies.*

Among foreign and international penological periodicals are the UN's *International Review of Criminal Policy,* the *Canadian Journal of Criminology and Corrections,* the *American Journal of Corrections, Federal Probation* (US), the *Prison Journal* (US) and the *International Journal of Offender Therapy,* a journal specifically concerned with so-called 'reality therapy'. Not strictly a periodical, but of great importance nonetheless, are the occasionally produced volumes entitled *Scandinavian Studies in Criminology* (Tavistock)—in particular, Vol. 2 (1969) and Vol. 3 (1971) both contain important papers reflecting the increasing interest in studying the activities of social control agents (see above).

Official publications

Naturally, Government organisations produce important series of publications relating to the penal system. One of the most important is the annual report on the prison and borstal system—this was known as the *Report of the Prison Commissioners* until 1962, and has been the *Report of the Prison Department* since 1964, with the intervening report entitled *Prisons and Borstals 1963.* All of these reports contain some statistical information, but the most important prison statistics, including reconviction data on borstal and detention centre trainees and on some prisoners, have since 1964 been published separately in volumes known as *Report of the Prison Department (Statistical Tables).*

Also very important, and rather more informative than Prison Department reports, are the annual *Reports* of the Parole Board, a series commencing in 1968 with the introduction of the parole system.

The Probation and After-Care Department of the Home Office, unlike the Prison Department, does not produce an annual report, but it does produce informative triennial surveys, the three so far published covering the years 1962–1965, 1965–1968 and 1969–1971, respectively. There are at present no published probation statistics, but annual unpublished statistics are compiled and made available to the Probation Service; serious research workers are allowed access.

Approved schools and other institutions for juveniles were formerly under the charge of the Home Office Children's Department. Important information is to be found in the 11 triennially produced Reports of that Department, the last published in 1970; additionally, from 1962 onwards, annual slim volumes of *Statistics relating to approved schools, remand homes and attendance centres*, with explanatory introductory notes, have appeared. These institutions are, however, in the process of merger into the new community homes system, and responsibility has been transferred to the Department of Health and Social Security from January 1971— information from 1971 is being incorporated in the published annual *Report* of that Department of State.

Publications by members of the Home Office's research and statistical sections have appeared in two HMSO series: most of the works are of a penological nature. The first series was named *Studies in the Causes of Delinquency and the Treatment of Offenders* (Nos. 1–13, 1955–1969); this was followed by *Home Office Research Studies* from 1969. Many individual items from these series are mentioned in the sections below. Two other series worthy of mention are the unpublished 'Psychologists' Monograph' and 'CP Report' series issued by the Office of the Chief Psychologist of the Prison Department.

Scottish penological affairs are covered in separate HMSO series, of which the most important are the annual reports entitled *Prisons in Scotland, Report of the Parole Board for Scotland* and *Social Work in Scotland* (from 1969).

Government policy documents and reports of official committees are also, of course, published by HMSO, but these are mentioned at appropriate points in the remainder of the chapter.

US official publications are beyond the scope of this chapter, but reference must be made to the penological sections of the very important Report of the President's Crime Commission, *The challenge of crime in a free society* (1967) and to the supporting Task Force reports of the Commission, especially those on *Corrections, Juvenile delinquency* and *Science and technology*.

FUNDAMENTAL ISSUES

Penal philosophy

Penal philosophy is fundamental to a study of penology, since it is imperative to be clear about the basis on which one is applying penal sanctions. The subject has, of course, been debated for hundreds of years: for selections from some especially influential eighteenth-century thinkers, see James Heath's *Eighteenth century penal theory* (Oxford U.P., 1963). Among modern writers, few have been more influential than H. L. A. Hart, whose *Punishment and responsibility* (Oxford U.P., 1968) collects together his most important papers on the subject. Among those who have disagreed with Hart on various issues are Barbara Wootton in *Crime and the criminal law* (Stevens, 1963) and Nigel Walker in the first chapter of *Sentencing in a rational society* (Allen Lane, 1969). An approach more akin to Hart's is taken by Ted Honderich in *Punishment: the supposed justifications* (Hutchinson, 1969; Penguin, 1971); while Mark Kennedy in the periodical *Catalyst*, Summer 1970 (N.Y. State University), develops a socially radical approach to penal philosophy which 'shows up the institutions and the political apparatus of the culture of capitalism'.

An extremely important recent collection of papers on the subject, mainly by British philosophers, is *The philosophy of punishment*, ed. H. B. Acton (Macmillan, 1969). Of less intellectual significance but full and readable is Sir Walter Moberly's *The ethics of punishment* (Faber, 1968).

The Continental approach to penal philosophy has been very different from the Anglo-Saxon tradition, and various 'schools' have emerged. One of the most important is that known as 'social defence'; and an explanation in English of the views of this school will be found in Marc Ancel's *Social defence* (Routledge, 1965). Enthusiasts may pursue this topic in the *Bibliographie de la défense sociale 1955–64* by S. Poitonniée which appeared in *Revue de science criminelle* for 1964.

English penal policy

The history of English policy in the first half of the twentieth century was largely a movement towards a reformative, individualistic approach, with an emphasis on the emergence of non-custodial penalties (see, generally, M. Grünhut's *Penal reform*, Oxford U.P.,

1948). This stage of policy development culminated in the *Criminal Justice Act 1948*. The first major subsequent policy statement was the 1959 White Paper *Penal practice in a changing society* (Cmnd. 645), which called for a replacement of antiquated prisons through a major rebuilding programme, and also pointed to the importance of research results in moving towards the determination of 'a fundamental re-examination of penal policy ... (which) could be a landmark in penal policy and illumine the way ahead for a generation'. A further policy statement published in 1964, *The war against crime in England and Wales, 1959–1964* (Cmnd. 2296), decided that the time for this fundamental re-examination had arrived, and announced the setting up of a Royal Commission on the Penal System. This, however, was disbanded without reporting in 1966, largely because the Commissioners felt that a single major review was inappropriate. Accordingly the Government established the Advisory Council on the Penal System (ACPS) to provide specific reviews of selected topics from time to time. This function was similar to that previously performed by the Advisory Council on the Treatment of Offenders (ACTO) from 1950 to 1964: many reports of both these Councils are listed in appropriate sections below. As for the Royal Commission, the only tangible remains are the five volumes of written and oral evidence it received (HMSO, 1967).

Among the penal policy documents of the 1960s, three were perhaps especially important. The first was the *Report of the Interdepartmental Committee on the Business of the Criminal Courts* (Cmnd. 1289, 1961: 'the Streatfeild Report'), which spelt out the need for courts to have adequate information before sentencing—this was implemented in most areas in 1963. Secondly, the ACTO report *The organisation of after-care* (1963) foreshadowed a massive increase in after-care for adult prisoners, and the assumption by the probation service (henceforth the 'probation and after-care service') of responsibility for all after-care functions. Thirdly, the so-called 'security crisis' within the prison system, which came to a head with the escape of the spy George Blake from Wormwood Scrubs in 1966, led to the setting up of the Mountbatten Inquiry, which reported later the same year (*Report of the Inquiry into Prison Escapes and Security*, Cmnd. 3175) and made recommendations for more sophisticated security measures and classification procedures.

A number of interesting critical questions about penal policy have been raised in recent years by members of House of Commons reviewing committees: see, in particular, the 1967 *Eleventh Report of the Estimates Committee* (on prisons, borstals and detention centres) and two reports of the Expenditure Committee in Session 1971–72, i.e. the *First Report* on *Probation and after-care* and the *Eighth Report* on relationship of expenditure to need.

The most recent general official statement on penal policy for those in custody is the White Paper *People in prison* (1969, Cmnd. 4214), which outlines in some detail the shape of a partially re-organised prison system facing an acute crisis of numbers. A stimulating unofficial look at penal policy, by a self-confessed 'armchair penologist', is to be found in Rupert Cross's Hamlyn Lectures, published as *Punishment, prison and the public* (Stevens, 1971).

Evaluation of penal measures

A fundamental academic problem which has to be considered before we turn to the practical aspects of the English penal system relates to how one can judge the success of particular measures. Too many discussions of efficacy are still content with producing simple 'success rates', i.e. rates of non-reconviction over a specified period, but this is over-simplified in two ways. First, it assumes that we are mainly concerned with the effect on the offender's behaviour, but many sentences are passed to deter *others*. As yet, we lack adequate research on deterrent efficacy—the best general discussion, with references, will be found in Nigel Walker's *Crimes, courts and figures*, Ch. 12 (Penguin, 1971). Second, even when we are primarily concerned with the effect on the offender, simple success rates are useless, since they take no account of the different types of offenders, with different 'risks' of reconviction, who are subjected to different treatments. There are two basic methods of trying to solve this problem: by randomly allocating offenders to different treatments, or by 'controlling' on certain variables, prefer-ably with a prediction instrument. Both methods have considerable technical difficulties, those of the former being especially well considered in R. V. G. Clarke and D. B. Cornish's *The controlled trial in institutional research* (HMSO, 1972). For discussions of the whole subject, see the excellent *Evaluating penal measures*, by Leslie Wilkins (Random House, 1969); also Chapter 13 of Walker's Penguin book (above) and Chapters 6 and 7 of Hood and Sparks's *Key issues* (see p. 110).

For obvious ethical reasons, prediction is more often used than random allocation, and has acquired a considerable literature. A classic in the field is H. Mannheim and L. T. Wilkins's *Prediction methods in relation to borstal training* (HMSO, 1955), which largely sparked off the post-war realisation of the importance of prediction in evaluation and can be regarded as one of the most influential penology books published. More recently, other techniques of prediction have been developed. For a recent extensive review and application to British probationers, see Frances Simon's *Prediction methods in criminology* (HMSO, 1971); for the use of a new technique of logistic regression in relation to a borstal sample, and a comparison with other methods, see Monica A. Walker's contribution in Bottoms, McClintock and Walker's *Working papers and supplementary data relating to the study on Criminals Coming of Age* (Cambridge: Institute of Criminology, 1973). American work on prediction (or 'base expectancy', as it is commonly there called) is well represented in the papers in the final section of Johnston's reader (see p. 110); this includes the review by D. M. Gottfredson, 'Assessment and prediction methods in crime and delinquency', which forms an appendix to the President's Commission Task Force report on *Juvenile delinquency* (see p. 112).

PROCESSING AND CLASSIFYING OFFENDERS

Police processing of offenders

Much of the newly developed interest in the way in which social control agents selectively perceive deviant acts, and the consequences of this, naturally centres around the police. Increasingly, police manpower deployment and police–citizen encounters are being seen as selective social interactions with relevance for processing. Very influential discussions in this area have been an article by Piliavin and Briar, 'Police encounters with juveniles' (*American J. Sociology*, **70**, 206, 1964; reprinted in several 'readers'); a further article by Werthman and Piliavin in *The police*, ed. D. J. Bordua (Wiley, 1964); *The social organisation of juvenile justice*, by Aaron Cicourel (Wiley, 1968); the discussion in Chapter 7 of David Matza's *Becoming deviant* (Wiley, 1969); and the essays in the first part of the book edited by Wheeler (see p. 110). These works in turn must be set in the context of general work on the sociology of the police, in which field the most important works are Jerome Skolnick's pioneering study, *Justice without trial* (Wiley, 1964), Michael Banton's *Policeman in the community*

(Tavistock, 1964), J. Q. Wilson's *Varieties of police behaviour* (Harvard, 1968), the book edited by Bordua (see p. 116) and A. J. Reiss's *The police and the public* (Yale U.P., 1971). Useful summaries of some of this work, with some additional perspectives, appear in John Lambert's *Crime, police and race relations* (Oxford U.P., 1970); and comparisons between urban and rural policing are made by Maureen Cain in an article in *Images of deviance*, ed. S. Cohen (Pelican, 1971) and her book *Society and the policeman's role* (Routledge, 1973).

All the above work except that of Banton, Cain and Lambert is American, and no British study equivalent to those of Piliavin or Cicourel exists. British interest has tended to centre upon a subsequent and probably less important stage in police processing, namely the decision whether to prosecute or to formally caution an offender who has been the subject of an official crime report. In relation to adults, the major work on cautioning is now David Steer's *Police cautions* (Blackwell, 1971); among juveniles, the main literature has been on so-called 'juvenile liaison schemes', in which supervision by a policeman follows a formal caution (see p. 140).

Sentencing

All offenders found guilty in this country must be 'allocated' by a court to a particular sentence, and the study of the use of this discretion is clearly of considerable importance.

In England the Court of Appeal has developed one of the most elaborate appellate sentencing jurisdictions in the world, and the principles and practice of the Court have been analysed in a major study by David Thomas, *Principles of sentencing* (Heinemann, 1969). A more general legal study of sentencing by higher criminal courts is Rupert Cross's *The English sentencing system* (Butterworths, 1970), one of the chief virtues of which is an attempt to analyse judicial practice critically in the light of theories of punishment.

By far the majority of English offenders are, however, sentenced in magistrates' courts. A useful legal introduction is Keith Devlin's *Sentencing offenders in magistrates' courts* (Sweet and Maxwell, 1970). More important is Roger Hood's empirical study of 12 magistrates' courts sentencing different proportions of defendants to imprisonment: these differences were more related to different policies and the type of area than to the types of defendants appearing before the various courts (*Sentencing in magistrates' courts*, Tavistock, 1962). Subsequently Hood has carried out further empirical research on magistrates' sentencing, mainly in relation to motoring offenders, and this is the first English study to obtain data on magistrates' personality and attitudes (*Sentencing the motoring offender*, Heinemann, 1972).

Empirical research on sentencing has also been carried out elsewhere. The two major studies are by Edward Green in Philadelphia (*Judicial attitudes in sentencing*, Macmillan, 1961) and by John Hogarth in Ontario (*Sentencing as a human process*, Toronto U.P., 1971). A useful summary and discussion of the literature will be found in Hood and Sparks's *Key issues in criminology* (Ch. 5).

Social enquiries before sentence were given great impetus in England by the *Streatfeild Report* (see p. 114). Academic study is, however, somewhat neglected: the main references will be found in Hood and Sparks's chapter already mentioned, although a subsequent paper by two probation officers is worth notice (D. A. Mathieson and A. J. Walker's *Social enquiry reports*, NAPO Probation Paper No. 7). An attack on the use of social enquiry reports and the whole concept of 'diagnostic' sentencing is contained in Chapter 7 of Nigel Walker's *Sentencing in a rational society* (Allen Lane, 1969), which is also important in relation to other aspects of sentencing.

A further result of the Streatfeild Report was the introduction of an official 'handbook for sentencers' in 1964, which was revised in 1969 (*The sentence of the court*, HMSO). Most of this slim volume consists of basic information about the various types of available sentence; by far the most interesting section is Part VI, which contains the only tables yet available in this country on the comparative efficacy of the main penal measures. Unfortunately, these tables are controlled on too few variables to tell us anything of real substance, although a different view is taken by Nigel Walker (*Crimes, courts and figures*, Ch. 13).

Classification for treatment purposes

In recent years increasing attention has been given to the notion that there are different kinds of offenders requiring different forms of treatment and to the operational implications of this. So far, however, more work has been done on offender typologies than on the matching treatment technologies. A good introduction is a collection of papers contained in a brief publication issued by the California State Board of Corrections in 1961, *Inquiries concerning kinds of treatment for kinds of delinquents*. It includes a rather general typology developed by Michael Argyle, and a summary by J. Douglas Grant of his work with Interpersonal Maturity Levels (I-level) at Camp Elliott. Grant's work, in more recent years, has been subject to very considerable refinement, particularly within the California Youth Authority (CYA). Of note are Carl Jesness's *The Preston typology study* (1969) (and see *J. Research in Crime and Delinquency*, **8**, 1971); and the many publications of the Community Treatment Project, of which two of the most important are M. Q. Warren's *Interpersonal maturity level classification: juvenile diagnosis and treatment of low, middle and high maturity delinquents* (1966), and *Report Number Ten of the Community Treatment Project*, by Ted Palmer (1970), which reviews the first three phases of the Project. In addition, the annual reports by Jesness and others of the *Youth Center Research Project* (1968–) (National Institute of Mental Health) are important. Jesness's own inventory has played an important part in these developments and his original work on this Inventory should be consulted (*The Fricot Ranch study*, Research Report No. 47, CYA, 1965), as should two attempts to apply it in a British context (Martin Davies's *The use of the Jesness Inventory on a sample of British probationers*, 1967, and Joy Mott's *The Jesness Inventory: application to approved schoolboys*, 1969, both HMSO).

A number of other schemes have been developed, although they have not usually found application within treatment settings. These include Don C. Gibbons's *Changing the lawbreaker* (Prentice-Hall, 1965), J. Roebuck's *Criminal typology* (C. C. Thomas, 1965) and M. B. Clinard and Richard Quinney's *Criminal behaviour systems* (Holt, Rinehart, 1967). The work of Herbert Quay (*J. Research in Crime and Delinquency*, **1**, 1964), which is based upon dimensions of behaviour, has received application at the Federal Youth Center at Morgantown, W. Virginia, described by R. Gerard and others (*Differential treatment: a way to begin*, 1969, mimeo). This has been published in 1970 by the US Department of Justice, Bureau of Prisons, Washington D.C. 20537; in this edition the authors' names are not given.) L. Hewitt and R. Jenkins's *Fundamental patterns of maladjustment* (Springfield, Ill.: State Printer, 1964) developed a threefold classification which has often been praised, and which has treatment implications, although few regimes seem to have used it explicitly. Some doubts about the typology arise, however, as a result of Elizabeth Field's study

Types of delinquency and home background (HMSO, 1967).

On the whole, it is the more sociological classification schemes which have been least applied in treatment practice. An exception to this was R. A. Cloward and L. E. Ohlin's *Delinquency and opportunity* (Free Press, 1960), which received massive implementation in preventive programmes within urban communities (*A proposal for the prevention and control of delinquency by expanding opportunities*, Mobilization for Youth, 1962), although this has subsequently been strongly criticised by, for example, Daniel Moynihan in *Maximum feasible misunderstanding* (Free Press, 1969).

A comprehensive overview of the whole range of the typological and differential treatment field can be obtained by reading four recent review articles: by Sparks and by Borjeson in Vol. 3 of *Collected studies in criminological research* (Council of Europe, 1968); by M. Q. Warren in *J. Criminal Law, Criminology and Police Science*, **62**, 1971; and by Bottoms in a paper to the Council of Europe in 1972. Earlier, more discursive surveys of some relevant work will be found in T. H. Ferdinand's *Typologies of delinquency* (Random House, 1966) and in S. and E. Glueck's *Towards a typology of juvenile offenders* (Grune and Stratton, 1970).

Classification and allocation practice is not well developed in the English penal system. On Borstal practice the *locus classicus* is R. L. Morrison's article in *British J. Delinquency*, **8** (1957), but the increasing numbers of subsequent years have made the system less elaborate and more rushed. Prison department psychologists have undertaken a good deal of work in this field and some interesting papers are contained in the unpublished *Borstal typology study* (1972). Within the approved schools, the classic statement of allocation practice was John Gittins's *Approved school boys* (HMSO, 1952); subsequent changes were outlined in the pamphlet *Aycliffe 1967*, by the same author, but further changes are now taking place as a result of the reorganisation of juvenile institutions.

Finally, two recent empirical approaches to developing typologies in relation to young offenders may be mentioned. They are, within an English borstal study, *Criminals coming of age*, by A. E. Bottoms and F. H. McClintock (Heinemann, 1973), and within an in-depth study of a hostel in Los Angeles, *The Silverlake experiment*, by LaMar Empey and Steven Lubeck (Aldine, 1971).

THE ADULT PENAL SYSTEM: A. IMPRISONMENT AND AFTER

The English prison system

The standard work, by the then Chairman of the Prison Commissioners, appeared in 1952 (L. W. Fox's *The English prison and borstal systems*, Routledge), and a new edition is badly required. A subsequent general view of the prison scene was provided by the former Secretary of the Howard League for Penal Reform (H. J. Klare's *Anatomy of prison*, Penguin, 1962) but this, too, is now dated. A brief official overview is given in the White Paper *People in prison* (see p. 115).

Among academic studies, two pieces of research carried out around 1960 are of interest, namely Terence and Pauline Morris's comprehensive sociological study of *Pentonville* (Routledge, 1963) and F. E. Emery's socio-psychological study of aspects of Bristol Prison, finally published in 1970 as *Freedom and justice within walls* (Tavistock). More recently, Richard F. Sparks's *Local prisons: the crisis in the English penal system* (Heinemann, 1971), based on research at Birmingham Prison, highlights the neglected problems of local prisons and shows how they must be set in the context of the prison system as a whole. Another relatively neglected matter is the perspective of the prison officer, but this is given an important if controversial airing in J. E. Thomas's *The English prison officer since 1850* (Routledge, 1972).

At a more journalistic level, Tony Parker's *The frying pan* (Hutchinson, 1970) and Tom Clayton's *Men in prison* (Hamish Hamilton, 1970) are perceptive and readable accounts of Grendon and Pentonville, respectively. Consumers' accounts also appear from time to time and among the best English ones to date are Frank Norman's *Bang to rights* (Secker, 1958), Peter Wildeblood's *Against the law* (Weidenfeld, 1955) and Zeno's *Life* (Macmillan, 1968).

A number of official publications on various aspects of the prison system are available—for example, *The organisation of the Prison Medical Service*, 1965; the Report of the Advisory Council on the Employment of Prisoners, *The organisation of work for prisoners*, 1961; and the internally circulated reports of the *Working Party on Communications*, 1963, and on *Group work in prisons and borstals*, 1966. On education in prisons there is a bibliography in the Cambridge Institute of Criminology series (by D. L. Howard); also available from Cambridge are short lists of references on prison work (comp. 1969), and on open prisons (comp. 1970). Short-term imprisonment and its alternatives are important topics, further considered below: among relevant literature is Robert Andry's *The short term prisoner* (Tavistock, 1963) and the report of the Scottish ACTO, *The use of short sentences of imprisonment by the courts* (1960), especially Appendix D, by W. H. Hammond.

Prison architecture and management both await more adequate attention than they have yet received. On architecture one may consult a special issue of *British J. Criminology* (1 (3), 1960); on management, see a paper presented by a former head of the English prison service (P. J. Woodfield in *Collected Studies in Criminological Research*, Vol. 5; Strasbourg: Council of Europe) and also an article on the recent management review in the Prison Department, by John Garrett and S. D. Walker in *O and M Bulletin*, 25 (1970). A major gap in the literature is a full study of an individual prison from an organisational perspective.

From this brief review it will be clear that there is in Britain no equivalent of the thorough research survey of an entire prison system as carried out by Daniel Glaser and his associates in the US Federal Bureau of Prisons (*The effectiveness of a prison and parole system*, Bobbs-Merrill, 1964).

Treatment regimes in prison

There is again a paucity of British descriptive material. The influential Maidstone regime of the 1950s is cursorily discussed in the autobiography of the then Governor, John Vidler (*If freedom fail*, Macmillan, 1965, Chs. 6 and 7). Among more recent regimes, an article on Blundeston Prison by the first Governor, E. A. Towndrow, should be consulted (in *Interaction*, ed. Paul de Berker, Cassirer, 1969), as should H. P. Tollington's account of Grendon prison in *British J. Criminology*, 6 (1966). For local prisons, Emery's full-length study on the introduction of the so-called 'Norwich scheme' at Bristol prison is important (see p. 121), and also useful is a review of treatment strategies at Swansea prison by the then Governor, W. Perrie, in *Howard J.* (1968). At the other end of the prison system, the ACPS report *The regime for long-term prisoners in conditions of maximum security* (HMSO, 1968) (chairman, Kenneth Younger; chairman of sub-committee, L. Radzinowicz) recommended dispersal of top security prisoners rather than their concentration in a particular prison, and also made many detailed points about the kind of regime required. The subjective perspective of prisoners facing long terms in maximum security conditions is discussed by Stan Cohen and Laurie Taylor in *Psychological survival* (Penguin, 1972).

Abroad, one of the most important approaches to the description of treatment strategies is contained in a book on young offenders' institutions, D. Street, R. Vinter and C. Perrow's *Organization for treatment* (Free Press, 1966), although a shorter comparative study undertaken by the same group in the University of Michigan is concerned with adult prisons (B. Berk's 'Organizational goals and inmate organisation', *American J. Sociology*, **71**, 1966).

With the attempt to apply the milieu therapy or therapeutic community approach within the prison there came a greater inclination to consider treatment within a total organisational context. Maxwell Jones, who pioneered the therapeutic community idea in Britain, was a consultant to the California Department of Corrections and for a few years he and his school, whose principles he described in *Social psychiatry in practice* (Penguin, 1968), had a significant impact. There has been little other British writing on this topic in a penological context, although the recent *Dealing with deviants*, by Stuart Whiteley and others (Hogarth, 1972), should be consulted. In contrast, there are several American publications which explore some of the organisational issues involved in developing milieu therapy or collaborative regimes. Dealing directly with the prison situation is *The correctional community*, ed. N. Fenton and others (U. of California P., 1967), and *C-Unit: search for community in prison*, by E. Studt and others (Russell Sage, 1968). Very close attention is given to what actually goes on inside the organisation, in a study of a hostel in Los Angeles by LaMar Empey and Steven Lubeck (*The Silverlake experiment*, Aldine, 1971). Additionally, useful description of group counselling in the prison setting is provided in a study of the California Men's Colony by G. Kassebaum and others (*Prison treatment and parole survival*, Wiley, 1971), and attempts at measuring the nature of staff–inmate interactions within the Hawthorne Cedar Knolls School in New York are reported by Polsky and Claster in *The dynamics of residential treatment* (U. of North Carolina P., 1968). Also worthy of note is the very different idea of *Reality therapy* (Harper and Row, 1965), developed by William Glasser and applied in the Ventura School for Girls in the CYA.

Recently there has been some emphasis on the development of refined tools so that the regimes of institutions can be more usefully compared. One important scheme was that of R. H. Moos, described in *J. Research in Crime and Delinquency*, **5**, 1968, which is one of a number of methods being used to describe the treatment regimes at two schools as part of the *Youth Center Research Project* (see p. 119). In Britain Roy King is carrying out research at Albany Prison using measurement techniques similar to those developed in an earlier study of institutions for handicapped children (*Patterns of residential care*, by Roy King and others, Routledge, 1971).

The sociology of imprisonment

The pioneering study, Clemmer's *The prison community* (1940; reissued by Holt, 1958), remains essential reading for those with an interest in the informal social world of the prison. Clemmer noted a wide variety of responses to imprisonment, and he accounted for these both in terms of environmental factors and as a function of the prison situation. There was a revival of sociological interest in the early 1950s followed by the publication of a number of important research papers. A survey of the scene at the time is provided by Lloyd Ohlin in his *Sociology and the field of corrections* (Russell Sage, 1956); two years later came the major American study of this period, Gresham Sykes's *The society of captives* (Princeton U.P., 1958). Sykes stressed the importance of the informal inmate code and the effectiveness of inmate solidarity in minimising 'the pains of imprisonment'. Subsequently, two very influential collections of papers were published, most of them similarly pointing to a functional response of oppositional solidarity (*Theoretical studies in the social organisation of the prison*, by R. A. Cloward and others, NY SSRC Research Pamphlet No. 15, 1960, and *The prison*, ed. D. R. Cressey, Holt, 1960); although McCleery's papers in these volumes view the prison from a pluralistic frame of reference.

The Michigan studies by Berk and by Street *et al.* (see p. 123) and Glaser's large-scale study of a number of institutions within the Federal Bureau of Prisons (see p. 122) question some of the earlier assumptions of solidarity and lay stress on differences between institutions. This theme also emerges from two studies of women's prisons, since these showed quite different types of response and pointed to the importance of cultural frames of reference imported into the prison (Rose Giallombardo's *Society of women*, Wiley, 1964; D. Ward and G. Kassebaum's *Women's prison*, Weidenfeld, 1966). Taking these ideas further, more recent studies have emphasised the pre-prison experience of inmates, the significance of imprisonment within society, and inmates' subjective perspectives of their inmate role and the situation on discharge: among influential studies are H. F. Cline's contribution in *Scandinavian studies in criminology*, Vol. 2; Martha Baum and Stanton Wheeler's 'Becoming an inmate' in *Controlling delinquents* (see p. 110); Thomas Mathiesen's *The defences of the weak* (Tavistock, 1965); Wheeler's essay in *Handbook of socialization theory and research*, ed. D. Goslin (Rand McNally, 1969); John Irwin's *The felon* (Prentice-Hall, 1970); Thomas Mathiesen's *Across the boundaries of organizations* (Glendessary P., 1971); and Cohen and Taylor's *Psychological Survival* (see p. 123).

The most thorough British study, Terence and Pauline Morris's *Pentonville* (Routledge, 1963), unfortunately largely antedates these newer perspectives. However, a distinctive contribution is its penetration of the informal world of the prison staff. Important in this connection also are Howard Polsky's researches in a private US reformatory, drawing attention to the collusive bargains between staff and inmates upon which social control often rests (*Cottage Six*, Russell Sage, 1962; and see the Polsky and Claster study, referred to on p. 123).

The recent *Prison treatment and parole survival* (see p. 123) notes the significance for informal social organisation of classification within a large prison system. Another recent, and highly unusual, book which should be consulted is A. J. Manocchio and J. Dunn's *The time game* (Russell Sage, 1970), which is presented through the eyes of an ex-inmate and a former correctional counsellor, and draws attention in particular to the implications of the castelike structure of most prison organisations. For a good literature review of the whole subject, Chapter 8 of Hood and Sparks (see p. 110) should be read.

Related to prison sociology, and likely quite soon to have a considerable impact on academic accounts of the prison, are the recent prisoners' protest movements. The literature on this is at present very fragmentary, but on the US scene see the important prison letters of George Jackson (*Soledad brother*, Penguin, 1971); an article by Frank Browning, 'Organizing behind bars' (*Rampart's Magazine*, Feb. 1972) (a book by the same author is forthcoming from Harper and Row); and, most importantly, the official report of the State of New York on the major riot at Attica prison in 1971, entitled *Attica* (1972). In Britain the movement Preservation of the Rights of Prisoners (PROP) emerged in 1972 and began its own magazine. For Scandinavia, see p. 144.

Parole and after-care

On parole in Britain, the only sources at present are the annual reports of the English and Scottish Parole Boards (see p. 111); a book of essays edited by D. J. West, *The future of parole* (Duckworth, 1972); and the January 1973 issue of *British J. Criminol.*

For the USA, Daniel Glaser's *Effectiveness of a prison and parole system* (Bobbs-Merrill, 1964; abridged ed., 1969) includes a review and broad evaluation of parole within the Federal system. A Californian attempt to assess different forms of parole is by J. Havel and E. Sulka (*Special Intensive Parole Unit* (SIPU), California Dept. of Corrections, 1962). Also in California have been two recent studies reflecting the focus on the career of the offender, what parole means to him, and the official arrangements concerning him after his release: these are *The felon* and *Prison treatment and parole survival* (see p. 125). The first of these arose from a research project conducted by Elliott Studt, the results of which are becoming available (*Parole Action Study, Final Narrative Report*, University of California, 1969) and which promises to be especially important in its consideration of the tasks facing both the parole and the parole officer. On US material generally, reference should be made to Keith Hawkins's excellent bibliography in the Cambridge bibliographical series, and also to his unpublished doctoral dissertation (University of Cambridge).

Adult after-care (other than on parole) has changed dramatically in England during the last decade, as a result of the major official statement in the ACTO report of 1963 (see p. 114), upon which the present framework is based. A chapter on the earlier history of after-care by J. P. Martin is contained in *Criminology in transition*, ed. T. Grygier and others (Tavistock, 1965). Also noteworthy is the earlier ACTO report *The after-care and supervision of discharged prisoners* (1958), which led to unimplemented provisions for compulsory after-care in the 1961 *Criminal Justice Act*.

Following on the 1963 reorganisation, a Working Party on the place of voluntary service in after-care produced two important reports, *Residential provision for homeless discharged offenders* (1966) and *The place of voluntary service in after-care* (1967). More recently, Hugh Barr has written a very full account of a pioneering approach to the use of volunteers in the Teamwork Associates project, *Volunteers in prison after-care* (Allen and Unwin, 1971); the Home Office Research Unit have reported on after-care units and hostels in *Explorations in after-care* (HMSO, 1971); C. H. Rolph has edited a brief report on five after-care hostels, *Homeless from prison* (Carnegie Trust, 1970); and a thorough enquiry into the need for accommodation for homeless prisoners is provided by Roy Walmsley in *Steps from prison* (Inner London Probation Service, 1972).

The links between *Prisoners and their families* were considered extensively in a book of that title by Pauline Morris (Allen and Unwin, 1965); a complementary short study is Kate Vercoe's paper for the National Association for the Care and Resettlement of Offenders (NACRO), *Helping prisoners' families*. Responsibility for the links between the prisoner and the outside world now rests with the probation and after-care service, and the National Association of Probation Officers (NAPO) have produced a short paper on this entitled *Probation officers in prison* (1970). A full study of this and other aspects of the treatment situation from a probation service viewpoint is Mark Monger's *Casework in after-care* (Butterworths, 1967).

NACRO produce annual reports which should be consulted, as should its series of occasional papers, including, for example, *In place of Skid Row*, by T. Cook and B. Pollak, a discussion of an experimental hostel for alcoholic ex-prisoners.

The difficulties of the ex-prisoner and the social consequences of his temporary exclusion from society are often popularly referred to. A pioneering research study which explored these issues for both ex-prisoners and those receiving non-institutional treatment was J. P. Martin and D. Webster's *Social consequences of conviction* (Heinemann, 1971). This research, however, was planned prior to the emergence of the interactionist perspective in this country, and a complementary study from this viewpoint would be helpful. Meanwhile, important practical proposals have been made for erasing certain old convictions from ex-offenders' records: see *Living it down*, a report of a committee set up jointly by the Howard League, NACRO and Justice (Stevens, 1972).

Evaluative studies of prison and parole

Many evaluative studies have already been mentioned in sections above: among the more important of these are *Prison treatment and parole survival*; Glaser's study; the *SIPU* project; *The Silver-*

lake experiment; and the Community Treatment Project. Other classic studies which should certainly be mentioned are Stuart Adams's paper on the Pilot Intensive Counselling Organisation Project (PICO), which is most easily accessible in Johnston *et al.* (see p. 110); the Intensive Treatment Project (ITP) (F. Fromm's *The I.T.P.*, Calif. Dept. of Corrections, 1966); and D. Knight's evaluation of a regime based on therapeutic community principles, *The Marshall program* (CYA reports Nos. 56 and 59, 1969–1970).

Inevitably such a catalogue has to rely very heavily on American and especially Californian material. For most penal systems, it remains true that evaluation of regimes and of parole is the exception rather than the rule—there is, for example, no full evaluative study of any regime for adult prisoners in England. It may be that this is in part due to the fact that most comparative studies which do exist are unable to demonstrate marked differences between treatments, although it is not true to say that all treatments are simply interchangeable. For the best general reviews, see Hood and Sparks's *Key issues*, Ch. 6, and an article by Walter Bailey, 'Correctional outcome: an evaluation of 100 reports', in *J. Criminal Law, Criminology and Police Science*, **57** (2), 153–160 (1966) (reprinted by Johnston and others, *op. cit.*).

THE ADULT PENAL SYSTEM: B. ALTERNATIVES TO IMPRISONMENT

Suspended sentence

The suspended sentence of imprisonment was introduced in England in the *Criminal Justice Act 1967*, so it has acquired little literature as yet. Essential background, however, are the 1952 and 1957 reports of the Advisory Council on the Treatment of Offenders, which both rejected the introduction of the measure—see *Alternatives to short terms of imprisonment* (1957), which includes both reports. A passionate advocate of the suspended sentence, whose lobbying was influential in its final acceptance, was Mr Brian Leighton, J.P.: see his Memorandum to the abortive Royal Commission on the Penal System (*Evidence*, Vol. IV). The somewhat unhappy experience of the sentence since the Act is usefully reviewed in an important article by R. F. Sparks in the *Criminal Law Review* (1971). *The Criminal Justice Act 1972* makes various important amendments to the suspended sentence: for a useful comment see Stephen White in the January 1973 *Criminal Law Review*.

Suspended sentence has, of course, a long Continental parentage, but this can only be understood in the over-all context of the relevant legal systems. A useful short introduction in English is Marc Ancel's *Suspended sentence* (Heinemann, 1971), although, like so much Continental penology, this is depressingly short on evaluative material. There has, however, been a more evaluative approach in Israel, on which one should consult articles by S. Shoham and M. Sandberg in *Crime and delinquency* (1964) and by L. Sebba in *Scripta Hierosolymitana*, **21** (1969).

Probation and the probation service

Probation has been described as the major penological innovation of the twentieth century, and not surprisingly a good deal of research and writing has been undertaken. A useful starting point is to be found in the volume edited for the National Association of Probation Officers by Joan King, now in its third edition (*The probation and after-care service*, Butterworths, 1970). A comparison with the first edition (1958) is also instructive in reflecting important developments in the service during that period.

Among early pieces of British research in probation were Max Grünhut's *Probation and mental treatment* (Tavistock, 1963) and the more general evaluative study *The results of probation* (Macmillan, 1958), prepared by F. H. McClintock for the Cambridge Department of Criminal Science. Unfortunately, the scope of the data collected in the latter study is very limited. More recently, the Home Office Research Unit's very large Probation Research Project has been at the centre of evaluative concerns in probation. The project's main reports are still awaited, but we have at present *Probation research: a preliminary report*, by S. Folkard and others (1966); *Trends and regional comparison in probation*, by H. Barr and E. O'Leary (1966); *A survey of group work in the probation service*, by Hugh Barr (1966); *Probationers in the social environment* (1969) and *Financial penalties and probation* (1970), both by Martin Davies; and *Hostels for probationers*, by Ian Sinclair; as well as Frances Simon's prediction study (see p. 116) and Davies's application of the Jesness Inventory (see p. 119). All these are published by HMSO in the two official research series (see p. 112). Sinclair's work is perhaps of special interest, being a thorough and self-contained evaluative study of probation hostels, and showing marked differences in absconding rates with different treatment styles, but very similar long-term effects on subsequent behaviour. A complementary, but less interesting research paper is by Mark Monger, *Probation hostels* (NAPO Probation Papers No. 6), and also relevant to this subject is the second report of the Departmental Committee on the Probation Service (1962, Cmnd. 1800).

Of American evaluative material, specially important are the various mimeographed reports of the San Francisco Project, by Lohman and his colleagues, obtainable from the School of Criminology, Berkeley. This still ongoing project is of a size comparable with the Home Office research effort in England and the results are not encouraging to probation officers. More generally on the US scene, see R. M. Carter and Leslie Wilkins's *Readings in probation and parole* (Wiley, 1970) and the bibliography *Probation since World War II*, by Dorothy Tompkins (Berkeley: Institute of Governmental Studies, 1964). A very thorough review of American and British literature is by R. F. Sparks and will be found in *Practical organisation of measures for the supervision and aftercare of conditionally sentenced and conditionally released offenders* (Council of Europe, 1970).

On administrative aspects of the English Probation Service, the main report of the Departmental Committee (1962, Cmnd. 1650) is still essential reading, although it now has a curiously dated air. This is not the Committee's fault, but reflects the very rapid changes which the service had to undergo in the 1960s as a result of the Streatfeild Report and the 1963 After-Care report (see p. 114), the introduction of the Parole System, and the beginning of a 'hiving off' of juvenile offenders to the child care service. Another very important unsettling influence was the series of discussions surrounding the possible merger of the probation service and other local authority social services: on this see the massive *Report of the Committee on Local Authority Social Services* (1968, Cmnd. 3703) (the Seebohm Report) and the subsequent *Local Authorities Social Services Act 1970*.

The outcome has been that the English probation service remains separate, at least for the time being, but with agonising problems of identity which can be traced in the journal *Probation*. In Scotland events have taken a different course: the probation service as such no longer exists, owing to the changes in Part I of the *Social Work (Scotland) Act 1968*. The background document to this is *Social work in the community* (1966, Cmnd. 3065); for a very informative account of how it came about, see Catherine M. Carmichael in *Applied Social Studies*, 1 (1969).

On probation treatment techniques, the fullest discussion is Mark Monger's *Casework in probation* (2nd ed., Butterworths, 1972). Also useful is Phillida Parsloe's *The work of the probation and after-care officer* (Routledge, 1967), mainly addressed to social work students, and the more journalistic account by Norman St. John, *Probation: the second chance* (Vista Books, 1961). Hugh Barr's HMSO study on group work contains a thoughtful appraisal of this type of treatment approach. Ancillary matters are dealt with in two NAPO Probation Papers, on *Case recording* (No. 5, 1968) and on *Aspects of training* (No. 2, 1965).

Community service and other alternatives to imprisonment

In England the 1957 report of ACTO, *Alternatives to short terms of imprisonment*, is an obvious first source. More recently the ACPS produced a lengthy and comprehensive report on *Non-custodial and semi-custodial penalties* (1970) which considered a wide range of measures, including the Swedish day-fine system, weekend imprisonment, adult attendance centres and day release schemes. One of its recommendations was for the introduction of community service as a means of dealing with offenders, and this, together with some other recommendations, e.g. on the introduction of the deferred sentence, has been given legislative force in the *Criminal Justice Act 1972*. For comments on these aspects of the Act and on the introduction of day training centres (not recommended by the ACPS), see the special issue of the *Criminal Law Review*, January (1973).

In the USA things have been taken rather further. One consequence of the results of the Californian Community Treatment Project has been legislation introducing the Probation Subsidy Scheme, which has successfully reduced committal rates and diverted many offenders away from institutions to the county probation departments (see *California's probation subsidy 1966–8*, CYA, 1968; also *Youth Authority Quarterly*, **21** (4) and **24** (2); for a brief introduction, see a note by Andrew Rutherford in *British J. Criminology*, **12** (2)). A more general review of developments in the USA as a whole is given by LaMar Empey in *Alternatives to incarceration* (US Dept. of Health, 1966). A detailed study of an experimental non-residential unit for adolescents is R. M. Stephenson and F. C. Scarpitti's evaluation of Essexfields (*The rehabilitation of delinquent boys*, Rutgers State University, 1967); and the

Silverlake study discusses in depth a residential hostel as an alternative to custody.

Fines and nominal measures

Although more than half of all adult indictable offenders in England are fined after conviction, we have very little information about this type of court order, and virtually none about those offenders sentenced to nominal measures such as conditional or absolute discharges. On fines, a useful article on the legal principles by Alec Samuels appears in the *Criminal Law Review* (1970), but, apart from the figures in *The sentence of the court* (see p. 118), we are forced abroad for an assessment of the preventive effect of fines, to P. Tornudd's interesting but inconclusive study on drunkenness offenders in Vol. 2 of *Scandinavian studies in criminology*. The use of fines in conjunction with probation is considered in the Home Office report already mentioned (see p. 129). Fine defaulters are an interesting group who are briefly considered by Richard Sparks in his book on *Local prisons* (see p. 121); a fuller research report by him is forthcoming.

Reparation and compensation

There is a growing interest in the idea of reparation by the offender being imposed as part of the court sentence. The 1972 *Criminal Justice Act* introduces provisions on this stemming from the ACPS report *Reparation by the offender* (HMSO, 1970).

A different idea is state compensation for the victim. This is provided for in relation to victims of crimes involving personal injury by the Criminal Injuries Compensation Scheme, introduced in 1964. The Board which administers the scheme produces an Annual Report published by HMSO. For the background to the scheme, see the White Paper *Compensation for victims of crimes of violence* (1964, Cmnd. 2323).

A full, though now dated, international survey is S. Schafer's *Restitution to victims of crime* (Stevens, 1960).

THE TREATMENT OF YOUNG OFFENDERS: A. YOUNG ADULTS

General

There has been an increasing consciousness in recent years of the special considerations relating to 'young adult offenders', a term at present used in Britain for convicted persons who are 17 and under 21 years. An international document reflecting this interest is *The young adult offender* (UN publication, 1965).

The whole range of provision for this age-group is currently under consideration by the Advisory Council on the Penal System, and a major report by them is expected in 1973. At present, apart from two senior attendance centres, in Greenwich and Manchester, no special features exist for non-institutional penalties, but a special linked system of institutions—detention centres, borstal and imprisonment—was fashioned by the 1961 *Criminal Justice Act* out of the earlier traditions of these treatments. The background to this is the ACTO report *The treatment of young offenders* (1959).

Borstals and detention centres have acquired a considerable literature and are dealt with separately below. There are few studies of young adults in imprisonment: see, however, Charlotte Banks's comparative study of the three types of institutions in *Changing concepts of crime and its treatment*, ed. H. J. Klare (Pergamon, 1966), and her article in *Current Legal Problems* (1964). For a bibliography, now a little dated, of all young offenders' institutions in Britain, see Keith Hawkins's *Select bibliography on deprivation of liberty as a means of treating juvenile delinquency in Great Britain 1940–1965* (Cambridge: Institute of Criminology, 1966).

Borstals

The borstal system was created in 1908 but acquired its major impetus from Alexander Paterson in the 1930s. The present system cannot be understood apart from its history, of which a good study is Roger Hood's *Borstal re-assessed* (Heinemann, 1965).

There have been several surveys of the characteristics of borstal trainees, including Gordon Rose's *Five hundred borstal boys* (Blackwell, 1954) and *Psychiatric studies of borstal lads*, by T. C. N. Gibbens (Oxford U.P., 1963). In a special category is H. Mannheim and L. T. Wilkins's *Prediction methods in relation to borstal training* (see p. 116), which contains not only a survey of characteristics and the famous prediction equation but an application of the equation to the comparative results of open and closed borstals.

Two major evaluative studies have been carried out in English borstals during the 1960s. The first was the Pooled Allocation Research Project, involving random allocation to three open borstals operating, respectively, group work, case work and traditional training: all that is so far available is a preliminary paper by Mark Williams ('Some aspects of borstal allocation', paper to British Association, 1970). The second study is A. E. Bottoms and F. H. McClintock's detailed evaluative study of the 'modified regime' of the closed institution at Dover: especial emphasis was laid on links between pre-institutional behaviour and problems, institutional assessments and subsequent outcomes (*Criminals coming of age*, Heinemann, 1973). An earlier, long-term follow-up of London borstal inmates was provided by T. C. N. Gibbens and Joyce Prince in 'The results of borstal training' (*Sociological Review Monograph* No. 9, 1965), and an exploratory study of social maturity levels in relation to borstal results by A. P. Sealy and Charlotte Banks is to be found in *British J. Criminology*, **11** (3), 245–264 (1971).

Other works on more detailed aspects of borstals include Erica Stratta's *The education of borstal boys* (Routledge, 1970); the official report on *Work and vocational training in borstals* (HMSO, 1962); Alan Little's unpublished London University doctoral dissertation (1961) on inmate attitudes to the borstal system and the staff; and Gordon Rose's important sociometric studies at North Sea Camp in the 1950s, published in three articles in the *British J. Delinquency* (**6** and **9**).

After-care on release from borstal is compulsory, but in comparison with institutional training has received little attention. Of special importance are two evaluative studies of special attempts to assist the homeless ex-trainee: Roger Hood's general study, *Homeless borstal boys* (Bell, 1966), and Derek Miller's account of a therapeutic post-release home, *Growth to freedom* (Tavistock, 1964). The Dover study contains the first account of the after-care received by a more general sample of ex-trainees. Also of some interest is David Lowson's *City lads in borstal* (Liverpool U.P., 1970), an interview study of trainees after their release.

Detention centres

Research on detention centres has been somewhat sporadic. An early study was carried out by Max Grünhut (*British J. Delinquency*, **10**, 1960). More recently, Banks has written a special paper on the detention centre boys in her comparative study (see p. 133): this appears in *Stephanos: Studies in psychology in honour of Cyril Burt*, ed. C. Banks and P. Broadhurst (U. of London P., 1965). A useful attitude study, though with a very poor follow-up, is Anne Dunlop and Sarah McCabe's *Young men in detention centres* (Routledge, 1965). A helpful review of recent research is provided by Elizabeth Field in *British J. Criminology*, **9** (1969).

The detention centre concept has long been extremely contentious, and, partly in response to criticism, the regimes have become decreasingly Spartan. The ACPS report on *Detention centres* (1969) is important in recommending the furtherance of this trend, though it is perhaps open to criticism in underplaying the extent of the deterrent emphasis in the original regimes. Most of the Council's detailed recommendations were implemented by circular in 1971. In an earlier report the Council had recommended the closure of the only detention centre for girls (*Detention of girls in a detention centre*, HMSO, 1968), and this was carried out in 1969. An important result of the main 1969 report was that it led directly to the current major review of all provisions for the young adult offender, as mentioned above (p. 133).

THE TREATMENT OF YOUNG OFFENDERS: B. JUVENILES

Juvenile courts and alternatives

In many countries the late nineteenth and early twentieth centuries saw the establishment of special tribunals for juvenile offenders, and since then argument has raged almost continuously about which precise composition and jurisdiction of court or panel is most appropriate.

In England special juvenile courts were established in 1908, with a very important additional Act in 1933. From then until 1969 the situation remained relatively static. A useful account of the principles and practice of this jurisdiction is Winifred E. Cavanagh's *Juvenile courts, the child and the law* (Penguin, 1967); and a research study of sentencing practice in different juvenile courts is Max Grünhut's *Juvenile offenders before the courts* (Oxford U.P., 1948). The situation is, however, now very substantially altered as a result of the *Children and Young Persons Act*

1969, which, even in its present partially implemented state, affects many aspects of juvenile court practice. Accounts of the Act will be found in an official Home Office document, *Part I of the Children and Young Persons Act 1969: A guide for courts and practitioners* (HMSO, 1970) and more discursively in J. A. F. Watson's *The juvenile court: 1970 onward* (Shaw, 1970) and in an article by Bottoms, McClean and Patchett in the *Criminal Law Review* (1970). Readers of all these accounts should, however, be aware that the present Conservative government has announced its intention not to bring into force certain parts of the legislation.

The 1969 Act was preceded by a very considerable amount of discussion, proposals and counter-proposals: these cannot be summarised here. Interested readers are referred, in chronological sequence, to the *Report of the Committee on Children and Young Persons* (1960, Cmnd. 1191: the 'Ingleby Report'); the Labour document *Crime, a challenge to us all* (1964); the Government White Paper of 1965, *The child, the family and the young offender* (Cmnd. 2742), containing proposals for 'Family Councils' which were subsequently abandoned; and, finally, the second White Paper *Children in trouble* (1968, Cmnd. 3601), on which the 1969 Act is largely based.

In Scotland special juvenile courts failed to develop as they had in England, except in four specific areas. The somewhat anomalous situation was reviewed in 1964 in the *Report of the Committee on Children and Young Persons (Scotland)* (Cmnd. 2306: the 'Kilbrandon Report'), which proposed a wholesale reform, including the setting up of special 'children's panels' to adjudicate on matters connected with juvenile offenders and others in need. A matching field-work organisation was also proposed. The Government accepted these proposals but broadened the second to include a comprehensive overhaul of Scottish social work services (see p. 130). This and the children's panel reforms were enacted together in the *Social Work (Scotland) Act 1968*, the background document to which is the White Paper *Social work in the community* (1966, Cmnd. 3065). This new system was fully implemented in 1971; see a useful article by Allison Morris in *Criminal Law Review* (1972).

Both the English and Scottish systems thus moved towards a 'welfare' and away from a 'criminal' jurisdiction. Precisely the opposite course has recently been taken in the USA, where a strong movement against the perceived jurisdictional excesses of the old informal *parens patriae* juvenile courts has emerged. A centrepiece of this trend towards greater safeguards of defendants' rights is the US Supreme Court decision in *In re Gault* 1966. The majority opinion of the Court is reproduced in Lerman's reader (see p. 110), which contains other excellent selections on the juvenile court. Other important literature relating to this trend includes the President's Commission Task Force Report on *Juvenile delinquency* (see p. 112) and the collection of essays in *In re Gault: what now for the juvenile court*, ed. V. D. Nordin (Ann Arbor, Mich.: Institute for Continuing Legal Education, 1968). Over and above these must be singled out two more theoretical books by sociologists, namely Anthony Platt's analysis of the origins of the old 'child-saving' movement, with a discussion of more recent trends (*The child savers*, U. of Chicago P., 1969), and E. M. Lemert's excellent discussion of sociological aspects of the enactment of California's new juvenile court law, which anticipated the *Gault* decision by several years (*Social action and legal change*, Aldine, 1970). Mention must also be made of the excellent analytic study of the social and institutional nature of the American juvenile court by Robert M. Emerson, *Judging delinquents* (Aldine, 1969), and of the sections on the courts in Cicourel's very important work, *The social organisation of juvenile justice* (Wiley, 1968).

In discussions of juvenile courts, the Scandinavian Child Welfare Boards are often mentioned; but little literature is available in English. An English translation of the text of the 1961 *Child Welfare Act of Sweden*, with an introduction, is, however, very useful (Ministry of Justice, Stockholm, 1965). A well-known work is Ola Nyquist's *Juvenile justice* (Macmillan, 1960), a somewhat legalistic study comparing Swedish and Californian systems in the 1950s: this still has many useful features, but it should be borne in mind that both systems have now been considerably altered by subsequent legislation (see above).

A Cambridge bibliography on juvenile courts and family courts by J. A. Sinclair is useful for the period up to 1966 but is now out of date.

Institutional treatment

The principal type of institutional treatment for juvenile offenders in this country has been the approved school. These grew out of the reformatory and industrial schools of the nineteenth century, a history which is usefully chronicled in Julius Carlebach's *Caring for children in trouble* (Routledge, 1970).

The only full-length study of approved schools is Gordon Rose's *Schools for young offenders* (Tavistock, 1967), which, however, suffers both from over-generality and from the fact that much of the detailed policy argument of the second part of the book has been overtaken by subsequent events. For approved school orders can, as a result of the 1969 Act, no longer be made; and all existing approved schools will be merged into the new and wider 'community home' system by 1974. Nor will this change be simply administrative, since it is based on a particular 'child-care' view of delinquency and of institutions. Some of the likely implications of full implementation of such concepts can be discerned from the official 'blueprint' for the three prototype community homes mainly for delinquents: *Care and treatment in a planned environment* (HMSO, 1970); for a wider presentation of the child-care approach which is being fostered, see Christopher Beedell's *Residential life with children* (Routledge, 1969). There are, however, many questions to be raised about the new system, and this is effectively done in two good collections of conference papers on the subject, namely *The residential treatment of disturbed and delinquent boys* (1968), ed. R. F. Sparks and R. G. Hood, and *Community homes and the approved school system* (1969), ed. R. G. Hood and R. F. Sparks, both obtainable from the Cambridge Institute of Criminology. The first of these collections is also notable as containing the distilled views of the senior Civil Servant who had most to do with the promotion of the 1969 changes—the late D. H. Morrell.

It is not impossible that some of the impetus for the 1969 reforms of institutions came from the bad publicity afforded to the approved schools during the 1960s, first by disturbances at Carlton School (see the official *Report* by Mr Victor Durand, 1960, Cmnd. 937), and then by alleged excessive punishments at Court Lees School (report of inquiry by Mr E. B. Gibbens, 1967, Cmnd. 3367). The first of these led directly to several legislative changes in the *Criminal Justice Act 1961*, as well as to the establishment for the first time of some closed units within the approved school system. Subsequent experience in the closed units has, however, shown that there is a small minority of highly disturbed and anti-social delinquents who need special medical treatment in a different environment, or else they disrupt the work of the closed units. Hence, the 1969 Act also contains provision for a small number of special national homes for these very disturbed children: an explanatory guide to this completely new venture is the Department of Health and Social Security pamphlet, *Youth treatment centres* (1971).

Surprisingly little research has been carried out in the approved school system, but reference should certainly be made to the very interesting experimental regime described by Derek Miller in *Changing concepts of crime and its treatment*, ed. H. J. Klare (Pergamon, 1966), although the promised full evaluation of this scheme still awaits publication. Also of interest are the accounts of the special regime for intelligent adolescents developed at Kneesworth Hall in the 1950s and 1960s (*Bright delinquents*, by Robert Brooks, NFER, 1972), and of an ongoing attempt to move a traditional approved school towards a therapeutic community model—especially as no attempt is made to hide the many resistances encountered (David Wills, *Spare the child*, Penguin, 1971). On a more specialised topic, the important report on *Absconding from approved schools* by R. V. G. Clarke and D. N. Martin (HMSO, 1971) should be consulted.

Not surprisingly, a good deal more research has been carried out in juvenile institutions in the USA. Most of the studies relevant to important current theoretical issues have been discussed in earlier sections, e.g. the studies at Fricot Ranch, Preston, Silverlake and Marshall, and the Michigan research by Street and others. An older study which remains of considerable importance is the Highfields Project: the treatment regime is described by L. W. McCorkle and others in *The Highfields story* (Holt, 1958), while a research evaluation is made by H. Ashley Weeks in *Youthful offenders at Highfields* (U. of Michigan P., 1958).

Non-institutional treatment

Sections on probation for juveniles will be found in many of the works on probation listed above (pp. 129–131), though it should be noted that probation as such no longer exists for juveniles, having been replaced by the 'supervision order'. The 1969 Act also abolishes the fine after so-called 'care proceedings' (which *may* contain a criminal element); but at present care proceedings are not compulsory in offence-based cases.

Some non-institutional treatments have been created specifically for juveniles. The most important example in England to date has been the attendance centre, which was the subject of a major piece of evaluative research by F. H. McClintock: *Attendance centres* (Macmillan, 1961). Proposals to widen the range of non-institutional treatments were considered and rejected by the Advisory Council on the Treatment of Offenders in 1962 (*Non-residential treatment of offenders under 21*, HMSO), in favour of a wider use by probation officers of their duty to 'take advantage of social, recreational and educational facilities'. This policy has been taken further by the 1969 Act, which contains provision for so-called 'intermediate treatment' conditions to accompany some supervision orders. These treatments will include such things as outward-bound schools and adventure courses: for an official account see *Intermediate treatment* (HMSO, 1972). A short bibliography has been compiled by the National Children's Bureau, London.

Delinquency prevention programmes

The most extensive delinquency prevention programmes have been carried out in countries other than Britain; the results tend to be depressing for the advocates of such programmes. The best general review is Nils Christie's lucid essay in *Collected studies in criminological research*, Vol. 1 (Council of Europe, 1967). Of the major studies, the most interesting are perhaps the Cambridge–Somerville study (E. Powers and H. Witmer's *An experiment in the prevention of delinquency*, Columbia U.P., 1951; W. and J. McCord's *Origins of crime*, Columbia U.P., 1959), the Midcity Youth Project (W. B. Miller in *Social Problems*, **10**, 1962) and Mobilization for Youth (see p. 120). Selections on preventive programmes appear in Johnston's reader (see p. 110) and a section on more general social planning in relation to juvenile delinquency is an important aspect of the final section of the book edited by Lerman (see p. 110). A more extensive collection of papers will be found in the important reader *Prevention of delinquency: problems and programs* (Macmillan, 1968), ed. J. R. Stratton and R. M. Terry.

In Britain there has been a very recent major publication which would seem to suggest that detached social work intervention can have a positive effect in delinquency prevention: C. S. Smith and others' *The Wincroft youth project* (Tavistock, 1972). This cautiously encouraging result could well lead to a revival of interest in the subject.

Other British work has tended to concentrate almost exclusively on the juvenile liaison officer schemes, on which see especially the pamphlet by Marilyn Taylor, *Study of the Juvenile Liaison Scheme in West Ham 1961 to 1965* (HMSO, 1971); and articles by J. B. Mays in *Sociological Review Monograph* No. 9 (1965), ed. Halmos, by J. A. Mack in *British J. Criminology*, **8** (1968) and by Gordon Rose and R. Hamilton in *British J. Criminology*, **10** (1970). More recently, attention has been paid to the wider aspects of possible police preventive functions in relation to juveniles, and here an influential article was by the late Sir Joseph Simpson, then Commissioner of the Metropolitan Police, in *British J. Criminology,* **8** (1968).

SPECIAL CATEGORIES OF OFFENDER

The persistent offender

One of the saddest stories of English penal history in the twentieth century has been the special persistent offender legislation. A special sentence of preventive detention was established in 1908, with the idea of providing long sentences for dangerous criminals. It was little used for technical reasons: also, it succeeded only in incarcerating petty persistent offenders for unjustifiably long periods. The story is chronicled in Norval Morris's *The habitual criminal* (London U.P., 1951). In 1948 a new, less technical, preventive detention sentence was created; but with dismally similar results. Its abolition was recommended by ACTO in 1963 (*Preventive detention,* HMSO), in a report notable for the use of two major research studies of preventive detainees, D. J. West's *The habitual prisoner* (Macmillan, 1963) and W. H. Hammond and Edna Chayen's *Persistent criminals* (HMSO, 1963). Preventive detention was duly abolished in 1967, and replaced by the extended sentence, which has been very little used.

Also in 1948 a sentence of 'corrective training' was established, intended for the incipient persistent offender in his twenties. On this see an unpublished study by R. S. Taylor in the Prison Psychologists' Monograph Series, and also an article by J. D. McClean in the *Criminal Law Review* of 1964. Corrective training was abolished in 1967.

Mentally abnormal offenders

On the historical aspects of the treatment of mentally abnormal offenders one should consult Nigel Walker's *Crime and insanity in England,* Vol. 1 (Edinburgh U.P., 1968); Vol. 2 of the same work will contain the author's recent research into persons sentenced to hospital orders. On psychiatric conditions of probation orders, see Grünhut's pioneering study (see p. 129). On the wider aspects of the subject perhaps the three most helpful works are collections of essays and papers, namely *Psychopathic disorders*, ed. M. Craft (Pergamon, 1966); the Ciba Foundation volume on *The mentally abnormal offender* (Churchill, 1968); and the Cambridge Institute's conference report, *Psychopathic offenders*, ed. D. J. West (1968). Specifically on institutional treatment, *Treating the untreatable*, by G. Stürup (Johns Hopkins P., 1968), should be consulted for its account of the famous Danish psychiatric prison, Herstedvester.

Women and girls

The literature on the treatment of female offenders is generally rather sparse. Ann Smith's *Women in prison* (Stevens, 1962) contains a historical discussion and an assessment of the modern situation. Nancy Goodman and Jean Price provide three short descriptive surveys of adolescent and adult women offenders in *Studies of female offenders* (HMSO, 1967); a follow-up study of the adolescents is J. Davies and N. Goodman's *Girl offenders aged 17–21* (HMSO, 1972). For juveniles a descriptive survey of approved schoolgirls is Cowie, Cowie and Slater's *Delinquency in girls* (Heinemann, 1968), and a more general work is Helen Richardson's *Adolescent girls in approved schools* (Routledge, 1969). Of rather more importance than any of these are the two American prison studies already referred to, by Ward and Kassebaum and by Rose Giallombardo (see p. 125). A treatment programme in a non-institutional setting is described in *Girls at vocational high*, by H. J. Meyer and others (Russell Sage, 1965).

Almost half the female prisoners in England are held at Holloway Prison. This is being systematically rebuilt to incorporate new treatment principles (see D. E. R. Faulkner in the *Howard Journal*, 1971; although the project has been subject to dissension in various quarters, e.g. *Alternatives to Holloway,* Radical alternatives to prison, 1972).

Drugs and drunkenness offenders

On the treatment of these groups in and out of the penal system, see Chapters 5 and 6, on 'Alcoholism and crime', by Timothy Cook and Celia Hensman, and 'Drug dependence', by James Willis.

OTHER TOPICS

Capital and corporal punishment

Although the terms of reference of the Royal Commission on Capital Punishment (1949 to 1953) did not include the question whether capital punishment should be abolished or retained, the huge *Report* of the Commission is undoubtedly the most comprehensive review of the whole subject.

The British abolition came in three stages: by the *Homicide Act 1957*, the *Murder (Abolition of Death Penalty) Act 1965* and parliamentary affirmative resolutions late in 1969. The statistics for murder during these periods are fully discussed in two Home Office publications, *Murder* (HMSO, 1961) and *Murder 1957 to 1968* (HMSO, 1969), both by Evelyn Gibson and S. Klein. The earlier historical movement against the penalty in this country is chronicled by Elizabeth Tuttle, *The crusade against capital punishment in Britain* (Stevens, 1961); leading proponents in the struggle were the Howard League, whose history is considered by Gordon Rose in *The struggle for penal reform* (Stevens, 1961). At a more popular level the abolitionist cause has thrown up a number of very good books, among them *A life for a life?*, in which the former Chairman of the Royal Commission, Sir Ernest Gowers, spelt out the reasons for his conversion to abolition; A. Koestler and C. H. Rolph's *Hanged by the neck* (Penguin, 1961), including a brief description of all murderers executed in Britain from 1949 to 1960; and the more recent book of essays produced by the Howard League, *The hanging question*, ed. L. Blom Cooper (1969).

For American experience on capital punishment one should consult T. Sellin's reader *Capital punishment* (Harper and Row, 1957); H. A. Bedau's *The death penalty in America* (Doubleday, 1964); and *Capital punishment*, ed. J. A. McCafferty (Aldine-Atherton, 1972). New Zealand experience from 1935 to 1962, during which hanging was abolished, restored and abolished again, is of particular interest and is well discussed in *Crimes, courts and figures*, by Nigel Walker (Penguin, 1971).

On judicial corporal punishment the major sources are two very thorough official enquiries, the *Report of the Departmental Committee on Corporal Punishment* (Cadogan Committee) (1938, Cmd. 2005) and the ACTO report of 1960, *Corporal Punishment*.

Foreign penal systems

A natural starting point is John P. Conrad's international survey of treatment attitudes and practices in the USSR, the USA, the UK, Continental Europe, and Scandinavia, *Crime and its correction* (Tavistock, 1965). The US system has been extensively noted above; but worthy of special note here is the critical appraisal of many aspects of American criminal and penal policy by Norval Morris and Gordon Hawkins in *The honest politician's guide to crime control* (U. of Chicago P, 1970).

For Europe, a very interesting comparative paper on *Aspects of the prison community*, by R. S. Taylor and T. Mathiesen (Council of Europe), should be consulted. Recently interest has centred on the inmates' rights movement in Scandinavian prisons: no full account exists in English, but the official view for Sweden is to be found in Bo Martinsson's *Prison democracy in Sweden* (Swedish Information Service, 1971), and a recent book by Thomas Mathiesen, a first-rank sociologist who is also a leader of the radical prison movement, is being translated from the Norwegian. For other countries, a useful source is the 'Chronique étrangère' in *Revue Pénitentiaire et de Droit Pénal*—for example, 'Chronique danoise', 1956, pp. 379–389; 1957, pp. 802–807; 1963, pp. 259–264; 1966, p. 439; 1970, pp. 647–650. See also the index to *Abstracts in Criminology and Penology*, under name of country. Short mimeographed bibliographies on the Scandinavian and Dutch penal systems are available from the Cambridge Institute of Criminology. A bibliography on criminology and treatment of offenders in Austria, the Democratic and Federal German Republics, and Switzerland, 1965–1970, is included in *Criminological research trends in Western Germany*, ed. G. Kaiser and T. Würtenberger (Springer, 1972).

The United Nations has been especially concerned with the *Standard Minimum Rules for the Treatment of Prisoners* (1955). These were extensively considered at the Fourth UN Congress on the Prevention of Crime and the Treatment of Offenders at Kyoto, Japan, in 1970: background papers to this include the *Working Papers* prepared by the Secretariat on the Rules in the light of recent developments (UN, 1970); an empirical study by Badr-El-Din Ali on the extent of implementation in nine selected countries, reprinted from the journal *Criminologica* for 1969; and an entire issue of the *International Review of Criminal Policy* (No. 26, 1968), devoted to the Rules and their implementation.

8

Criminal law and the administration of criminal justice

David A. Thomas

Unlike many countries, England has no code of criminal law or criminal procedure. Both the substantive law (the law defining those forms of behaviour which are prohibited) and the adjectival law (the law prescribing procedures, and regulating what evidence is admissible in a trial) are to be found in a collection of Acts of Parliament and judicial decisions which span the centuries from the Middle Ages to the present day. The law of treason, for instance, still depends primarily on a statute of 1351; the law of damage to property was re-defined in 1971. The starting point in a search for a criminal law must therefore be the statute book; but the statute book tells only part of the story and much of the law can only be found in decisions of the courts. There are still a significant number of offences whose definitions can only be found in case law; most of the general principles of criminal liability are also defined only in this way; and, of course, judicial decisions frequently place a vital gloss on the meaning of a statute. Secondary sources, such as textbooks, play a very important part in guiding the lawyer to the most up to date information; but textbooks are not treated as authoritative and a court would normally base its decisions on its own interpretations of the statutes and judicial decisions cited to it.

THE SUBSTANTIVE LAW: MAJOR TEXTBOOKS

The leading modern textbook on the substantive criminal law of England is undoubtedly J. C. Smith and B. Hogan's *Criminal law* (3rd ed., Butterworths, 1973). This text, which offers a detailed analytical discussion of the general principles of criminal liability and of the definition of a wide variety of indictable offences, is probably the textbook in use in the vast majority of university courses in the subject and can be recommended as a reliable and comprehensive guide to substantive law. Another popular university textbook is Cross and Jones's *Introduction to criminal law*, now in its seventh edition (Butterworths, 1972), by Sir Rupert Cross and P. Asterley Jones. This work, shorter and less detailed than Smith and Hogan, aims to present the law in a straightforward way and is an excellent introduction to the subject for the layman or less ambitious student. For many years the standard textbook on the criminal law was C. S. Kenny's *Outlines of criminal law*, originally published in 1902, and last published in its nineteenth edition in 1966, edited by the late Dr J. W. C. Turner (Cambridge U.P.). Inevitably a book which has passed through so many editions loses something of its original vitality, and the many changes in the substantive criminal law which have taken place in the last 7 years mean that this text must now be considered out of date. Other texts which should be mentioned include S. F. Harris's *Criminal law* (22nd ed., by McLean and Morrish; Sweet and Maxwell, 1973) and I. G. Carvell and E. Swinfen Green's *Criminal law and procedure* (Sweet and Maxwell, 1970). Both of these texts are designed to provide somewhat concisely for the needs of students preparing to follow professional examinations. The large two-volume *W. O. Russell on Crime* (12th ed., by J. W. C. Turner; Stevens, 1964) is still used occasionally for reference.

Books dealing with more specialised aspects of the criminal law include Glanville Williams's *Criminal law: the general part*, first published in 1954 and republished in its second edition in 1961 (Stevens). Although it cannot be considered entirely up to date, it is still regarded as the most important and lucid exposition of the general principles of criminal liability; it does not deal, except incidentally, with the definitions of particular offences. A comparable American text by an equally distinguished author is Jerome Hall's *General principles of criminal law*, first published in 1947 and republished in its second edition in 1960 (Bobbs-Merrill). Other texts dealing with particular aspects of the general principles of liability include Colin Howard, *Strict responsibility* (Sweet and Maxwell, 1963); J. Ll. J. Edwards, *Mens rea in statutory offences* (Macmillan, 1955); H. L. A. Hart, *Punishment and responsibility* (Clarendon P., 1968), and F. G. Jacobs, *Criminal responsibility* (Weidenfeld, 1971). The problem of mental disorder in criminal law has been the subject of a considerable amount of literature; recent works of particular interest include *Crime and insanity in England*, by Nigel Walker (Edinburgh U.P., vol. 1, 1968; vol. 2, with S. McCabe, 1973); *Criminal responsibility and mental illness*, by F. A. Whitlock (Butterworths, 1963); *Law and psychiatry: cold war or 'entente cordiale'?*, by Sheldon Glueck (Tavistock, 1963); and *The insanity defence*, by Abraham S. Goldstein (Yale U.P., 1967). *Studies in criminal law*, by Norval Morris and Colin Howard (Clarendon P., 1964), is a collection of essays dealing with a number of different aspects of criminal responsibility, and Glanville Williams's *The mental element in crime* (Jerusalem: Magnes P., 1965) is a brief account of some of the basic principles.

There are fewer texts dealing with specific parts of the law relating to the definitions of criminal offences. Two important works on the law of theft, with particular reference to the *Theft Act 1969*, are J. C. Smith's *The law of theft* (2nd ed., Butterworths, 1972) and Edward Griew's *The Theft Act 1968* (Sweet and Maxwell, 1968). Ian Brownlie's *Law relating to public order* (Butterworths, 1968) is a detailed account of the law of riot, affray, public nuisance and disorderly behaviour. Leonard Leigh's *The criminal liability of corporations in English law* (Weidenfeld, 1969) is an analysis of the development of the principles upon which limited companies can be convicted of criminal offences committed by their officers on their behalf.

Introductory books intended for the layman or student at the beginning of his legal studies include P. J. Fitzgerald's *Criminal law and punishment* (Clarendon P., 1962) and G. T. Giles's *The criminal law* (3rd ed., Penguin, 1963), both now somewhat dated. The general theory of criminal law, and the function of criminal law in society, are discussed from a variety of positions by a number of authors—in particular, by H. L. A. Hart in *Punishment and responsibility* (see above), Herbert Packer in *The limits of the criminal sanction* (Oxford U.P., 1969) and Lord Devlin in *The enforcement of morals* (Oxford U.P., 1965). Barbara Wootton's *Crime and the criminal law* (Stevens, 1963) probably comes into this category also.

Casebooks fall into two patterns—the English and the American. English casebooks on criminal law tend to be simply collections of extracts from the decisions of courts in leading cases, and are intended mainly to provide the student with a convenient form of reference. The principal casebooks in criminal law at present available are R. Cross and P. A. Jones's *Cases on criminal law* (4th ed., Butterworths, 1970) and J. W. C. Turner and A. L. Armitage's *Cases on criminal law* (3rd ed., Cambridge U.P., 1964). Although the second of these is now clearly somewhat dated, both serve as quite useful collections of extracts from some of the leading cases. American casebooks, on the other hand, attempt a much more critical presentation of the criminal law in its social context, although they are often also useful as sources of reference to otherwise difficult-to-find American cases. Particularly worth mentioning are S. H. Kadish and M. G. Paulsen's *Criminal law and its processes* (2nd ed., Little, Brown, 1969; with suppt., 1972); and *Criminal law: problems for decision*, by R. C. Donnelly, J. Goldstein and R. D. Schwartz (Free Press, 1962). Each of these texts presents a body of material from which the student can form his own ideas of what the general principles of the law are, rather than a series of dogmatic propositions. An earlier casebook on the same lines was J. Michael and H. Wechsler's *Criminal law and its administration* (Foundation P., 1940). A supplement prepared by Wechsler was published in 1956. The other leading American casebook is *Cases and readings on criminal law and procedure*, by J. Hall and G. O. W. Mueller (2nd ed., Bobbs-Merrill, 1965). Some classic judgements, still referred to in textbooks, are dropped from later editions of casebooks, and it is therefore worth consulting earlier editions on occasion.

FINDING THE LAW

The main works of reference on criminal law used by practising lawyers are Archbold's *Criminal pleading: evidence and practice*, now in its thirty-eighth edition, edited by T. R. F. Butler and M. Garsia (Sweet and Maxwell, 1973), which deals with the law relating to indictable offences, and Stone's *Justices' manual*, published annually by Butterworths, dealing with offences triable by magistrates. Each of these works is an indispensable tool of reference for the professional lawyer. Acts of Parliament are published separately by the Stationery Office in what is known as the King's Printer's Copy, but most libraries will contain one of the various collections of statutes which are available. The user of these statutes needs to know the difference between them. First, there is the series known as *Statutes at Large*, which becomes *Public General Statutes* in 1851. This series, like the *Law Reports (Statutes)*, presents the statutes in their original form as enacted; they are thus not necessarily an accurate guide to the condition of a statute at the present time. The *Statutes Revised* is a collection of statutes printed as they stood with amendments and repeals in 1950; again, this series must be used with considerable care. A more up to date collection of statutes on criminal law is contained in Halsbury's *Statutes*, now in its third edition (Butterworths). Volume 8, dealing with criminal law generally, was published in 1969, and Vol. 21, dealing with law relating to magistrates, in 1970. Halsbury reprints the statutes as amended at the date of publication and with notes setting out related sections and referring to cases decided on the provisions of the section in question or similar sections in other statutes. Up to date information on the latest statutory developments can be found either in the supplementary service issued with Halsbury's *Statutes* or in *Current Law*, a monthly publication dealing with legal developments, including case law. Another way to check the status of a particular statute is to consult the *Chronological Table of the Statutes*, published annually by the Stationery Office. This index gives the subsequent history of every statute ever enacted, and it is a simple matter to check whether the statute one is concerned with has been amended, extended or repealed up to the date of the publication of the index. Appointed Day Orders, bringing new legislation into force, are listed in the weekly *New Law Journal*, and new Statutory Instruments in *Solicitors' Journal*.

Court decisions of importance for the development of the law are reported in a number of series of law reports. Apart from the general *Law Reports*, which report all kinds of cases, there are the *Weekly Law Reports*, and the *All England Law Reports*. Cases on criminal law are reported in the *Criminal Appeal Reports*, the *Justice of the Peace Reports*, and, in summary, in the *Criminal Law Review*. An earlier series of reports dealing exclusively with criminal cases is Cox's *Criminal Cases*, which ended in 1940. The very earliest law reports dealing with criminal law are reprinted as Vols. 168 and 169 of the *English Reports*, a series of law reports reprinting all the early short series of law reports which were published up to the 1860s. Apart from using reference books, there are a number of ways of ascertaining the position in relation to case law. Each volume in a series of law reports normally contains an index to its own contents, and each series normally produces an index to the whole of the series at particular intervals.

For instance, the *All England Law Reports* published a consolidated index covering the years from 1936 (when the series began) to 1965; each year a further short volume is produced covering the period from 1966 onwards. Similarly, the *Criminal Appeal Reports* published in 1968 an index to the first 51 volumes in that series. The most up to date information on case law can be found by checking either *Current Law* or the cumulative index of the *Criminal Law Review*. Some of the textbooks—in particular, *Archbold*—publish periodical supplements dealing with the latest information.

THE HISTORICAL BACKGROUND

The best general account of the history of the English Criminal Law is undoubtedly Sir James Fitzjames Stephen's *A history of the criminal law of England*, published in 1883. (A reprint is available from Burt Franklin of New York.) This three-volume work, whose author was one of the leading scholars in the field of criminal law in the late nineteenth century as well as being a distinguished, if somewhat conservative, criminal judge, traces the history of criminal law and criminal procedure from Anglo-Saxon times onwards. A student of the history of English law could also consult some of the major treatises of the past. These really begin in 1557 with Sir William Staunford's *Les plees del coron*, the first textbook concerned exclusively with what were then called Pleas of the Crown. The powers and duties of magistrates at roughly the same period are set out in William Lambard's *Eirenarcha* (1581). A slightly later book on the same subject is Dalton's *Countrey justice* (1618). This book was the standard guide-book on the law relating to justices of the peace for almost 150 years. The eighteenth century saw three major textbooks on criminal law published. The first and probably the most important is Sir Matthew Hale's *History of the pleas of the crown*, first published posthumously in 1736, although probably written as much as 60 years earlier. This text, considered one of the greatest works of legal scholarship in the English language, offers a comprehensive historical account of the law and procedure in relation to the trial of serious offences up to the beginning of the eighteenth century. Published a few years earlier, although written slightly later, was William Hawkins's *Pleas of the crown*, which appeared between 1716 and 1721. The exploits of Bonny Prince Charlie led indirectly to the third eighteenth century textbook of note: Foster's *Dis-*

courses, originally published as an appendix to an account of the trials of the Scottish rebels. Finally, before turning to those nineteenth century works which are still in print in later editions— *Archbold* and *Russell*—the historical student would turn to East's *Pleas of the crown*, first published in 1803. All of these works are, of course, long since out of print in their original editions, but a reprint of all the texts mentioned above and a number of others of less importance is being undertaken by Professional Books Ltd., of London, under the editorship of P. R. Glazebrook.

Specialised historical discussions of particular branches of the criminal law are rare, but deserving of mention are Jerome Hall's *Theft, law and society* (2nd ed., Bobbs-Merrill, 1952), an examination of the evolution of the law relating to theft and dishonesty, and Nigel Walker's *Crime and insanity in England*, vol. 1 (see p. 147), in which the evolution of the McNaghten Rules is discussed.

PERIODICALS

Although articles relating to criminal law are carried in all the major series of legal periodicals, including the English *Law Quarterly Review*, *Modern Law Review* and *Cambridge Law Journal*, there are two periodicals specifically devoted to criminal law and the administration of criminal justice. One is the *Criminal Law Review*, a monthly published by Sweet and Maxwell Ltd., which began in 1954. (A reprint of the complete series is currently available.) This periodical carries articles by academic and practising lawyers, reports and commentaries on recent decisions of importance, book reviews and other material intended to keep the reader abreast of developments. The other periodical worth particular mention is *Justice of the Peace,* which is published weekly and addresses itself primarily to magistrates and clerks to justices, but contains material of interest to all those interested in developments in the criminal law. The *Journal of Criminal Law* is an independent publication which consists exclusively of summaries of recent decisions of the criminal courts; it seldom contains any articles or other discursive material. A reader wishing to trace periodical literature on the criminal law is best advised to consult the H. W. Wilson *Index to Legal Periodicals*, an American publication issued monthly and cumulated quarterly, annually and in volumes covering 3-year periods. This index lists articles under subject matter and the name of the author, and matters of interest to the criminal lawyer will be found under such headings as Abortion, Accomplices, Administration of justice, Admissions, Assaults, Arrest, Arson, Bail, Burglary, etc., as well as Criminal law and Criminal procedure. The index covers all legal periodicals of any significance published in the English language, including those published in the UK and the British Commonwealth as well as the very large number of law reviews published by university law schools in the USA. Periodicals published in foreign languages are indexed in the *Index to Foreign Legal Periodicals*, published by the Institute of Advanced Legal Studies of the University of London in co-operation with the American Association of Law Libraries. Articles are also indexed here by subject and author headings, although in this case the two indexes are kept separate.

LAW REFORM

Projects to reform or codify the criminal law have been a feature of English life for well over a century; and while they have until recently had very little success, they have produced a considerable volume of literature in the form of reports of Royal Commissions and other public enquiries. Apart from the reports of the commissioners appointed at various times during the nineteenth century to consider the problem of codifying the criminal law as a whole, important reports of more recent date include the report of the Royal Commission on Capital Punishment 1949–1953, which examined in great detail the law of murder as it then stood, and the reports of the Criminal Law Revision Committee (in particular, the seventh report entitled *Felonies and misdemeanours*; the eighth report entitled *Theft and related offences*; the eleventh, *Evidence (general)*; and the twelfth, *Penalty for murder*). Both the seventh and eighth reports were followed by legislation of great importance. More recently the task of preparing proposals for a codification of the criminal law has been entrusted to the Law Commission, a law reform agency established by Parliament in 1965. This body had produced a number of published working papers, dealing with such topics as forgery, damage to property, the general principles of criminal responsibility, and the implications of strict liability in criminal law on the enforcement of regulatory legislation. Undoubtedly, both the Criminal Law Revision Committee and the Law Commissioners will produce a series of further reports in the future. Justice, the British section of the International Commission of Jurists, produces frequent reports proposing reforms; these are obtainable from Justice or the publishers, Stevens.

Efforts at the revision of the criminal law in North America have also resulted in the publication of a substantial body of literature. The most significant individual item is the Model Penal Code prepared by the American Law Institute. The code, originally published over a period from 1953 to 1961 as a series of tentative or provisional drafts, was finalised in 1962. This draft code has had considerable influence on criminal legislation in a number of American states in subsequent years. More recently, an effort to revise the Federal Criminal Laws of the USA has resulted in the publication of several substantial working papers discussing those provisions, notably the National Commission on Reform of Federal Criminal Law's *Study draft of a new Federal criminal code* (US GPO, 1970). Additionally, a considerable number of the individual states, each of which has its own system of criminal law, have published in recent years proposals for the revision of their criminal law with commentaries. All these papers provide useful material for those concerned with the reform of the criminal law; however, they are not easy to obtain outside specialised libraries. The study of comparative criminal law has been facilitated by the *American series of foreign penal codes*, sponsored by New York University School of Law and published by Sweet and Maxwell.

CRIMINAL PROCEDURE AND THE ADMINISTRATION OF CRIMINAL JUSTICE

Until quite recently, criminal procedure was a topic which attracted relatively little literary attention; in the last few years, however, the library of the subject has increased quite considerably. The best general introduction is R. M. Jackson's *Enforcing the law* (Macmillan, 1967; rev. ed., Penguin, 1972) or the relevant chapters in the same author's *Machinery of justice* (6th ed., Cambridge U.P., 1972), and a stimulating criticism of the system of trial is to be found in Glanville Williams's *The proof of guilt* (2nd ed., Stevens, 1958). For those who require a succinct account of legal technicalities, the best brief guide is J. D. Devlin's *Criminal courts and procedure* (2nd ed., Butterworths, 1967). Much of the rest of the literature is best arranged in relation to different stages in the administration of criminal justice; one useful exception is Delmar Karlen's *Anglo-American criminal justice* (Clarendon P., 1967), which offers a comparative description of English and American criminal courts and procedure. A valuable presentation of American problems in the administration of criminal justice can be found in *Criminal justice administration: materials and cases*, edited by F. J. Remington and others (Bobbs-Merrill, 1968), and in the series of the American Bar Association—*Arrest*, by W. LaFave (1965), *Conviction*, by D. Newman (1966), *Detection of crime*, by Tiffany and others (1967), *Sentencing*, by R. Dawson (1969), and *Prosecution*, by F. W. Miller (1969), all published by Little, Brown. The periodicals mentioned earlier also carry articles on procedure and administration.

THE POLICE, CRIMINAL INVESTIGATION AND PROSECUTION

The police system has been described from a variety of perspectives in a number of works. The history of the English police system has been discussed at length by Sir Leon Radzinowicz in his *History of the English criminal law* (4 vols., Stevens, 1948–   ) and, more briefly, T. A. Critchley's *A history of police in England and Wales 1900–1966* (Constable, 1967). The constitutional status of the police is discussed by Geoffrey Marshall in *Police and government* (Methuen, 1965) and the report of the Royal Commission on the Police (HMSO, 1962, Cmnd. 1728).

Sociological studies of the English police include M. Banton's *The policeman in the community* (Tavistock, 1964), John R. Lambert's *Crime, police and race relations* (Oxford U.P., 1970) and *The police: a study in manpower*, by J. P. Martin and G. Wilson (Heinemann Educational, 1969). The most recent addition is Maureen Cain's *Society and the policeman's role* (Routledge, 1973). More popular descriptions of the police system include Whitaker's *The police* (Penguin, 1964), *The police and the public*, ed. C. H. Rolph (Heinemann, 1962), Peter Laurie's *Scotland Yard* (Bodley Head, 1970) and *A man apart*, by Anthony Judge (Barker, 1972). Other books, now rather dated, but sometimes useful from a historical point of view, include J. Coatman's *Police* (Oxford U.P., 1959) and Jennifer Hart's *The British police* (Allen and Unwin, 1951). The law regulating police activity is set out succinctly and clearly in J. D. Devlin's *Police procedure, administration and organisation* (Butterworths, 1966) and in the traditional police training manual, C. C. H. Moriarty's *Police law* (20th ed., Butterworths, 1970).

The English law relating to police operations has received very little systematic treatment, apart from the now somewhat dated account by Sir Patrick Devlin in *The criminal prosecution in England* (Oxford U.P., 1960). The operation of the Judges' Rules is described by G. Abrahams in *Police questioning and the judges' rules* (Oyez, 1964). Articles on police investigation and related topics can be found in the periodicals mentioned earlier, particularly the *Criminal Law Review*.

The machinery of prosecution in England has rarely been described in detail. J. Ll. J. Edwards's *The law officers of the crown* (Sweet and Maxwell, 1964) is a full-length historical study of the offices of the Attorney General and Solicitor General, and a brief account of the Director of Public Prosecutions by the late Sir Theobald Matthew was published under the title *The office and duties of the Director of Public Prosecutions* (U. of London, Athlone P., 1950). More recently (1970), Justice, a body of lawyers concerned with law reform, have published a booklet entitled *The prosecution process in England and Wales*, which makes suggestions for reform. A description of the process of prosecution from the viewpoint of a former Chief Constable can be found in A. E. Wilcox's *The decision to prosecute* (Butterworths, 1972).

THE TRIAL

The standard texts on trial procedure have already been mentioned; they are Archbold's *Criminal pleading: evidence and practice* and Stone's *Justices' manual*, both works of reference which are republished in fresh editions at fairly frequent intervals. Introductory works for the student include R. Arguile's *Criminal procedure* (Butterworths, 1969), I. G. Carvell and E. Swinfen Green's *Criminal law and procedure* (Sweet and Maxwell, 1970) and Celia Hampton's *Criminal procedure and evidence* (Sweet and Maxwell, 1973). Both are primarily for the professional student and deal with the main outlines of technical legal aspects of the trial procedure. A comprehensive scholarly account of criminal procedure in England does not exist, but there are a number of works dealing with particular parts of the subject. On the work of the magistrates' courts, a valuable reference book, apart from Stone, is Brian Harris's *The criminal jurisdiction of magistrates* (2nd ed., Barry Rose, 1972)—again, a work of legal reference rather than description. There are a number of textbooks on the law of evidence—in particular, R. Cross on *Evidence* (3rd ed., Butterworths, 1967), the leading scholarly text on the English law of evidence; and R. Cross and N. Wilkins's *An outline of the law of evidence* (3rd ed., Butterworths, 1971), a more concise version intended for students. Another popular description of the law of evidence is G. D. Nokes's *An introduction to evidence* (4th ed., Sweet and Maxwell, 1967); the most detailed practitioner's reference book is *Phipson on Evidence* (11th ed. by D. W. Elliott; Sweet and Maxwell, 1970). The eleventh report of the Criminal Law Revision Committee on *Evidence (general)* (HMSO, 1972) is essential reading, especially with regard to safeguards for the accused. The English jury system is the subject of books by Sir Patrick Devlin (*Trial by jury*, 2nd ed., Stevens, 1966) and W. R. Cornish (*The jury*, rev. ed., Penguin, 1971), as well as an important Government enquiry published as the Report of the Departmental Committee on Jury Service, 1965 (Cmnd. 2627). Two interesting American studies of the jury system are H. Kalven and H. Zeisel's *The American jury* (Little, Brown, 1966) and R. J. Simon's *The jury and the defense of insanity* (Little, Brown, 1967). The important procedural principle of double jeopardy is described by M. L. Friedland in his book *Double jeopardy* (Clarendon P., 1969). The history and functions of the magistracy are discussed in Sir Frank Milton's *The English magistracy* (Oxford U.P., 1967) and Esther Moir's *Justice of the Peace* (Penguin, 1969), in addition to the Report of the Royal Commission on Justices of the Peace (HMSO, 1948, Cmd. 7463).

JUVENILE COURTS

Recent changes in the law relating to Juvenile Courts mean that many works on this subject are now out of date. The standard practitioner's reference work is Clarke Hall and Morrison's *Law relating to children and young persons* (8th ed. by L. Goodman, Butterworths, 1972), an essential guide to the extremely complex legislation. There is also a useful *Supplement on The Children and Young Persons Act 1969* (HMSO, 1971). More general accounts of the juvenile court can be found in W. E. Cavenagh's *Juvenile courts: the child and the law* (rev. ed., Penguin, 1967) and John Watson's *The child and the magistrate* (3rd ed., Cape, 1965).

SENTENCING

Sentencing is the subject of a number of works investigating the matter from different points of view. A basic text is the official publication *The sentence of the court* (2nd ed., HMSO, 1970), which sets out the legal provisions governing courts' powers to sentence, and describes briefly the purposes of the different sentences and institutions available. This is generally considered basic reading for any student of sentencing in England. Also for the beginner is R. Cross's *The English sentencing system* (Butterworths, 1971), a critical account of the law and practice of sentencing in England. A more detailed account of judicial attitudes in sentencing is found in D. A. Thomas's *Principles of sentencing* (Heinemann Educational, 1970), a description of the principles and policies adopted by the English Court of Appeal in dealing with appeals from higher courts. Keith Devlin's *Sentencing offenders in magistrates' courts* (Sweet and Maxwell, 1970) deals with principles applicable to sentencing in summary trials. Nigel Walker's *Sentencing in a rational society* (Allen Lane, 1969) offers a radical critique of present sentencing practices and a number of provocative proposals for possible changes. Empirical studies of sentencing in England are few; the most important are both by R. G. Hood. The first is *Sentencing in magistrates' courts* (Stevens, 1962) and the second, more recent, *Sentencing the motoring offender* (Heinemann Educational, 1972). Important empirical studies of sentencing in other jurisdictions include E. Green's *Judicial attitudes in sentencing* (Macmillan, 1961), a study of sentencing in Philadelphia, and J. Hogarth's *Sentencing as a human process* (U. of Toronto P., 1972), a very detailed empirical assessment of sentencing attitudes and behaviour among Canadian magistrates. *Criminal sentences* by M. Frankel (Hill and Wang, 1973) is an interesting general discussion of sentencing by an American federal judge, and an Australian judge's view on related matters can be found in Sir John Barry's *The courts and criminal punishments* (Government Printer, New Zealand, 1969).

APPEAL

Criminal appeal has now a significant literature of its own. The work of the Court of Criminal Appeal was the subject of two interesting investigations, the first of which was published as a report by Justice entitled *Criminal Appeals in 1964*. This was followed by the report of the Interdepartmental Committee on the Court of Criminal Appeal (HMSO, 1965, Cmnd. 2755). More recently, D. R. Thompson and H. W. Wollaston have published *Court of Appeal Criminal Division* (Knight, 1969), a practitioner's reference book dealing with the work of that court, and a similar text has been published by P. Morrish and I. McLean entitled *A practical guide to appeals in the criminal courts* (Sweet and Maxwell, 1971). This text deals with all sorts of appeals, including appeals from Magistrates' Courts. A critical survey of the work of the Court of Appeal Criminal Division and its predecessor, the Court of Criminal Appeal, is to be found in Michael Knight's *Criminal appeals* (Stevens, 1970). D. J. Mendar's *Criminal appeals: English practice and American reforms* (U. of Virginia P., 1973) is a fascinating comparative study.

EMPIRICAL STUDIES

Empirical studies of the administration of criminal justice in England and Wales are an innovation, but a number of small-scale research projects have been reported in recent years. Studies of the administration of legal aid have been published by the Institute of Judicial Administration of Birmingham University (*Legal aid in criminal proceedings*, 1970), Justice (*The unrepresented defendant in the magistrates' courts*, Stevens, 1971) and Susanne Dell (*Silent in court: the legal representation of women who went to prison*, Bell, for Social Administration Research Trust, 1971). Other projects, conducted by Michael Zander, have been reported in article form in the *Criminal Law Review*: see particularly *Crim. L.R.* 632 (1969) and *Crim. L.R.* 132 (1972). These should be read in conjunction with the report of the Interdepartmental Committee on Legal Aid in Criminal Proceedings (HMSO, 1966, Cmnd. 2934). Studies of the working of the bail system include *Prison before trial* (Bell, 1970), by Keith Bottomley, and the Cobden Trust Report, *Bail or custody*, 1972, directed by Michael King. A series of occasional papers published by the Penal Research Unit of Oxford University include David Steer's *Police cautions: a study in the exercise of police discretion* (Blackwell, for Penal Research Unit, 1970) and *Bypassing the jury: a study of changes of plea and directed acquittals in higher courts*, by R. F. Purves and S. McCabe (Blackwell, for PRU, 1972). Other projects are reported in the *Criminal Law Review* and the *British Journal of Criminology*.

BIBLIOGRAPHICAL GUIDES

More detailed information about law literature, as well as law libraries, is given by D. J. Way, a librarian, in *The student's guide to law libraries* (Oyez, 1967) and Glanville Williams, an academic lawyer, in *Learning the law* (7th ed., Stevens, 1963). A more recent guide, though with a North American bias, is M. A. Banks's *Using a law library* (U. of Western Ontario P., 1971). *A bibliographical guide to the law of the United Kingdom, the Channel Islands and the Isle of Man* (2nd ed., U. of London Institute of Advanced Legal Studies, 1973) has sections listing selected works on criminal law and criminology. The editor is A. G. Chloros. A useful check-list is 'The statement of minimum library holdings for law libraries in England and Wales', by J. C. Smith, in *J. Society of Public Teachers of Law*, **11** (2), 90–103 (1970). For legal terminology, *Mozley and Whiteley's Law Dictionary* is useful. The eighth edition, by J. B. Saunders, was published by Butterworths in 1970.

9

Police literature

Dennis T. Brett

Police literature comprises works written for, about and sometimes by the police. Regrettably, and understandably, much is restricted to police and related personnel—some, indeed, to the most senior police officers and government officials. However, the bona fide researcher, and even the general reader, can be agreeably surprised at the quantity and scope of literature available to him through the public library system and, by courteous and tactful enquiry, from elsewhere. The literature is, of course, too vast for exhaustive treatment here. What follows is therefore a historical outline of the police, with reference to major—and sometimes minor—primary and secondary information sources.

GENERAL WORKS

J. Coatman's *Police* (Oxford U.P., 1959) is a discursive example of a book with the broadest approach. J. Cramer's *The world's police* (Cassell, 1964) is more systematic, providing historical, constitutional, statistical and photographic information under police forces. It is therefore incidentally useful as a directory.

Theoretical matters concerning, for example, the police role, purpose, ethics, are generally diffused within the literature of other police subjects such as history, office of constable, police powers, procedure, sociology and autobiography, and the reader must examine this when exhaustive research is required. Many early force instruction books carry inspiring words from chief constables indicating the conduct expected of the police. Other notable works

160

are: J. Tobias's 'Origins of the police role' (*Criminologist*, May 1969, 106–112); G. Marshall's *Police and government* (Methuen, 1965); and several of C. Reith's—for example, *Police principles and the problem of war* (Oxford U.P., 1940) and his *New study of police history* (Oliver and Boyd, 1956), containing the 'Nine principles of policing'. Separate treatment of police ethics is given in D. Kocken's *Ethics in police service* (C. C. Thomas, 1957) and D. A. Hansen's *Police ethics* (C. C. Thomas, 1973); and other American views are given in the many police administration and procedure manuals.

HISTORY

The police equivalents in ancient and classical times are covered briefly in general encyclopaedias and police histories. There are a few helpful periodical articles on the police of Rome—and, for further research, there are the resources of ancient history literature.

For long, the outstanding general history of the English police was W. Melville Lee's *A history of police in England* (Methuen, 1901), which, covering the period from Anglo-Saxon times to the end of the nineteenth century, omits a large and important part of the story. The matter has now been rectified by the publication of T. Critchley's completely new and comprehensive *A history of police in England and Wales, 900–1966* (Constable, 1967). Other notable histories are: E. Glover's *The English police: its origin and development* (Police Chronicle, 1934); A. Solmes's *The English policeman, 871–1935* (Allen and Unwin, 1935); C. Reith's *British police and the democratic ideal* (Oxford U.P., 1943) and *Short history of the British police* (Oxford U.P., 1948); and G. Howard's *Guardians of the Queen's peace* (Odhams, 1953). Several contemporary accounts of constables' duties and encounters, showing their part in the sixteenth and seventeenth century machinery of justice, are contained in *The Elizabethan underworld*, by A. V. Judges (2nd ed., Routledge, 1964). Goddard's *Memoirs of a Bow Street Runner* (Museum P., 1956) describes the work of one of these early nineteenth century detectives, trained under the system initiated by the reformer and magistrate Henry Fielding, and later his brother John. There are also several attractive junior histories covering a rather wider subject field, for example J. Tobias's *Against the peace* (Ginn, 1970); J. Dumpleton's *Law and order: the story of the police* (2nd ed., Black, 1970). An unusual but excellent book of excerpts is B. Naunton's *A tree of law and order*

(Justice of the Peace, 1970), a wide-ranging work comprising original and other texts over several hundred years. Useful display material is contained in D. Johnson's *London Peelers and the British police* (Jackdaw, 1971), which consists of a folder of facsimile reproductions of police documents and posters, with notes and transcripts, from 1668 to 'modern times'.

There were many proposals for penal and police reform in the eighteenth and early nineteenth centuries. These were often moral and humanitarian in tone, discussing the incidence and nature of contemporary crime and making recommendations for its alleviation. The more important are: H. Fielding's *Enquiry into the causes of the late increase in robbers* (1751); J. Fielding's *Plan for preventing robberies within twenty miles of London* (1753) and *Account of the origin and effects of a police set on foot ...* (1758); J. Hanway's *Defects of police ...* (1775); W. Blizard's *Desultory reflections on police ...* (1785); and P. Colqu'houn's treatises *The police of the metropolis* (1796), proposing a centrally coordinated police force, and *Commerce and police of the River Thames* (1798), which led to the establishing of Harriot's Marine Police. Two works appeared in 1821: G. Allen's *Brief considerations on the present state of the police of the metropolis*, and G. Mainwaring's *Observations on the present state of the police of the metropolis*. Details of the many reports of Parliamentary Committees from about 1750 are to be found in the official lists of parliamentary papers, those edited by P. and G. Ford, and those listed in L. Radzinowicz's *History ...* (see below).

There is ample literature on the century prior to 1829, the most recent being: A. Babington's *A house in Bow Street* (Macdonald, 1969); G. Howson's *Thief-taker general: the rise and fall of Jonathan Wild* (Hutchinson, 1970); and P. Pringle's *Henry and Sir John Fielding* (Dobson, 1968), *The thief-takers* (Museum P., 1958), and *Hue and cry* (Museum P., 1955). L. Radzinowicz's comprehensive and detailed *History of the English criminal law*, especially Vols. 2, 3 and 4 (Stevens, 1956–1968), is a major work of research containing an extensive bibliographical section.

The fairness and tact of the police gradually won a grudging public respect, and reform outside London was effected by the *Lighting and Watching Act 1833* and the *Municipal Corporations Act 1835*. After the First Report of the Constabulary Force Commissioners in 1839, the *County Police Act 1839* permitted, and later the *County and Borough Police Act 1856* compelled, justices to maintain police forces. Regular government inspection was established, the first annual report appearing in 1857. A valuable historical account of inspection is provided by F. Tarry's unpublished *A century of police inspection.*

The following cover the 'modern period' as a whole: J. Hart's *The British police* (Allen and Unwin, 1951); J. Martin and G. Wilson's *Police: a study in manpower* (Heinemann, 1969); and C. Pulling's *Mr. Punch and the police* (Butterworths, 1964), a judicious selection of cartoons and texts from 1841, considered to 'form links in the story of the police'.

Pay and morale were low after World War I and there were police strikes in 1918 and 1919, historically treated in G. Reynolds and A. Judge's *The night the police went on strike* (Weidenfeld, 1968). The Desborough Committee reported in 1919 and 1920 on personnel matters and the *Police Act 1919* adopted many of its recommendations: improved pay; establishment of the Police Federation as a negotiating body for ranks below superintendent; formation of the Police Council; and the empowering of the Home Secretary to make regulations on pay and conditions. These latter are published by HMSO as statutory instruments and are also available from the Federation. The *Report of the Royal Commission on Police Powers* (HMSO, 1929, Cmd. 3297) followed some public criticism of police methods—for example, non-adherence to the 'Judges' Rules,' a revised version of which was published by HMSO as Appendix A to Home Office circular 31/1964 in 1964. The rules are reprinted, with notes, in G. Abrahams's *Police questioning and the judges' rules* (Oyez, 1964). The most important history for this period is the unpublished *Home Office and the police between the two world wars,* an account of the 'principal changes which took place in the 20 years' when 'the service was transformed' and a new structure was framed for the future. The author, Sir Arthur Dixon, was Principal Assistant Under-Secretary of State, Home Office.

During the latter half of the 1950s, a number of unfortunate incidents and their resultant publicity severely weakened public confidence in the police. In 1956, for example, disciplinary action concerning force administration was taken against the Chief Constable of Cardigan (*Report of the enquiry into the administration and efficiency of Cardiganshire Constabulary and the state of discipline in the force,* HMSO, 1957, Cmnd. 251), and in 1957 in Thurso, Scotland, a provocative boy was beaten by the police: *Report,* Cmnd. 718 (Edinburgh: HMSO, 1959). In 1960 the Royal Commission on the Police was appointed. 'Its genesis was, basically, concern about the means of controlling the police and bringing them to account when things went wrong' (Critchley). But its terms of reference were wide. Its *Interim report* (HMSO, 1960, Cmnd. 1222) led to a substantial pay rise. The *Final report* (HMSO, 1962, Cmnd. 1728) was followed in 1964 by the *Police Act*. An authoritative record of recent events is provided by the *Annual reports of Her Majesty's Chief Inspector of Constabulary*, published by HMSO. Recent issues of the main police periodicals, and the Annual Reports of Chief Constables, are also useful.

Some 180 force histories are listed in the Police College Library's bibliography, *The police of England and Wales*. Researchers should consider the following local sources when covering new ground: archivists, history societies, newspaper offices, public libraries and, if necessary, force public relations officers. Quarter Sessions order books can be helpful and local police committees maintain detailed police records. Written local history can be of value. Thus, A. Redford's *History of local government in Manchester* (Longmans, 1939–40) contributes much to the history of the Manchester Police. Little has been written about the Commonwealth forces, the main work being C. Jeffries's *The colonial police* (Parrish, 1952). Some individual force histories have been produced but few have been published. The R.C.M.P. is, apparently, the most popular force and the one most written about.

ORGANISATION AND PROCEDURE

W. Hewitt's *British police administration* (C. C. Thomas, 1965) describes our national administrative structure and includes a section on police statutes. Chapter IV of F. Newsam's *The Home Office* (2nd ed., Allen and Unwin, 1955) covers police administration from the viewpoint of the Home Office, where the author was Permanent Under-Secretary of State. Home Office circulars 198/1972 and 154/1973 cover arrangements for the new police areas from 1 April 1974 (Local Government Act, 1972). Police organisation and procedure manuals, used by police studying for the promotion examinations, can be useful guides for others. Works in current use include a series of four frequently revised books in Butterworths' 'Police Promotion Handbooks' series, ed. E. Baker and G. Wilkie. Moriarty's *Police law* has been a basic textbook for more than 40 years and is now in its 21st edition (Butterworths, 1972). Some books become slightly dated by administrative and legislative change, yet retain their general value: for example, J. Conlin's *Local and central government—police administration*

(Cassell, 1967); J. Devlin's *Police procedure, administration and organisation* (Butterworths, 1966); and J. Thomas's *Police organisation and administration* (5th ed., Police Review, 1965). Official works include the Home Office *Manual of guidance* (2nd ed., HMSO, 1970), which covers the requirements of the Police Promotion Examinations Board; the Home Office *Consolidated circular to the police on crime and kindred matters* (1969); and a basic training school textbook, *The training of probationary constables: students' lesson notes* (HMSO, 1969). All forces issue instructions to their members concerning policy and procedure. For example, the Metropolitan Police have in use *The Metropolitan Police guide* (1939), *The instruction book ...* (1963) and *General orders and regulations* (1969). In addition, they issue the bulletin *Metropolitan Police orders* twice weekly.

Police powers

Incidents in which police exceed their powers continue to occur; see, for example, *The Challenor Report* by A. James (HMSO, 1965, Cmnd. 2735). The subject is treated in S. Bowes's *The police and civil liberties* (Lawrence and Wishart, 1966) and in National Council for Civil Liberties pamphlets. However, most serious works on the problems of police power are American. The *Knapp Commission report* (Braziller, 1973), a recent official statement resulting from 'allegations of police corruption', also examines New York's anti-corruption procedure. C. Sowle's *Police power and individual freedom ...* (Aldine, 1962) covers arrest, detention, search and seizure, interrogation and self-incrimination. J. Creamer's *Law of arrest, search and seizure* (Saunders, 1968) covers similar ground; and W. LaFave's *Arrest: the decision to take a suspect into custody*, an American Bar Foundation Report published by Little, Brown in 1965, is a comprehensive general work on police policies and methods in the USA. Two works on police review boards—a system in which civilian boards review police activities, especially relations with minority groups—are notable. The first, cited by Cray as 'the single, most comprehensive survey of present reviewing agencies', is H. Beral and M. Sisk's 'The administration of complaints by civilians against the police' (*Harvard Law Review*, 77, 1964); and a useful select list of material, geographically arranged, is E. Cray's 'Annotated bibliography on police review boards' (*Law in Transition Quarterly*, 197–205, 1966).

Criminal investigation

The history of scientific crime detection is fully treated in J. Thorwald's three volumes, published by Thames and Hudson: *The marks of Cain* (1965); *Dead men tell tales* (1966); and *The proof of poison* (1966). Individual ability and flair were for long the detective's main qualities. To these co-operation and system have gradually been added. The *Report of the Home Office Committee on Detective Work and Procedure* (1938) led to radical reforms, including national co-ordination of resources, use of the latest scientific aids and proper detective training. The *Report of the Home Office Committee on the Prevention and Detection of Crime* (1965) covered similar matters. The *Police Gazette*, an internal police circular giving descriptions of wanted persons, derived from *Public Hue and Cry*, itself a development from Sir John Fielding's notices of thefts and persons wanted in *The Public Advertiser* and other papers. In 1800 it was published as *Hue and Cry and Police Gazette*, and in 1828 as the weekly *Police Gazette*. Scotland Yard issued it from 1883, since when it has developed into the present daily issue, with supplements.

There are several manuals of crime detection, the best-known being those by Söderman and Gross. N. Morland's *Outline of scientific criminology* (Cassell, 1971) describes the present state of the science and the quarterly periodical, *The Criminologist*, contains articles by experts on a variety of crime subjects. Books about detectives and their work are numerous, a recent example being P. Deeley's *The manhunters* (Hodder and Stoughton, 1970), which describes cases from five countries. Many collections of detectives' cases are autobiographical, an early example being J. Caminada's *Twenty-five years of detective life* (2 vols., Heywood, 1895, 1901); and a recent example is G. Hatherill's *A detective's story* (Deutsch, 1971). D. Brett's *Crime detection* (Cambridge U.P., 1959), an annotated reading list covering scientific detection, criminal cases and the police in action, is a reader's guide to selection.

Interrogation

There are several manuals—for example, A. Aubrey and R. Caputo's *Criminal interrogation* (C. C. Thomas, 1965); P. Deeley's *Beyond breaking point* (Barker, 1971), which discusses various methods in past and present use; and *The third degree*, by C. Franklyn (Hale, 1970), on practices unacceptable in a temperate, western democracy.

Police and public

In 1960 the Government Social Survey questioned both police and public for the Royal Commission on the Police, detailed results being later published as Appendix IV to the *Minutes of evidence* (HMSO, 1962). Even at this difficult time, nearly 83% of informants had 'great respect for the police.' In the same year, Heinemann published a collection of essays: *The police and the public: an enquiry*, edited by ex-police inspector and journalist C. H. Rolph. M. Banton's *Police–community relations* (Collins, 1973) is an elementary manual for police and others; see also the White Paper *Police/immigrant relations in England and Wales*, Cmnd. 5438 (HMSO, 1973).

Notable American works include essays edited by A. Brandstatter and L. Radelet entitled *Police and community relations: a sourcebook* (Collier-Macmillan, 1968); J. Marx's *Officer tell your story: a guide to police public relations* (C. C. Thomas, 1967); H. Earle's *Police–community relations: crisis in our time* (2nd ed., C. C. Thomas, 1970); and A. J. Reiss's *Police and the public* (Yale U.P., 1971). Two important works have been prepared for the President's Commission on Law Enforcement. The first is the report of a research study by Michigan State University National Center on Police and Community Relations entitled *A national survey of police and community relations* (US GPO, 1967); and *The police and the community: the dynamics of their relationship in a changing society*, by the Dean and Staff of the School of Criminology, University of California (2 vols., US GPO, 1966), the latter work including much detailed information and verbatim reports of police–public dialogues. *A bibliography on police and community relations*, from the National Center on Police and Community Relations, East Lansing, 1966, is one of the few known bibliographies on the subject.

Relations with special groups

J. Kenny and D. Pursuit's *Police work with juveniles* ... (C. C. Thomas, 1970) is a classic now in its 4th edition. M. Holman's *The police officer and the child* (C. C. Thomas, 1962) instructs the police in child interrogation; and D. Bouma's *Kids and cops: a study in mutual hostility* (W. Eerdmans, 1969) shows from survey results 'how police and youth felt about each other in medium sized cities in midwest.' England's juvenile liaison scheme, in which the police take a preventive role, is described by its pioneers, Liverpool Constabulary, in *The police and children* (2nd ed., 1962 with later amendments). A. Richardson's *Nick of Notting Hill* (Harrap, 1965), a policeman's story of his attempts to 'tackle crime at its source,' exemplifies the value of individual police effort.

J. Lambert's *Crime, police and race relations* (Oxford U.P., 1970) is based on the results of a Birmingham study. It finds coloured immigrants 'not in the main responsible' for crime and emphasises the importance of the police role in crime prevention. Further evidence for this is provided by the House of Commons Select Committee on Race Relations and Immigration: *Minutes of evidence: police/immigrant relations*, and the *Report* (HMSO, 1972). Among the predominating American works on police relations with racial groups are: C. Epstein's *Intergroup relations for police officers* (Williams and Wilkins, 1962) and D. Bayley and H. Mendelsohn's *Minorities and the police* (Collier-Macmillan, 1969).

Personnel

Career literature is available from local police forces and from the Home Office. Two frequently revised booklets are useful for this purpose: *Choice of careers, No. 80: Police*, issued by the Central Youth Employment Executive, and the Central Office of Information's *The police service in Britain*. Career literature can be biographical, as in P. Nobes's *A policeman's lot* (Educational Explorers, 1973).

There are two official reports on police manpower: that issued by the ACPO in 1962 entitled *Methods of assessing police establishments* and the Police Advisory Board's *Working Party Report on Police Manpower*, published with two other reports by HMSO in 1967. J. Martin and G. Wilson's *Police: a study in manpower* (Heinemann, 1969) is a historical study, using social accounting techniques and covering 'the evolution of the Service in England and Wales, 1829–1965', with special emphasis on personnel and finance. There is also an official study by J. Stokes, *Some aspects of man-management in the police service*, a survey carried out on behalf of the Home Office by the Government Social Survey in 1967–1968 (Office of Population Censuses and Surveys, 1971) analysing police opinion on welfare, conditions of service, and the service generally. Recent American works include: A. Bristow's *Police supervision readings* (C. C. Thomas, 1971), for police super-

visors 'covering subjects least available under in-service training';
W. Melnicoe and J. Mennig's *Elements of police supervision* (Glencoe P., 1969), valuable as a synthesis of 'the best thought and practice'; and N. Iannone's *Supervision of police personnel* (Prentice-Hall, 1970).

Education and training

P. Alagendra's *Police training techniques* (Royal Malaysia Police, 1969) outlines the various methods practised in different parts of the world and G. Cedermark's *Selection and training of police personnel in England, France and Sweden* (1970) is a Council of Europe Research Fellowship Report.

Recruiting and training in England have been discussed by several committees already mentioned. In addition, the Central Conference of Chief Constables' Reports *Review of arrangements for probationer training* (1954 and 1969) and the First Report to the Police Training Council by the Home Office Working Party on Police Probationer Training (Home Office, 1971) are notable. Part 1 of the Metropolitan Police Working Party's Report on *Probationer training* appeared in 1969, and Part 2, *Field Training*, in 1971. For recent changes, see Home Office circulars. Promotion examination syllabuses are issued by the Local Government Training Board; examination papers by the Civil Service Commission.

Official thought and policy on central higher training are recorded by the following papers and reports: Police Council Sub-Committee on the Establishment of a Police College (HMSO, 1930); Home Office Committee on Higher Training ... (HMSO, 1947, Cmd. 7070); Home Office, *Police training in England and Wales* (HMSO, 1961, Cmnd. 1450); Police Council on Higher Police Training (HMSO, 1962) and its *Second Report ...* (Senior Staff Course) (HMSO, 1963); *Supplementary Report ... on the Senior Staff Course* (1963); and the *Second Supplementary Report on the Special Course* (1963). The position in Scotland is covered by the Police Advisory Board for Scotland's Working Party Report, *Higher police training in Scotland* (Edinburgh, HMSO, 1968).

Truncheons and tipstaves

The main published works are E. Clark's *Truncheons* (H. Jenkins, 1935); and E. Dicken's *The history of truncheons* (A. Stockwell, 1952). There are also several periodical articles.

Modern use of the truncheon in America is shown in the handbooks: *Koga method: police baton technique*, by R. Koga and J. Nelson (Collier-Macmillan, 1968), and *The Yawara stick and police baton*, by J. Moynahan (C. C. Thomas, 1963).

BIBLIOGRAPHY

Throughout this chapter, bibliographies relating to particular subjects have been mentioned in context. The following therefore describe general works, but readers are reminded of the many useful lists contained in books themselves, the outstanding example being L. Radzinowicz's *History of the criminal law* (see p. 162).

The International Police Association's *International bibliography of selected police literature* (2nd ed., M. and W. Pubns. for I.P.A., 1968) provides an impressive collection of modern police literature, arranged under country by broad subject headings.

Most of the remaining English-language bibliographies are American. D. Culver's *Bibliography of crime and criminal justice, 1927–1931* (H. W. Wilson, 1934) is a wide-ranging work containing some European material in its 60-page police section; S. Greer's *A bibliography of police administration and police science* (Inst. of Public Admin., Columbia U., 1936) is a major work of professional quality but listing American literature in the main; W. Hewitt's *A bibliography of police administration* ... (C. C. Thomas, 1967) uses an alphabetico-classed subject arrangement for its 11 000 entries; H. Becker and G. Felkenes's *Law enforcement: a selected bibliography* (Scarecrow P., 1968) is 'broader in scope and more dynamic in its contribution to research', with systematically arranged entries in a specially numbered series. An annotated bibliography, *Police literature*, by A. L. McGehee, was published in 1970 by the Police Science Division, Institute of Government, University of Georgia, Athens, Georgia.

Sir John Cumming's *A contribution towards a bibliography dealing with crime* (3rd ed., Metropolitan Police, 1935) is mainly English in content. Despite its title, 32 of its 107 pages are on police matters and it remains the basic police bibliography for the nineteenth and early twentieth centuries. *The police of England and Wales: a short bibliography*, issued by the Police College Library, is frequently revised but limited to history and general matters. The Government Publications *Sectional List No. 26: Home Office* (HMSO, latest issue) contains a police section showing works currently available from HMSO.

PERIODICAL LISTS, INDEXES, ABSTRACTS

There is no established police abstracting service for this country; the Police College Library's monthly *Additions to the Library* is the most comprehensive of its kind, and some periodical articles are included. However, some abstracts covering a wider or related field contain police entries, for example *Abstracts on Criminology and Penology* (formerly *Excerpta Criminologica*), published bi-monthly in the Netherlands by A. Kluwer for the Criminologica Foundation. From April 1973, the sections dealing with police science and forensic science have been published separately as *Abstracts on Police Science* (also by Kluwer). In addition, Oakland, California, Police Department's Police Research and Development Institute provides an abstracts service by annual supplements to its main work issued in 1965 and the US Department of Justice, LEAA, National Criminal Justice Reference Service, Washington, disseminates information about publications of police interest. Interpol's *Semi-annual list of selected articles* contains very brief notes of articles in the police periodicals of its member countries, arranged under subject headings.

LIBRARIES

There are no published catalogues of police libraries except for the occasional listing of force holdings. Notable British police libraries include those of the Police College, Scottish Police College, Metropolitan Police, Home Office and a few of the larger forces outside London. Also relevant are the libraries in related subject fields and, for older material, the large national and university libraries.

PERIODICALS

The most important and widely read English police periodicals are: *Police Review*, dating from 1893, a weekly, commonly read throughout the Service; *Police Journal* (1928–), containing authoritative police and legal articles and comment; *Police*, issued by the Police Federation; *Police College Magazine*, providing serious articles on police subjects as well as news of College activities; *Police Research Bulletin*, covering new equipment and techniques; *Criminal Law Review*, for legal notes on new legislation and cases and for topical contributed articles; *Police Gazette*; *Police Reports*; and *Criminologist*. In addition, there are the many magazines issued by police forces, ranging from those limited to local domestic matters to those containing serious articles by experts on police and legal subjects. Many of the newer force magazines, e.g. *The Job* (Metropolitan Police), *Constables County* (Suffolk), *Thames View* (Thames Valley), are attractively produced and help force morale considerably by keeping the men informed of police policy and developments. In addition, many forces issue to the public road safety periodicals for information and educational purposes. Notable overseas periodicals are: *Australian Police Journal*; *Deutsche Polizei*; *F.B.I. Law Enforcement Bulletin*; *International Criminal Police Review* (Interpol); *Journal of Police Science and Administration* (see p. 45); *Police Chief*; *Polizia Moderna*; *R.C.M.P. Quarterly* and *Revue Moderne de la Police*. Two lists of police periodicals may be quoted: the Police College Library's *List of periodicals currently received*, which lists some 280 items; and J. Vandiver's *Police periodicals* (1970), containing 208 titles.

DIRECTORIES

The annual *International security directory* (Security Gazette Ltd.), provides details of top personnel in government departments, associations and police forces throughout the world, although most of the book is concerned with fire and industrial security services. Another annual, the *Police and constabulary almanac* (R. Hazell, Ltd.), is limited to police and other departments of the British Isles, and in its 366 pages provides much personnel detail. The *Police guide* (Police Review, annual) is an expanded version of the general information section in the late *Police Review Diary*. In addition, many forces have their own directory. In America there are several directories of police departments, personnel and equipment in use.

POLICE ORGANISATIONS AND ASSOCIATIONS

The International Police Association, a non-political society, was formed in Great Britain in 1950. Its publications include the *International Police Journal*. Other international organisations are: The International Association of Chiefs of Police, Washington, and

The International Federation of Senior Police Officers, Paris. Statutory organisations for England and Wales include the Police Federation, whose history and function are described in A. Judge's *The first fifty years* (Police Federation, 1968), the Police Council and the Police Advisory Board. Further information is contained in the *Report of the Police Council Committee on Police Representative Organizations and Negotiating Machinery* (HMSO, 1952) and J. Gaskain's *Consultative organs in the police service* (Cheltenham Office of HM Inspector of Constabulary, 1966).

ANNUAL REPORTS AND STATISTICS

Under the *Police Act 1964*, all chief constables must issue an annual report covering activities and policy concerning administration, personnel, crime, traffic and other matters; they are, therefore, a source of local statistics. Nationally, the *Annual Report* of Her Majesty's Chief Inspector of Constabulary presents a similar account, and the sequence from the first, 1857, is basic research material. *Police force statistics*, an annual prepared by the Institute of Municipal Treasurers and Accountants and the Society of County Treasurers, provides statistical tables on population, police strengths and expenditure. The American *Police yearbook*, issued by the International Association of Chiefs of Police, contains annual conference proceedings and papers on many police problems.

SPECIAL TYPES OF POLICE

Policewomen

Reports of official committees on policewomen and their duties appeared in 1920 (Cmd. 877) and 1924 (Cmd. 2224); then, in 1929, came C. Owing's *Women police: a study of the development and status of the women police movement* (Patterson Smith reprint, 1969), with world coverage. The following memoirs are valuable for the information provided on this subject: M. Allen's *Pioneer policewoman* (Chatto, 1925) and *Lady in blue* (S. Paul, 1936); L. Wyles's *A woman at Scotland Yard* (Faber, 1951); S. Condor's *Woman on the beat* (Hale, 1960); J. Hilton's *Gentle arm of the law* (Educational Explorers, 1967; revised ed., Transworld Pubs., 1973); and J. Lock's *Lady policeman* (M. Joseph, 1968).

Special Constabulary

Official reports include Sir E. Ward's on the Metropolitan Special Constabulary, 1914 (HMSO, 1920, Cmd. 536); and the *Fourth Report* of the Police Post-War Committee. Other works are: J. Muddock's *All clear* ... (Everitt, 1920); W. Reay's *The specials* (Heinemann, 1920); and R. Seth's *The specials* ... (Gollancz, 1961).

Other kinds of police

The powers of some police are limited to the premises or area served—for example, railway, airport and dock police. A. Lynford discusses them in 'Britain's other police forces' (*Illustrated London News*, April 15, 1967). For railway police, readers may refer to J. Whitbread's *The railway policeman* (Harrap, 1961) and H. Dewhurst's *The railroad police* (C. C. Thomas, 1955). The Service police were merged to form the Ministry of Defence Police in 1971. Military police are described in A. Lovell-Knight's *History of the office of Provost Marshal and the Corps of Military Police* (Gale and Polden, 1945). Private police work varies from solitary detection to highly organised, large-scale contract work. F. Oughton's *Ten guineas a day* (Long, 1961) describes the former and T. Clayton's *The protectors* (Oldbourne, 1967) discusses the multi-million-pound security industry. There are several manuals of industrial and commercial security, including: K. Knight's *Shopkeeper's security manual* (T. Stacey, 1971), R. Cole's *The application of security systems and hardware* (C. C. Thomas, 1970), T. Carter's *Crime prevention* (Police Review, 1965), and E. Oliver and J. Wilson's *Security manual* (Gower Press, 1969).

Totalitarian police

Dictatorship and political police, by E. Bramstedt (Kegan Paul, Trench and Trubner, 1959) and *The police state*, by B. Chapman (Pall Mall P., 1970) provide a suitable background. There is ample further reading matter on the secret police of Nazi Germany, Russia and some other countries. *The Okhrana: The Russian Department of Police—a bibliography*, an extensive compilation by E. Smith and R. Lednicky was published by the Hoover Institution, Stanford University, in 1967, and was based on the holdings of the Institution's library.

POLICE RESEARCH

The establishment of the Police Research and Planning Branch at the Home Office in 1963 followed a Royal Commission recommendation. The Summer 1971 issue of the *Police Research Bulletin* is particularly valuable for its review of methods and equipment employed in recent years. Research is done also by police forces and other bodies—for example, Lamsac, The Local Authorities Management Services Computer Committee, Police Applications Group. An important three-part volume was published by HMSO in 1967: the Police Advisory Board's *Reports of three working parties on police manpower, equipment and efficiency*. In America The Center for Law Enforcement Research Information issues a quarterly bulletin under the auspices of the IACP.

There is a growing body of serious and even scholarly literature on the police function in society and the emergent sociological, ethical and legal problems, of which the following are representative: M. Banton's *The policeman in the community* (Tavistock, 1964), P. Devlin's 'Police in a changing society' (*Police J.*, 1966), B. Whitaker's *The police* (Eyre and Spottiswoode, 1964), and several papers from two recent conferences—The Fourth National Conference on Research and Teaching in Criminology, Cambridge, 1970, and the Bristol University Seminar on the Sociology of the Police, 1971. *The police we deserve* edited by J. C. Alderson and P. J. Stead (Wolfe, 1973) is a collection of essays on current police problems. Another police viewpoint is provided by A. Judge's *A man apart: the British policeman and his job* (Barker, 1972).

The following are typical of the better American writings: H. Becker's *Issues in police administration* (Scarecrow P., 1970); D. Bordua's collection of *Six sociological essays* (Wiley, 1967); *Law and order: police encounters*, ed. M. Lipsky (Aldine, 1970), six essays reprinted from *Transaction*, describing the 'potential usefulness of social science in working out alternatives to the enforcement of order by violence'; A. Niederhoffer's *Behind the shield: the police in urban society* (Doubleday, 1967); J. Skolnick's *Justice without trial: law enforcement in democratic society* (Wiley, 1966); W. Turner's *The police establishment* (Putnam, 1968); The President's Commission on Law Enforcement and Administration of Justice Task Force Report: *Police* (US GPO, 1967); N. Watson and J. Sterling's *Police and their opinions* (IACP, 1969), a wide-ranging sociological study based on the results of a survey; W.

Westley's *Violence and the police* (MIT Press, 1971) which examines the inner character of the police, their attitudes, behaviour, relations with the public and day-to-day duties as revealed by a study of a midwestern municipal force 20 years ago; and J. Wilson's 'Police and their problems' (*Public Policy*, **12**, 1963, Harvard University Graduate School of Public Administration) and his *Varieties of police behaviour: the management of law and order in eight communities* (Harvard U.P., 1968).

10

Criminal and related statistics

N. Howard Avison

INTRODUCTION

The word 'statistics' and the thought of columns and columns of figures very frequently seem to cause a blocking of people's thought-processes. In the case of statistics about crime and criminals, this is particularly unfortunate; because while the statistics involved are of the simplest kind, they remain one of the most important sources of information about criminality in society. This chapter sets out to describe the form of British statistics in this field, and the sorts of information which can be gleaned directly from them. It goes on to consider what the figures mean, and how further information in related areas may be gathered. A shorter section deals with foreign material, and discusses the difficulty of comparing different countries. Finally, there is a brief discussion of prediction in criminology.

Three main groups use statistics of crime and criminals. First, members of Parliament and local officials see them as measures of the extent to which the criminal law is broken, and of the sentences imposed on offenders. Secondly, administrators see them as some measure of the effectiveness of the police and penal system; from statistics such as these, plans may be made for the future of the various provisions for dealing with offenders. Thirdly, criminologists study them, comment on them and interpret them in an effort to gain a better understanding of the social processes leading to the defining of members of society as criminals, the disposal of these offenders in courts, and the future conduct of such offenders.

THE FORM AND CONTENT OF CRIMINAL STATISTICS

For two centuries criminologists have provided a vast literature relating to criminal statistics, and it is impossible to do more than indicate a fraction of the bibliography dealing with the subject. In its historical section, the book by Sellin and Wolfgang[50] traces the development of criminal statistics, which in Britain grew from an irregular account of convictions in courts, to the modern compilation with an extensive classification of crimes known to the police, with additional details relating to sentences imposed in courts.

Every year Her Majesty's Stationery Office publishes the *Criminal Statistics*.[5] Looking at a typical volume, it seems full of statistical tables. How are they gathered, and what do they mean? Let us take a typical example. A crime is reported to an English police station and the complainer tells a policeman what has happened—suppose that someone jostled him in a bus queue and later he found his wallet missing. The policeman fills in a 'crime report form', and the start of the process of recording this event begins. It looks as though a theft has been committed, and accordingly 1 will be added to that police force's record of the number of thefts they know about. Had it seemed like a robbery, 1 would have been added to the total of robberies, and so on. Each month the running total of all crimes made known to the police is sent to the Home Office Statistical Branch, giving the classification of the crime (as the police know it) and the number of crimes under each classification. At the Home Office these figures are added together to provide a monthly total for the whole of England and Wales; each quarter a preliminary document is circulated to appropriate officials, giving the total for the year so far; and at the end of the year preparations are put in hand for the publication of figures of crimes known to the police during that year. This document is eventually published, about 6 months after the year to which the figures refer. However, this is not the only information the police provide. If, for example, the theft referred to above was attributed to an alleged offender, it would be counted as detected, or 'cleared-up'. And if the offender came to court, the police would provide information about his age, sex, number and type of previous convictions, and the sentence imposed. Other information about the legal process—for example, whether he was granted bail, or how long he remained in custody —and details of any appeal against conviction or sentence are also collected, and some of these details are eventually incorporated in a summary form in *Criminal Statistics*.

PROBLEMS OF INTERPRETATION: THE 'DARK FIGURE'

All this is perfectly straightforward and easy to understand. The difficulties arise only when one tries to interpret the figures thus collected. From the foregoing it may be thought that every crime committed in the community is eventually recorded in the annual *Criminal Statistics*, and that by reference to this volume a sort of 'political barometer' could be read. This, indeed, was Jeremy Bentham's hope when he urged the Government to start collecting criminal statistics, so that the health of the body politic might be ascertained. Unfortunately, this is far from being the true position. Long suspected by criminologists, and now revealed by enquiries in the United States, a substantial number of crimes are committed—and recognised by the victims as crimes—but are not reported to the police. This is the 'dark figure' of crime and an American survey suggests that it is at least as large as the numbers of crimes recorded by the police[11, 12]. Here, then, is the first problem of interpretation. When (as is the usual case) this year's crime figures are larger than last year's, does this mean that *actual* crime has increased? If only a relatively few more people who were victims of crime decided to report the facts of the crime to the police, this year, rather than deciding not to report them (as last year), the number of *recorded* crimes would increase, without there necessarily being any increase in criminal acts. There is no certain answer, but criminologists have tended to assume that there must be *some* real increase in crime, although there may be, in addition, an apparent increase owing to people having a greater readiness to report crime. An increased readiness to report crime might come from factors such as its being easier to do so— by the use of '999' systems; by an increased 'sensitisation' to crime, such as violent crime; or by the necessity to report crime for insurance claims to be successful. The American material suggests that people refrain from reporting crime because they feel that the police cannot do much about it, anyway; or that it was not sufficiently serious to warrant involving the police. Other reasons range from embarrassment at being the victim of certain types of crime to fear of reprisals from offenders. Some crimes are extremely rarely reported by victims, and the recording of such crimes is directly related to police activity. All these factors show that the figure of 'crime made known to the police' can be no more than an indication of the amount of crime committed in the community. McClintock's survey of the 'dark figure' of crime[31] is an invaluable reference source and contains an extensive bibliography.

Attempts to ascertain the actual amount of crime committed in a community and the number of criminals living there have been made along three broad avenues.

First, it was thought possible to ascertain details of particular crimes from other sources of statistical data. Thus, the Registrar-General gives details of deaths caused by homicide. These should tally with the numbers of murders recorded by the police. For various reasons they do not, and the Registrar-General's figures are also susceptible to error. Again, the number of housebreakings might be ascertained from insurance company claims. Problems of access to material have prevented this approach being fruitful.

The second main line of attack on the problem of the 'dark figure' has been victim surveys. The most extensive literature comes from the USA[11, 12].

A third approach to the problem has been that developed by researchers who have, by questionnaire or by interview, asked individuals about crimes or offences they have committed in the past. It appears that, in conditions of confidentiality, a high proportion of people will admit to committing criminal offences[2, 9, 10, 19, 53]. Despite the methodological difficulties in these techniques, the evidence has been so overwhelming that the main emphasis of studies in criminology has been changed. Earlier studies on causes of crimes considered individual factors (poverty, child-rearing practices) as causes of crime. Later, multiple factor theories, or theories relating to basic sociological forces, were popular. Now many criminologists see these as largely irrelevant, preferring to concentrate on the reasons why people from particular backgrounds are labelled as officially delinquent or criminal, and see the interaction between the individual and the state agencies as crucial.

The literature on victim-surveys and on self-report studies is synthesised by Hood and Sparks[26], who also provide an excellent commentary on the difficulties in interpreting the results of these surveys.

The assessment of seriousness

A further problem in relation to the problem of the 'dark figure' arises from the fact that, in England and Wales, the police are not required to count all crimes made known to them; only those on the 'standard list' are recorded and reported for statistical purposes. Standard list offences are thought to be more serious than those not on the list. Non-standard list offences are recorded only when proceedings are brought against persons accused of them, and an unknown number of undetected non-standard list offences should be added to the total of crimes made known to the police, to give a more complete picture of crime. However, the concept of 'seriousness of crime' brings other problems in its wake. These arise most acutely when we try to compare one police area with another, or a police area now with what it was like 10 years ago. Direct comparisons between areas are difficult. Clearly, it is ridiculous to compare crime in the Metropolitan Police Area, involving a total population of more than 8 million, with any other police area, having a much smaller population. One way round this is to divide the number of crimes made known by the population and then (to make the answer a bigger number, without too many decimal places) multiply by 100 000: this gives a crime rate 'per hundred thousand', and allows comparisons to be made more easily. But it does not solve the problem of seriousness. If two police areas each have an over-all crime rate of 2500 per 100 000, but one has twice as many murders as the other, this fact is concealed by the over-all figure. Again, if a police area seems to have twice the crime rate as it had 10 years ago, without any information about the seriousness of crime in the area, the increase is difficult to interpret. Comparison over time is also made more difficult by changes in police practices, and (owing to dependence on legal classification systems) by changes in the law. Such changes, whether by creation of new criminal offences, by decriminalisation of old offences, or by redefining old offences, make long-term trends in crime very difficult to interpret. One solution is to give a series of figures or rates of crime for each of the categories of crime in which one is interested. This would lead to forty or fifty figures, which would have to be compared with a similar list; a difficult enough task in itself, but when more than two areas are to be compared, overwhelming. It would be more reasonable to give a rating of seriousness to each crime, add up the weighted scores and compare the final weighted rates. One difficulty in this is to find someone capable of deciding just how serious one crime is compared with another. Who would judge? Sellin and Wolfgang[50] found a way round the difficulty by asking many people—students, police and judges—to rate the seriousness of criminal incidents and averaging the results. This provided a 'delinquency index', in which a murder was rated as 26, as compared with theft of $5, which was rated as 1. This approach clearly overcomes the objections to one person doing the assessment but a different rating might be given by the other sections of the community. For proper comparability, the Sellin and Wolfgang approach needs a rating group from a cross-section of society and needs updating regularly—an expensive procedure, which still can be objected to on other methodological grounds[46]. A second approach, devised by McClintock and Avison[32], compares each police area with the average for the whole country, on four dimensions—rates of violent crime, breaking offences and theft, and 'serious crime', judged by the legal classification of the crime. Originally, with over 100 different areas in England and Wales, this approach had some utility, but with successive amalgamations to form a total of less than 50 police areas, each area is so heterogeneous that the McClintock–Avison 'criminotype' is no longer a good measure of seriousness of crime in an area.

THE CLASSIFICATION OF CRIME

Another great objection levelled at the *Criminal Statistics* arises because the classification of crimes used in their compilation is based purely on legal concepts. Thus, crimes of violence are divided into murder, manslaughter, felonious wounding and so on; many criminologists argue that these classifications are of little value in determining what is really occurring in sociological terms. The nature of the relationship between offender and victim, and the circumstances in which the crime was committed, would provide an extra dimension of realism to the figures. This problem is particularly acute in robbery, which can range from a well-organised and planned venture with many thousands of pounds at stake to a trivial assault and theft of pocket-money in a school playground. To add one of each of these incidents together and speak of 'two robberies' is thought by many to be a ridiculous servitude to a legal classification system. Furthermore, no less than 1 in 5 crimes falls under the heading of 'other theft'—a catch-all category so heterogeneous as to defy analysis. The criticism of the basis of classification in the *Criminal Statistics* can be answered only by provision of much extra information, which, while of great utility, would swell the volume to many times its present size.

Apart from criticism of the classification system, there are other major complaints about the absence of linking material in the *Statistics*. There are details of social transactions in criminal courts, arranged by age (in broad groups), sex and type of court, with certain details of sentences of those found guilty. Again, there is no statistical sophistication: the number of 'persons' appearing is all that is recorded. A person, for this purpose, counts as one every time he passes through the court, and a man appearing for public drunkenness 60 times in a year is indistinguishable from 60 people each appearing once. Unfortunately, there is no distinction drawn between persons who are found guilty and those who plead guilty; thus, information as basic as the proportion of persons who plead not guilty and are acquitted cannot be derived[34]. Furthermore, in England and Wales a person is classified according to the crime as it was known to the police. This leads to anomalies. For example, a woman may complain that she has been raped; the offender, charged with rape, may plead guilty to, and be sentenced for, the 'lesser' offence of indecent assault on a female. Reading the statistics, he appears still under the classification of rape, and the (probably) much less severe penalty imposed seems as though it was imposed on a man found guilty of rape. This anomaly prevents assessments of the sentencing process and debars comparisons of sentences for different types of crime. Only in cases of murder which are reclassified by the courts before the *Statistics* go to press is the revised classification recorded. In Scotland all offences which are revised in the judicial process are classified under the new classification. Neither approach is seen by criminologists as wholly satisfactory, and a full documentation of the criminal legal process is called for.

These criticisms, both major and minor, have been directed at the British *Criminal Statistics*. They can be directed at any compilation which purports to record the numbers of crimes known to the police, or the criminal legal processes which ensue. The published volumes for Britain contain introductory material which, since World War II, has been fairly minimal in interpretation. Thus, while each contains descriptions of the bases for the statistics, with information on changes in the legal system which may influence trends in the figures, and some information on murder, we no longer have the long and informative details of 40 and more years ago. Before the war, introductions had much material on recidivism, and in the first decades of this century attempts were made to relate the incidence of crime to factors such as the temperature at Kew Gardens and the cost of living.

OTHER STATISTICAL PUBLICATIONS

Further information for England and Wales may be found in the annually printed, but not published by the Stationery Office, groups of *Supplementary Statistics*[23]. Here may be found information about particular police areas, and, in addition, details of offences taken into consideration or made the subject of additional charges. Here, too, more details of police cautioning (as an alternative to taking proceedings in courts) are given.

In an effort to provide information about particular crimes in more detail, two less well known annual publications are also issued. These relate to drunkenness[56] and to motoring offenders[57]. There is also an annual return regarding drug addiction[23a].

The single best introduction to the English material is given in Walker[66], while the most wide-ranging attempt to synthesise the material contained in *Criminal Statistics* is McClintock and Avison[32] for England and Wales; for Scotland, see Shields and Duncan[52]. The defects in *Statistics* have been commented on, and proposals made for their improvement, by many writers. Recently, however, two Government reports were issued, for England and Wales and for Scotland[42], the recommendations of which have been accepted in principle by the Government. The full implementation of the far-reaching changes suggested is likely to take several more years, although initial revisions of certain sections of the *Statistics* may well come sooner.

If a more detailed account of crime in a particular area is sought, reference must be made to the individual Chief Constables' *annual reports*. These are printed and frequently circulated to the press. Copies may be found in public libraries, or on application to the Chief Constables concerned. One of the most important of these reports, containing as it does information about crimes not recorded even in the *Criminal Statistics*, is that of the British Transport Police. Here are recorded many thefts of goods which took place 'in transit'. Because so little information is known about the undetected thefts in transit—not even, with certainty, the police area in which the theft took place—the thefts are unaccounted in the official publication. A second major series of reports, analogous to those of a Chief Constable, are those issued by the Commissioner of the Metropolitan Police[41]. Because the Home Secretary has ultimate responsibility for this force, the reports are issued as Command Papers by H.M. Stationery Office. Finally, to complete the survey of British statistics relating to the incidence of crime, it should be noted that details in a summary form relating to Northern Ireland are contained in an annual publication of the Ministry of Home Affairs[35a], while the Chief Constable of the Isle of Man gives a summary of crime recorded on the island. Interestingly, in an area regularly receiving an influx of visitors and holiday-makers, a distinction is drawn, for detected crimes and offences, between those attributable to residents and to non-residents[40].

More information about particular crimes, giving analyses of trends in crime over periods of years, can be derived from various research reports. Murder has been the subject of two Home Office reports[14] and these details relate to the whole of England and Wales. The later one has an annexe relating to Scotland. Further information for more distant periods of time may be found in the various reports on Capital Punishment. In 1969 the Howard League for Penal Reform published K. Vercoe's short survey *Murder in Western Europe* (mimeographed). Less useful, because they deal with limited areas of the country, but invaluable for the light thrown on the relationship between the social event of the crime and its legal classification, are the Cambridge series of reports on sexual offences[38], robbery[29] and violence[30]. Work has also been done on criminal fraud[21] and breaking offences[3]. Murder[69] and shoplifting[13] have also been dealt with by research writers.

The most important research work on the sentencing process is Hogarth's[22] dealing with Canadian magistrates; unfortunately, there is no comparable British material. Reference may be made to Thomas's work on the English Court of Criminal Appeal[61] and Hood's work on magistrates[24, 25]. A Government publication, *The sentence of the court*[51], provides an overview of the possible sentences which may be imposed, while Walker's book[65] gives an important philosophical perspective in addition. Material from the USA includes Green's study of the Philadelphia court[20] and the American Bar Association's survey of sentencing[8].

When an offender is sentenced to be handled by some official agency, he again becomes the object of social accounting procedures. These take the form of official reports from various departments of the Home Office, and reference may be made to these as appropriate.

Thus, the Prisons Department provides a two-volume annual report dealing with offenders in its care[44]. These include prisoners, borstal and detention centre inmates, and those ordered to attend

Senior Attendance Centres. The first volume deals with general developments in the Prison Department, giving an overview of the operation of the prison system, and a few details of population trends among inmates, employment and punishments in institutions. The second volume, of statistical tables, gives greater details of the background of inmates received, by length of sentence, previous record and types of offence. It also provides information about re-convictions of different categories of ex-inmates, from which may be calculated the 'success rate' of different sentences for the carrying out of which the Prison Department is responsible. There is a corresponding volume dealing with Scotland[37]. Information about the prison system, not readily compiled from the annual reports, is given at the end of the White Paper *People in prison* (HMSO, 1969, Cmnd. 4214) and in the periodical *Social Trends*; both these present information in diagrammatic form.

Again, about such figures there is much dispute, not usually about the accuracy of the figures but rather about their interpretation. For a proper understanding of 'success' in a penal setting, and for meaningful comparisons to be drawn, an evaluation has to be made not only in terms of the sentence served but also on factors such as the offender's previous record, and so forth. An overview of the 'success' of different sentences can be found in *The sentence of the court*[51]. Clearly, 'success' measured only in terms of subsequent re-conviction is dependent not only on outcomes of treatment or punishment but also on the effectiveness of the police in again detecting the recidivist offender. Some apparent 'successes' of a particular measure may be no more than undetected failures.

Associated with, but not part of, the Prison Department is the Parole Board, which produces an annual report giving details of persons paroled and the outcome[36, 43].

Statistics are also issued relating to the institutional treatment of children and young persons[55a].

Other series of official statistics relating to different sentences appear less regularly—such as those dealing with community homes (approved schools), attendance centres and remand homes[55] and Probation and After-Care[58]. The annual *Probation and after-care statistics* are not published, but are circulated by the Home Office to interested bodies. For particular areas, reference may be made to the Principal Probation Officer, who can usually provide some statistical information. Statistics relating to Welfare services, police forces and Children's services are issued by the Institute of Municipal Treasurers and Accountants and, for Greater London, in the *Annual abstract of Greater London statistics* (1966–).

Demographic and other data can be found in annual reports of Medical Officers of Health.

It is a defect of our present statistical system that no statistics are available in relation to the effectiveness of fining, discharge or suspended sentence, which make up the majority of sentences imposed by magistrates' courts. These deal with the great bulk of offenders and here two out of three found guilty of indictable offences, and nine out of ten found guilty of non-indictable offences, are dealt with by fine or by discharge. The Home Office does, however, compile a quarterly *Comparison of fines for speeding offences*, county by county, for England and Wales (mimeographed).

Full discussion of the problems surrounding *Criminal Statistics* are included in most textbooks, and there is a large journal literature on the topic. Most articles include a discussion of improvements which may be made in the official system of collecting such figures[4, 45, 49, 72]. Attempts are occasionally made to utilise information contained in such statistics to provide further information about, for example, causes of crime and linkages between crimes. Among the most important is Wilkins's demonstration of a delinquent generation[70]. This statistical model has been used in other countries[26a] but the methodology used has been criticised[48, 68]. Rose avers that the existence of the 'delinquent generation' is a statistical artefact generated by Wilkins's technique of calculation. Links between thefts from cars and the numbers of vehicles on the road and between different types of crime have been demonstrated. An attempt to factorise the variance in recorded crime[1] has been severely criticised[63]; but if criteria for identification of factors can be refined, this technique may yet have something of theoretical value to offer. Other calculations have been made to assess the incidence of recorded criminality[26, 32] and the number of persistent offenders in the community[47], while relationships between the recorded crime rate and demographic factors have been considered by correlational analysis[20a, 32]. Unfortunately, the findings have not been particularly valuable in the development of theoretical understandings, and Lander's attempt[27a] to demonstrate for Baltimore a connection between certain factors and anomie has been criticised[21a] for the circularity of its argument. An elegant overview of the earlier literature of ecological studies is contained in Morris[35]. However, ecological studies have suffered from the fact that the over-all recorded crime rate has been taken as the dependent variable, and it will be interesting to see how an assessment of the sociological background to offences can be related to demographic factors. Work along these lines is being carried out at Sheffield by Bottoms and colleagues. To put criminal statistics in perspective, more general information is often necessary. Much of this is issued (through HMSO) by the Registrar-General, notably the *Annual Abstract of Statistics,* and the journal *Social Trends*; but local sources should not be overlooked, and a key to these is *Local government statistics: a guide to statistics on local government finance and services in the UK at August 1964,* compiled by W. Barker (London: Institute of Municipal Treasurers and Accountants, 1965). It lists publications and organisations from which various types of information may be obtained, including welfare services and police.

FOREIGN STATISTICS

As has been mentioned, most governments now publish statistics relating to crime and criminals. These can be obtained, with more or less difficulty, from the respective Government Printing Offices. The Uniform Crime Reports is a compilation derived by adding figures from most civil police agencies in the USA. The classification system is discussed in Sellin and Wolfgang[50], and there is an extensive critical literature[4, 45, 49, 72]. European Governments produce criminal statistics which vary in their completeness. Most embassy libraries carry runs of these publications, which may be consulted there. Some provide headings in English, but a dictionary is likely to be needed. J. A. Adler has attempted to compile a *Dictionary of criminal science* in eight languages (Elsevier, 1960), but since it gives one-word equivalents with no definitions, it is impossible to assess to what extent the terms in different languages correspond with one another and the dictionary is correspondingly limited in use. A good two-language dictionary and a detailed knowledge of the system of classifying offences in the country concerned are the only safe guide to foreign statistics.

Attempts to compare recorded crime in different countries have been common since regular series of criminal statistics have been published by different governments. As will have been noted, all will suffer from the artefacts related to uneven recording of crime and from the different legal interpretations which are placed on similar acts in different jurisdictions. This problem was regarded as insuperable from the days when, in 1853, a General Statistical Congress was held in Brussels. An extensive literature has been devoted to the problems of international criminal statistics, characterised by a uniform pessimism about the probability of achieving anything useful. However, a fresh attempt was made in 1957 under the auspices of the Social Defence Section of the Bureau of Social Affairs of the United Nations. A working paper attempted to synthesise the elements of homicide, aggravated assault, and robbery and burglary by a world-wide survey of literature relating to criminal law. The statistical classifications of crimes to be included and excluded are listed by the relevant criminal law statutes. The Secretariat believe 'that such world-wide or near-world-wide figures could be established without undue difficulty'.

Some of the difficulties in this approach have been considered by T. S. Lodge[28], who attempted a comparison of English and Scottish criminal statistics. Even where the same statutory provisions apply (as, for example, in Road Traffic legislation), variation can occur in the extent of police enforcement. Where there are differences in legal provision, minute comparisons will be fruitless. However, broad generalisations can be offered, but the value of such generalisations is still in doubt. When comparisons are to be made at an international level, the variation between different areas of one country may be as great as, or greater than, variations between countries[14]. The most frequent discussion of international crime rates has been with regard to murder, and in a recent survey of violence Wolfgang and Ferracuti[74] were obliged to use the international classification of medical causes of death rather than figures derived from national criminal statistics. It seems that in the present state of criminal statistics much work will have to be done before useful comparisons between countries can be made.

PREDICTION STUDIES

Prediction in criminology refers to two main objects: first, the prediction whether certain individuals in the community will be convicted of crime; and second, whether individuals released from particular treatments or punishments will be again convicted of crime. Professor Walker gives an excellent and relatively non-statistical overview of each of these[64], while Frances Simon not only provides a commentary on early attempts at prediction but also includes a discussion of the predictive power of techniques of prediction, and of the attempt to develop an instrument to predict success in probation[54]. Miss Simon's bibliography gives an indication of the breadth of criminological literature in this field. Important contributions in the field of prediction of incidence of criminality have come from the Gluecks in the USA[15, 17]; their techniques have been extensively criticised[27, 39, 60, 62, 67] and they have attempted to answer these criticisms[16, 18]. A major British predictive instrument in this field is that of D. H. Stott[59]. The work of Mannheim and Wilkins[33] in relation to English borstals has been of seminal importance in the area of relapse prediction, while the ongoing work of C. Nuttall in the Home Office research unit on prediction of parole success and subsequent outcome continues to demonstrate the utility of these instruments. Different statistical techniques have been used in an effort to refer and to strengthen prediction instruments, and it is evident that prediction will be one of the major growth points of criminology in the future.

The usage of criminal statistics is fraught with difficulties. However, even if the system of recording crime is improved, so that, for example, the dark figure is reduced to insignificance, the interpretation of the figures will still be problematic. Until each classification of crime is meaningful in sociological terms—showing, for example, relationship between offender and victim, and the circumstances in which the crime took place—the interpretation of the figures can only be misleading.

REFERENCES

1. Ahamad B. (1967). 'An analysis of crime by the method of principal components', *Applied Statistics*, **16**, 17–35
2. Belson, W. A. *The extent of stealing by London boys and some of its origins*, London School of Economics, Survey Research Centre, 1968
3. Chappell, D. (1965). 'The development and administration of the English Law relating to breaking and entering', University of Cambridge unpublished Ph.D. thesis
4. Cressey, D. R. (1967). 'The state of criminal statistics', *National Probation and Parole Assoc. J.*, **3**, 230–41
5. *Criminal Statistics, England and Wales* (annual), HMSO, London
6. *Criminal Statistics, England and Wales* (1928) (Cmd. 3581, Introduction)
7. *Criminal Statistics, Scotland* (annual), HMSO, Edinburgh
8. Dawson, R. D. (1969). *Sentencing*, Little, Brown, Boston
9. Elmhorn, K. (1965). 'Study in self-reported delinquency among school children in Stockholm', in: Christiansen, K. O. (ed.), *Scandinavian Studies in Criminology*, Vol. 1, Tavistock, London
10. Empey, L. T. and Erickson, M. L. (1966). 'Hidden delinquency and social status', *Social Forces*, **44**, 546–54
11. Ennis, P. H. (1967). *Criminal victimization in the United States* (President's Commission on Law Enforcement and Administration of Justice, Field Surveys II. Washington, mimeog.)
12. Field Surveys I, II and III, Vol. 1: President's Commission on Law Enforcement and Administration of Justice (1967), US GPO, Washington
13. Gibbens, T. C. N. and Prince, Joyce (1962). *Shoplifting*, ISTD, London

14. Gibson, Evelyn and Klein, S. (1961, 1969). *Murder; Murder 1957 to 1968* (HMSO)
15. Glueck, S. and E. T. (1950). *Unraveling juvenile delinquency*, Commonwealth Fund, New York
16. Glueck, S. (1960). 'Ten years of unraveling juvenile delinquency, an examination of criticism', *J. Criminal Law, Criminol. & Police Sci.*, **51**, 283
17. Glueck, S. and E. T. (1960). *Predicting delinquency and crime*, Harvard U.P., Cambridge, Mass.
18. Glueck, S. and E. T. (1964). 'Potential juvenile delinquents can be identified: what next?', *Brit. J. Criminol.*, **4**
19. Gold, M. (1966). 'Undetected delinquent behaviour', *J. Res. in Crime & Delinquency*, **3**, 27–46
20. Green, E. (1961). *Judicial attitudes in sentencing*, Macmillan, London
20a. Greenhalgh, W. F. (1964). *Police correlation analysis*, Home Office Scientific Advisory Branch, London, mimeog.
21. Hadden, T. (1967). 'The development and administration of the English law of criminal fraud', University of Cambridge, unpublished Ph.D. thesis
21a. Hirschi, T. and Selvin, A. C. (1967). *Delinquency research: an appraisal of analytical methods*, Free Press, New York
22. Hogarth, J. (1972). *Sentencing as a human process*, U. of Toronto P.
23. *Home Office Supplementary Statistics Relating to Crime and Criminal Proceedings* (annual), Home Office, London, mimeog.
23a. Home Office Drugs Branch. *Report to the United Nations ... on the working of the international treatise on narcotic drugs* (annual), London, Home Office
24. Hood, R. (1962). *Sentencing in magistrates' courts*, Stevens, London
25. Hood, R. (1972). *Sentencing the motoring offender*, Heinemann, London
26. Hood, R. and Sparks, R. (1970). *Key issues in criminology*, Weidenfeld, London
26a. Jasinski, J. (1966). 'Delinquent generations in Poland', *Brit. J. Criminol.*, **6**, 170–182
27. Kahn, A. J. (1965). 'The case of the premature claims', *Crime and Delinquency*, **11**
27a. Lander, B. (1954). *Towards an understanding of juvenile delinquency: a study of 8,464 cases ... in Baltimore*, Columbia U.P., New York
28. Lodge, T. S. (1956–57). 'A comparison of criminal statistics of England and Wales with those of Scotland', *Brit. J. Delinquency*, **7**
29. McClintock, F. H. and Gibson, Evelyn (1961). *Robbery in London*, Macmillan, London
30. McClintock, F. H. (1963). *Crimes of violence*, Macmillan, London
31. McClintock, F. H. (1969). 'Criminological and penological aspects of the dark figure of crime and criminality', Sixth European Conference of Directors of Criminological Research Institutes, Council of Europe, Strasbourg
32. McClintock, F. H. and Avison, N. H. (1968). *Crime in England and Wales*, Heinemann, London
33. Mannheim, H. and Wilkins, L. T. (1955). *Prediction methods in relation to borstal training*, HMSO, London
34. Mark, R. (1965). 'The rights of wrongdoers', *The Guardian*, May 18
35. Morris, T. P. (1957). *The criminal area*, Routledge, London

35a. Northern Ireland *Report on the administration of Home Office services* (annual), HMSO, Belfast

36. *Parole in Scotland* (annual), HMSO, Edinburgh

37. *Prisons in Scotland* (annual), HMSO, Edinburgh

38. Radzinowicz, L. (ed.) (1957). *Sexual offences*, a report of the Department of Criminal Science, University of Cambridge, prepared by F. J. Odgers and F. H. McClintock, Macmillan, London

39. Reiss, A. J. (1951). 'Unraveling juvenile delinquency II: an appraisal of research methods', *American J. Sociology*, **57**, 115

40. *Report of the Chief Constable of the Isle of Man* (annual), Chief Constable's Office, Douglas

41. *Report of the Commissioner of the Police of the Metropolis* (annual), HMSO, London

42. *Report of the Departmental Committee on Criminal Statistics* (Chairman, W. Perks) (1967). HMSO, London, Cmnd. 3448
Crime recording: report of Departmental committee on Scottish Criminal Statistics (Chairman, A. Thompson) (1968). Cmnd. 3705

43. *Report of the Parole Board, England and Wales* (annual), HMSO, London

44. *Report on the work of the Prison Department* (annual, 2 vols., report and statistical tables), HMSO, London

45. Robison, S. M. (1966). 'A critical review of the Uniform Crime Reports', *Michigan Law Rev.*, **64**, 1031–54

46. Rose, G. N. G. (1966). 'Concerning the measurement of delinquency', *Brit. J. Criminol.*, **6**, 414–21

47. Rose, G. N. G. and Avison, N. H. (1966). 'Note on estimate of recidivism', in: Radzinowicz, L., *Ideology and crime*, Heinemann, London, 129–32

48. Rose, G. N. G. (1968). 'The artificial delinquent generation', *J. Criminal Law, Criminol. & Police Sci.*, **58** (3), 370–85

49. Sellin, T. (1951). 'The significance of records of crime', *Law Quart. Rev.*, **67**, 489–504

50. Sellin, T. and Wolfgang, M. E. (1964). *The measurement of delinquency*, Wiley, New York

51. *Sentence of the Court. A handbook for Sentencers* (2nd ed., 1970). HMSO, London

52. Shields, J. V. M. and Duncan, Judith A. (1964). *The state of crime in Scotland*, Stevens, London

53. Short, J. F. (Jr) and Nye, F. I. (1958). 'Extent of unrecorded delinquency', *J. Criminal Law, Criminol. & Police Sci.*, **49**, 296–302

54. Simon, Frances H. (1971). *Prediction methods in criminology*, HMSO, London

55. *Report on the work of the Children's Department* (triennial), HMSO, London

55a. *Statistics relating to approved schools, remand homes and attendance centres in England and Wales* (annual), HMSO, London

56. *Offences of drunkenness* (annual), HMSO, London

57. *Offences relating to motor vehicles* (annual), HMSO, London

58. *Report on the work of the Probation and After-Care Department* (triennial), HMSO, London

59. Stott, D. H. and Sykes, E. G. (1956). *The Bristol Social Adjustment Guides*, U. of London Press

60. Stott, D. H. (1960). 'The prediction of delinquency from non-delinquent behaviour', *Brit. J. Delinquency*, **10**   —
61. Thomas, D. A. (1970). *Principles of sentencing*, Heinemann, London
62. Voss, H. L. (1963). 'The predictive efficiency of the Glueck Social Prediction Table', *J. Criminal Law, Criminol. & Police Sci.*, **54**
63. Walker, Monica, A. (1967). 'Some critical comments on "An analysis of crimes by the method of principal components", by B. Ahamad', *Applied Statistics*, 36–9
64. Walker, N. D. (1968). *Crime and punishment in Britain*, rev. ed., Edinburgh U.P.
65. Walker, N. (1969). *Sentencing in a rational society*, Allen Lane, London
66. Walker, N. (1971). *Crimes, courts and figures: an introduction to criminal statistics*, Penguin, Harmondsworth
67. Walters, A. A. (1956). 'A note on statistical methods of predicting delinquency', *Brit. J. Delinquency*, **6**
68. Walters, A. A. (1963). 'Delinquent generations', *Brit. J. Criminol.*, **3**
69. West, D. J. (1965). *Murder followed by suicide*, Heinemann, London
70. Wilkins, L. T. (1960). *Delinquent generations*, HMSO, London
71. Wilkins, L. T. (1964). *Social deviance*, Tavistock, London
72. Wilkins, L. T. (1965). 'New thinking in criminal statistics', *J. Criminal Law, Criminol. & Police Sci.*, **56**, 277–84
73. Wolfgang, M. E. (1967). 'International criminal statistics: a proposal', *J. Criminal Law, Criminol. & Police Sci.*, **58**, 1
74. Wolfgang, M. E. and Ferracuti, F. (1967). *The subculture of violence*, Tavistock, London

11

The history of prisons and penal practices

S. D. M. McConville

This chapter refers mainly to the penal history of England and Wales in the last three centuries, although some reference is made to other countries and to earlier centuries. No modern terminal date has been fixed, the approach being that history is also contemporaneous and that in any case a reference to the present will often assist a historical study in much the same way that a historical understanding heightens contemporary research. It has further been assumed that the reader will be a newcomer to the historical study of penal institutions and practices.

GENERAL

The researcher will wish to review a broad sweep of institutions and developments in order to obtain a perspective of his more specialised field. For this purpose reference should be made to one of the general histories or surveys. George Ive's *A history of penal methods* (S. Paul, 1914) is a vigorously written (though, at times, over-emotional) account of penal methods and subjects from mediaeval times to the beginning of the twentieth century. In 20 chapters he covers an area ranging from witch trials and treatment of the insane to problems of classification and reform; there are subject and author indexes.

An unchallenged example of scholarship in its field and, despite its own disclaimer, an excellent bibliographical guide, is Sidney and Beatrice Webb's *English prisons under local government* (Longmans, 1922; Cass, 1963), which gives a detailed account of developments in common gaols, bridewells (houses of correction) and penitentiaries under local government from the sixteenth century until nationalisation in 1877, concentrating mainly on the eighteenth and nineteenth centuries.

With a largely legal and parliamentary emphasis, general and frequent digressions and an enormous time-span, *A history of crime in England*, by L. Owen Pike (2 vols., Smith, Elder, 1873), is in some ways unsatisfactory even as a general review. But for the researcher who is looking only for the origin or development of any one penal practice, such as branding or whipping, it is a fair starting point. Also going back to an early historical period, but covering a more limited area is *Imprisonment in medieval England*, by Ralph B. Pugh (Cambridge U.P., 1968), which makes extensive use of newly researched primary sources and is excellently written, footnoted and indexed.

Two books to be read in tandem are *Eighteenth century penal theory*, by James Heath (Oxford U.P., 1963), and John Howard's still vivid *State of the prisons* (1777 and successive editions to the abridged Everyman Library edition, Dent, 1929). Heath, on the one hand, provides a short guide in the form of translations and texts to penal theorists ranging from Montesquieu and Fielding to Romilly and Colquhoun. Howard's work provides, on the other hand, a wealth of detail of contemporary practices, including diets and dimensions of cells. (Although the Dent edition is useful, researchers who can should consult the early editions. The Fourth Edition (1792) is particularly recommended.)

A product of the mid-Victorian interest in prisons and things penal, *Criminal prisons of London*, by H. Mayhew and J. Binny (Griffin, 1862), is a detailed survey which includes the function, location, dimensions and regime of all the London criminal prisons of the time. As with Mayhew's other works, the illustrations are realistic and informative.

Of more limited use to the serious student is *The roots of evil*, by Christopher Hibbert (Weidenfeld, 1963, and in Penguin), which covers an enormous area in its 500-odd pages with a journalistic rather than a scholarly orientation. Advantages are its index and bibliography, which may be helpful at the introductory stage. Making good use of parliamentary material in particular, Giles Playfair's *The punitive obsession* (Gollancz, 1971) give an interesting, if polemical, history of the English prison system from the early nineteenth century to date, and also provides a good bibliography and index.

Paralleling Howard as an incisive contemporary comment on the prison system, *English prisons today*, ed. Stephen Hobhouse and A. Fenner Brockway (Longmans, Green, 1922), is the report of the comprehensive and influential investigations of the Prison System Enquiry Committee. This is essential complementary reading to the official Prison Commission and Home Office publications of the time. It was published simultaneously with the Webbs' work on prisons. Gordon Rose's *The struggle for penal reform* (Stevens, 1961) looks at the development of penal policy in England during the last 100 years and the influence of voluntary societies—chiefly the Howard League and its predecessors. As an appendix, there is a useful listing of the publications of the penal reform societies.

By a one-time chairman of the Prison Commission, Sir Lionel W. Fox, *The English prison and borstal systems* (Routledge, 1952) is interesting as a description of the prison and borstal systems as they existed at the time of writing, and as an insight into the views of a leading prison administrator. There is a brief historical introduction, a very brief bibliography and a number of useful addenda.

A picture of our present penal system is given in *The English penal system in transition*, by J. E. Hall Williams (Butterworths, 1970), which includes sections on sentencing, imprisonment and the treatment of young offenders. Although a criminological work, Nigel Walker's *Crime and punishment in Britain* (revised ed., Edinburgh U.P., 1968) has much to interest a historian as a study of the present ways of defining, accounting for and disposing of offenders. It has an index and (largely criminological) bibliography. Similarly useful to the student as an introduction to the development of modern practice and problems is *Borstal reassessed*, by Roger Hood (Heinemann, 1965). The bibliography of this work is very useful. Gordon Rose's *Schools for young offenders* (Tavistock, 1967) performs a similar task of description and evaluation for Approved Schools. The first chapter gives a brief historical outline of developments since the nineteenth century, and the bibliography should provide starting references for historical research.

Sir Leon Radzinowicz's *History of English criminal law* (4 vols., Stevens, 1948–68) is an excellent introduction to penal history, and because of its own broad scope should prove interesting to many with more limited and specialised interests. There are extensive footnotes and bibliographies.

CAPITAL AND CORPORAL PUNISHMENT

There is a proliferation of books of dubious motivation and value in this area, and the discerning reader may, after a time, begin to recognise some favourite and reappearing passages. The selection given here has been restricted to the more useful works.

George Ryley Scott has published several works in this field. His *The history of capital punishment* (Torchstream, 1950) discusses past and contemporary methods of capital punishment in technical, sociological and psychological terms, and attempts to summarise the abolitionist and retentionist arguments. This work is illustrated, with bibliography and index. More limited in scope, *A history of capital punishment*, by John Laurence (Sampson Low, n.d.), refers particularly to the British experience, but has a rather unsatisfactory bibliography.

Giving no bibliography at all, but with a number of historical and modern references in the text, is *A handbook on hanging* (revised ed., Putnam, 1961). Here Charles Duff, from a dedicated abolitionist standpoint, carries out a satirical examination of hanging and some other forms of execution. *Hanging in chains*, by Albert Hartshorne (Fisher Unwin, 1891), examines the practice of gibbeting from ancient times to the most recent British occasion in 1834. Powerfully argued abolitionist views are expressed in *Hanging by the neck*, by Arthur Koestler and C. H. Rolph (Penguin, 1961), while the companion volume, Leslie Hale's *Hanged in error* (Penguin, 1961), examines some cases where doubt of guilt existed.

With considerable detail, James Berry tells us of *My experiences as an executioner* (Lund, 1892; second facsimile ed. with introduction by Jonathan Goodman, David and Charles Reprints, 1972). Items include his method of calculating 'drops' in tabulated form, and some memorable cases and clients. Justin Atholl's biography of Berry, 'the scientific hangman', although written in a sometimes irritating narrative style, contributes sufficient extra information to Berry's own book, on which it is in part based, to be worth reading (*The reluctant hangman*, J. Long, 1956). *The hangmen of England*, by Horace Bleackley (Chapman and Hall, 1929), is of a different level of writing altogether from the previous two titles. It is well-researched, using contemporary journals and books and Guildhall records in its account of the London hangman from the beginning of the eighteenth century to the end of the nineteenth.

George Ryley Scott makes a further contribution with his *The history of corporal punishment*, subtitled *A survey of flagellation in its historical, anthropological and sociological aspects* (Torchstream, 10th imp., 1954). The book is illustrated and has an index and bibliography. Outside the immediate scope of this chapter, but none the less of probable interest to a researcher in British penal history, is *Red Hannah*, by Robert Graham Caldwell (Oxford U.P., 1947). This is a history of public whippings in the State of Delaware, with photographic illustrations of the apparatus. Other books that may be of interest are *The flogging craze*, by Henry S. Salt (Allen and Unwin, for the Humanitarian League, 1916), which has a particularly clear photograph of the pinioning apparatus then in use at Wormwood Scrubs prison; *Flagellation and the flagellants*, by Wm. M. Cooper* (1868), which seems to be extensively used as a source book, and has been reprinted many times; *Under the lash*, by Scott Claver (Torchstream, 1954), a history of corporal punishment in the British armed forces with an informative bibliography.

Torture has been a recognised and established penal procedure, and therefore comes within our area. Despite the title, John Swain's *The pleasures of the torture chamber* (1931) is, in fact, worth consultation. Chapter V discusses various devices for shaming offenders, such as cages, repentance stools, the ducking stool, the drunkard's cloak, finger-stocks, pillories and so forth. There is a rather unsatisfactory index. George Ryley Scott completes a trio of histories with his *The history of torture through the ages* (Luxor P., 1959), which is illustrated, with bibliography and index. Although a general history, it does give details of devices such as branks, thumbscrews, wooden horses and other instruments.

It is worth remembering that besides these specialised titles, the general works noted above also often contain information on particular past penal practices. For a student seeking details of just one instrument or custom, they may be the best start. Radzinowicz (*op cit.*, Vol. I, Chs. 6 and 7), for example, discusses the various modes of executing capital sentences, including several aggravated forms of the death penalty.

---

* Nom de plume of James Glass Betram, see George Ryley Scott, *op. cit.* (1954).

HULKS AND TRANSPORTATION

Probably the best starting point for a study of transportation would be *Convicts and the colonies*, by A. G. L. Shaw (Faber, 1966). The author has carried out considerable work from primary sources in this study of transportation to Australia and other parts of the British Empire, and provides an extensive bibliography and index. A useful first book for a study of the hulks, on the other hand, is W. Branch Johnson's *The English prison hulks* (Phillamore, 1970), which contains digests of the several Select Committees and a bibliography with a strong emphasis on parliamentary papers. Rather more specialised are: *John Grant's journey*, by W. S. Hill-Reid (Heinemann, 1957), a biographical account of 7 years' transportation; *Recollections of the Jersey prison ship* (Corinth Books, 1961), an account of the treatment of American prisoners of war upon a notorious British prison ship; and *The convict ships, 1787–1868*, by Charles Bateson (Brown Son & Ferguson, 1959), a history of the convict ships which transported prisoners to Australia from England and Ireland.

PRISONS: TYPES OF SOURCE MATERIAL

The titles listed above as 'general' do refer, in large part, to prisons. As this is the area of penal history which is probably of interest to most students, an outline of the *types* of material which would be worth investigating in the course of research or in the construction of a bibliography may be of benefit.

Memoirs and biographies*

The *Dictionary of national biography* (Oxford U.P.), which now extends up to 1960, should be consulted in the first place. This provides basic information and (usually) a list of further readings. But some individuals who are of interest will have no entry. A search will then have to be made for works of biography or reminiscences.

Virtually every casual browser has seen volumes of memoirs relating to crime and imprisonment in bookshops or libraries. As with biographies, in the strict sense, these works can be discursive,

* See also Chapter 1, pp. 18–19.

uneven in their attention to detail, and possibly misleading if considered in isolation. But within a programme of broader reading they can be informative and helpful. It is interesting to compare, for example, the account of a particular prison given by two authors—one serving there as a governor or officer and the other as a prisoner. While it is said, with some justification, that prisoners' accounts are likely to be distorted with a sense of grievance or injustice, there seems no reason to suppose that some officials' memoirs may not similarly be distorted by self-righteousness or even callousness. Both types need careful and comparative evaluation.

Well-known governors' memoirs are: *Quod*, by Major Wallace Blake (Hodder, n.d., c.1926), which gives an impression (often humorous) of governorship as a post-military occupation in the first part of the twentieth century; *If freedom fail*, by John Vidler (Macmillan, 1964), has 30 years of prison experience behind it, including the author's innovating 10 years at Maidstone; *Prison screw*, by L. Merrow-Smith (H. Jenkins, 1962), spans a similar length of service, over roughly the same years, from the point of view of an officer who rose to the rank of Chief Officer. As a former serving prison officer and General Secretary of the Prison Officers' Association, Harley Cronin contributes an important viewpoint in his *The screw turns* (J. Long, 1967).

Memoirs of prisoners are available from the early nineteenth century and beyond, and are so prolific that only the briefest mention is possible. Of modern volumes with interest beyond the usual, there are: *Against the law*, by Peter Wildeblood (Weidenfeld, 1955); *Time out of life*, by Peter Baker (Heinemann, 1961); and *Life*, by 'Zeno' (Macmillan, 1968).

Prison chaplains do not aspire to authorship as often as other staff members, but this fact and the comparative isolation of their jobs gives their reminiscences extra interest. *A prison chaplain on Dartmoor*, by Rev. Clifford Richards (E. Arnold, 1920), and *The prison chaplain*, by W. L. Clay (1861), both have merit, the latter, in particular, giving information on administration, regime, and so forth, in early Victorian prisons.

Arthur Griffiths's *Fifty years of public service* (Cassell, 1905), while only in part an account of Griffiths's prison career, is of value not only to a researcher interested in the details of administration, etc., in late-Victorian prisons, but also as a guide to the views and attitudes of a senior official of the time. (Griffiths attained the office of Inspector of Prisons. He was a prolific writer on prison and military history. His *Memorials of Millbank*, 2 vols., Henry

S. King, 1875, and *The chronicles of Newgate*, 1884, are well worth attention.) Biographies or memoirs and other writings of senior officials are generally not very informative on the minutiae of prison life, but they do provide a broader perspective, particularly of developments in prison policies. Unfortunately, *Sir Evelyn Ruggles-Brise*, by Shane Leslie (Murray, 1938), is badly constructed and has a personal rather than penological interest, but it is an introduction to the man who founded the borstal system during his chairmanship of the Prison Commission. S. K. Ruck's *Paterson on prisons* (Muller, 1951) is misleadingly subtitled *The collected papers of Sir Alexander Paterson* and is, in fact, *selections* from Paterson's papers, but it does introduce Paterson's approach to penal matters. The 1971 Hamlyn Lectures, delivered by Rupert Cross, look at penal reform in the twentieth century and briefly assess the policies of Du Cane, Ruggles-Brise, Paterson and Fox. They are published as *Punishment, prison and the public* (Stevens, 1971).

Biographies of penal reformers can be very tedious, and some are remarkably uninformative, being for their authors a means of communicating some personal religious or other philosophy. The various 'tract' societies were particularly guilty of this approach. While care should be taken in their use, as they can waste hours of valuable time, this field should at least be surveyed by the student. Elizabeth Fry has been much written about in the past, but the best account is John Kent's *Elizabeth Fry* (Batsford, 1962), which is particularly concerned with her prison work. The same title has been used by Georgina King Lewis (Headley Brothers, 1909), Laura E. Richards (Appleton, 1928) and Janet Whitney (Harrap, 1937), but they may be found rather repetitive and of limited value for the student. *Elizabeth Fry's journeys 1840–1841*, by Elizabeth Gurney, ed. R. Brinley Johnson (Bodley Head, 1931), although mentioning visits to various continental prisons, is chiefly of interest for the light it throws on the outlook of this famous Quaker family, so much a part of penal history. Although not a publication of the usual kind, D. Johnson's Jackdaw folder *Elizabeth Fry and prison reform* (Jackdaw No. 63, Cape) is concise in its information and useful at an early stage.

There are numerous biographies and studies of John Howard. The Webbs (*op. cit.*, 1963 ed., p. 32 fn) list a number of contemporary and later works. *John Howard: prison reformer*, by D. L. Howard (C. Johnson, 1958), although lacking a bibliography, provides an encouraging introduction and will assist those who intend to read further. J. C. Rowe's short book of the same title

(Epworth P., 1927) is also a useful introduction.

Alexander Maconochie of Norfolk Island, by John Vincent Barry (Oxford U.P., 1958) is a detailed study of Maconochie's involvement with the British penal system. It discusses his mark system of prison discipline and the various stages in his career, including his governorship of Birmingham Prison. Well-annotated, it has a bibliography, illustrations and short index, and is of general interest to those studying mid-nineteenth century prisons. *Romilly*, by Patrick Medd (Collins, 1968), has two helpful chapters on criminal law reform in an otherwise general biography. Beccaria, Bentham and Romilly are the subjects of *Three criminal law reformers*, by Coleman Phillipson (Dent, 1923), each of them dealt with biographically and in relation to law and penal administration. Finally, *Margery Fry*, by Enid Huws Jones (Oxford U.P., 1966), gives some useful information on the course of twentieth century penal reform, and is worth selective reading.

Parliamentary papers

Parliamentary papers are a major resource area for students of prison and penal history, and are still underused to a surprising degree. For those new to their use, much time and effort will be saved if the series of publications by P. and G. Ford are consulted in the preliminary stages of research (all are published by Blackwell, Oxford, so date alone is shown). Their *Guide to parliamentary papers* (1956) defines the area, sorts out the various terms and descriptions, helps location and gives practical advice on use —including correct methods of citation. They have also produced several breviates of parliamentary papers. *A breviate of parliamentary papers, 1917–1939* (1951), for example, covers more than 1200 Royal Commissions and other committees of enquiry, giving terms of reference, argument, conclusions and recommendations made. The student can thus, with some safety, decide whether the particular report is likely to be of interest to his work without going through all the time-consuming business of locating and reading for himself. It also permits a wider area of headings to be surveyed, enabling one to use material from fields which otherwise might not have been of obvious relevance. Under the heading *Legal Administration, Police and Law* in the volume cited above, there are sub-sections on police, prisons and prisoners, listing reports on prison officers' pay, allegations against the Acting-Governor of Wandsworth Prison, the Dartmoor Mutiny, and so forth. Other volumes cover the years 1900–1916 (1957) and 1940–1954 (1961). The whole series is extended by a facsimile reproduction (with an introduction by the Fords) of *Hansard's catalogue and breviate of parliamentary papers, 1696–1834* (1953) and its companion volume, *Select list of parliamentary papers, 1833–1899* (1953). As the authors themselves comment, 'The two volumes together give access to the main streams of Parliamentary inquiry over two centuries.'

An addition to the work of the Fords is *British official publications*, by John E. Pemberton (Pergamon, 1971), which deals with official publications in general, of which parliamentary papers are, of course, only a part. For students not having access to copyright libraries or other good collections of parliamentary papers, the Irish University Press project to reprint some seven hundred volumes of British parliamentary papers should eventually be helpful. The reprints will be facsimile, edited, indexed and classified volumes, and will thus also overcome some of the difficulties and irritations caused by the erratic indexing and classifying practices of former compilers.

Examples of some reports which may be of interest are: *Reports of House Committee into the Management of the Fleet* (1729, Vol. XXI, p. 274); *Select Committee on the Laws Relating to Penitentiary Houses* (1810/11, Vol. III, p. 567); *An Account of All the Gaols, Houses of Correction or Penitentiaries in the United Kingdom* (1819, Vol. XVII, p. 371); *Report of the Departmental Committee on Prisons* (1895, C-7702—known as the Gladstone Committee). There are a multitude of others.

It is worth remembering that relevant information will be found under a variety of headings, and some time should therefore be spent in drawing up a list of reports, etc., for preliminary investigation. The *Eleventh Report from the Estimates Committee* (1967), for example, contains considerable information on prisons, borstals and detention centres. One other word of warning. Minutes of evidence can be exciting and rewarding for the researcher, yielding just the kind of detail on day-to-day prison life that is the essence of much good work. But this material is voluminous and often difficult to assess. It should be used wherever possible in conjunction with other sources of evidence. This principle can be justified by even the briefest glance at the chaplains' enthusiastic contributions to the annual reports of the Directors of Convict Prisons, which enthusiasm would not seem to be justified by other contemporary evidence. (See Playfair, *op. cit.*, who makes this point effectively; also S. and B. Webb, *Methods of social study*,

Longmans, 1932, p. 155.) One should therefore be rendered more cautious in the use of governors' and other officials' contributions to reports.

Public Record Office and other archives

Before consulting any documents in the Public Record Office (PRO) or other depository, it is most advisable to have undertaken a thorough search of printed material, which often summarises a range of documents that would take considerable time to consult first hand. (See Griffiths, *op. cit.*, 1875, for example.) While the process of using original documents can be very engrossing, the actual amount of material that can be read and noted in a full working day is very limited—especially as handwritten documents are usual until comparatively recently. For those who reside outside London, or at a distance from the depository in question, there is also the extra time and expense of travelling.

Indispensable to the use of the PRO is the *Guide to the contents of the Public Record Office* (2 vols., HMSO, 1963), which provides a survey of the materials held in relation to various departments of government, and of the categories into which they are organised. Information of interest is to be found under certain main Home Office and Prison Commission categories, of course, but much may be found under seemingly peripheral headings: in exchanges between departments on legal, penal and criminal matters. The three London prisons linked to specific courts—King's Bench, the Fleet and Marshalsea (later the Queen's Prison)—all have records catalogued under an individual heading (PRO Pris. 1–11). In general, some thought on the processes of imprisonment—staffing, financing, pardoning, and so on—and a little imagination, will direct the student to less obvious headings and occasional finds of interesting documents.

There are numerous private and local government collections of documents which can also be of use. Papers of politicians, civil servants, philanthropists, authors and others can have direct or indirect reference to the topics of interest. The National Register of Archives, Quality House, Quality Court, Chancery Lane, London, WC2, aims to record the location, content and availability of all collections of documents, large and small, in England and Wales, except central government papers. They hold indexes to the collections of documents of which they have been notified, and the information given includes the names and addresses of custodians, a selective contents index, and a rather limited subject index. The National Register of Archives (Scotland), General Register House, Edinburgh 2, performs the same function for Scotland. A useful publication is their *Record repositories in Great Britain* (3rd ed., HMSO, 1968), which gives addresses, telephone numbers, custodian's name, hours of opening and other details. Published annually is the *List of accessions to repositories* (HMSO) covering MS accessions to repositories in England, Scotland, Wales and N. Ireland. From personal experience of the London Office, it should be added that staff are unusually welcoming, helpful and friendly. The intending visitor will find it especially useful to have a previously worked-out list of headings—politicians' names, institutions and even localities. When eventually a visit to certain archives is decided upon, it is helpful to write in advance, stating the time of the intended visit, material which is of interest and the general field of research. The staff can then have the relevant documents ready, and much time will be saved.

Newspapers and journals

Students will be familiar with the journals of their own disciplines and will consult modern historical journals and monographs; here, therefore, it is mainly intended to mention journals and newspapers which provided contemporary comment on prison and other penal matters. Useful sources available in copyright libraries and other collections include: *The Edinburgh Review, The Gentleman's Magazine, The Westminster Review, The Quarterly Review, The Nineteenth Century* and *The Fortnightly Review. The Pamphleteer* is not really a journal, but a series of pamphlets published in periodical form from 1813 to 1828, and has the advantage of an index. Four or five issues appeared each year, with the years between 1816 and 1824, in particular, having a good content of penal matters. *The Times* has the enormous asset of continuity and an index, even for earlier periods: *Palmer's index to The Times newspaper*, covering the years 1790 to 1941, and the *Official index to The Times* (1906–). Again, look also at less obvious headings. Obituary notices can be useful. To those who intend a detailed search of journals, such as those mentioned above, the *Wellesley index to Victorian periodicals, 1824–1900*, ed. Walter E. Houghton (U. of Toronto P.; Routledge, 1966), provides invaluable assistance. It consists of a table of contents and identification of contributors to eight of the most important Victorian journals, with a bibliography of the contributors and an index of initials and pseudonyms. Further volumes are planned. Other guides are listed in Chapter 1, and more fully in Sellin and Savitz's *Bibliographic manual for the student in criminology* (see p. 6).

The *Howard Journal*, produced by the Howard League, should receive attention, while on corporal and capital punishment the journal of the Humanitarian League—*The Humanitarian*—is of interest together with *Humane Review* and *Humanity*. For the early part of the nineteenth century the publications of the Society for the Improvement of Prison Discipline are often important. The files of the *Prison Officers' Magazine* (1910–   ) are valuable, if somewhat tedious at times, and the modern *Prison Service Journal* (1960–   ) carries historical articles from time to time.

Literature*

Contemporary or near-contemporary works of literature might also profitably be consulted, as contributions to penal reform and debate were often made in this way. Fielding's *Amelia* (1751) is relevant to the process of imprisonment of the time—particularly for debt. T. Holcroft's *Memoirs of Bryan Perdue* (1805) deals with Newgate, while Marcus Clark uses life in an Australian penal colony for his *For the term of his natural life* (1874; Collins, 1953). Of recent interest is Brendan Behan's *Borstal boy* (Hutchinson, 1958) and the short story by Alan Sillitoe, also set in borstal, *The loneliness of the long distance runner* (W. H. Allen, 1959). Other books include *Somewhere like this*, by Pat Arrowsmith (W. H. Allen, 1970), which deals with life, particularly emotional and sexual life, in a women's prison, and Steven Slater's *Approved school boy* (Kimber, 1967). The list of titles is extremely long, and the task of locating suitable material by no means easy in this field. A book that may help is *Dickens and crime*, by Phillip Collins (Macmillan, 1962), which discusses Dickens's work in relation to crime and the penal system in chapters on Newgate, the Silent System, the Separate System, Pentonville and the like. It has an index and extensive bibliography. A similar type of book is Keith Hollingsworth's *The Newgate novel, 1830–1847* (Wayne State U.P., 1963). This is primarily concerned with the history of fiction in the first part of the nineteenth century. However, Hollingsworth's approach to his writers—Bulwer Lytton, Ainsworth,

* Miss N. M. Macdonald, Newnham College, Cambridge, made some helpful suggestions for this section, for which I am grateful.

Dickens and Thackeray—gives this work a relevance to students of penal history. Extensive footnotes, index and bibliography (including works of fiction, criticism, law and penology) are provided. Also of possible interest is *Social elements in English prose fiction between 1771 and 1832*, by C. B. A. Proper (1929).

Theses

Theses can be difficult to consult, as conditions for their use vary from institution to institution, but a preliminary search in this area is essential for students, particularly those whose research will be submitted for a degree. This should be done by consulting the *Index to British Theses* (Aslib, 1950–   ), which is an annual listing of postgraduate theses accepted by universities in England, Wales, Scotland, N. Ireland and the Republic of Ireland. The *Index* is classified and has subject and author indexes, although the subject index is inadequate. Once again, imagination should be used when searching under particular headings. Penal historians may find relevant theses listed under Ninteenth century English history, or under Sociology, English literature, Criminology, Politics or even Architecture. As the number of theses is not so great, a thorough search can be carried out in a few hours. For those who wish to invest more time, *Dissertation Abstracts International* (University Microfilms, 1952–   ) performs a similar function for the USA. Lists exist for other countries, but particular attention might be paid to the Commonwealth countries. Useful theses include E. A. L. Moir's 'Local government in Gloucestershire, 1775–1800: a study of the Justices of the Peace and their work' (Cambridge, 1955/56); A. G. Rose's 'The history of the Howard League for Penal Reform' (Manchester, 1959/60); L. Johnstone's 'Attitudes towards poverty and crime in the eighteenth century English novel' (Cambridge, 1961/62); and D. S. Thomas's 'Fielding's Amelia: a critical survey of its themes ...' (Birkbeck, 1962/63). Clifford Dobb's 'Life and conditions in London prisons, 1553–1643 ...' (Oxford, 1953) and J. E. Thomas's 'The English prison officer, 1850–1968' (York, 1970) are further examples of specialised topics which may be of interest. A particularly helpful feature of most theses is the bibliography, and it may be worth while consulting a thesis in a slightly less relevant area in order to begin the snowball process of reference compilation.

Universities keep lists of their own accepted dissertations, which may be found useful for earlier works, and in some cases for undergraduate dissertations.

Finally, it is hoped that the student who uncovers a new source of information, whether in a little-known published work or in a collection of private papers, will consider its interest to others. A good piece of research is all the more valuable if some attention is paid to guiding others in a field successfully navigated by oneself, and steps should be taken to list new material in some publicly accessible manner.

12

Illustrations in criminological and penological literature

Clare M. Sheridan

The following list is intended to be of use to those engaged in research on the historical aspects of criminology to whom illustrative material would be of some value. The examples, chiefly English, are from eighteenth, nineteenth and twentieth century books that deal with or touch upon the history of crime, criminals and related fields. A separate section on French prisons and prisoners is included.

The original sources of these drawings, engravings, woodcuts, etc., include the British Museum, the National Portrait Gallery, the London Library, the Guildhall Library, the *Radio Times* Hulton Picture Library, the Mansell Collection, the Mary Evans Picture Library and various university libraries. Much local illustrative material can be obtained through the public library.

With a few exceptions no attempt has been made to include material not in the Institute of Criminology Library. Annotations are given where the title is insufficient to describe the illustrations.

For a general guide to sources, see Hilary and Mary Evans's *Sources of illustration 1500–1900* (Adams and Dart, 1971). This attractively produced book includes reproductions of, for example, female convicts in Brixton prison in 1862; but unfortunately it is not indexed.

PRISONS AND PRISONERS

Adam, Hargrave Lee. *The story of crime from the cradle to the grave* (London [1908]). Photographs of Broadmoor and Dartmoor prisons, prisoners at work and play, and an attempted prison escape.

Ashton, John. *The Fleet: its river, prison, and marriages* (London, 1888). Illustrations from the original eighteenth and nineteenth century drawings and engravings of women prisoners beating hemp, a pass room, a prisoner in irons, the common side of the Fleet, the introduction of a new prisoner, prisoners at play and Fleet weddings.

Atholl, Justin. *Prison on the moor: the story of Dartmoor Prison* (London, 1953). Photographs of Dartmoor Prison including convicts in dress marked with broad arrows.

Bateson, Charles. *The convict ships, 1787–1868* (Glasgow, 1959). Paintings and photographs of the ships.

Chesney, Kellow. *The Victorian underworld* (London, 1970). Prisoners on a treadmill and at exercise, and burglar tools.

Cook, Charles. *Personal experiences in the prisons of the world with stories of crime, criminals, and convicts* (3rd ed., London, 1902). Nineteenth century engravings of exterior of Holloway Gaol, Newgate, Pentonville, Wormwood Scrubs, Wandsworth Prison, Millbank.

East, W. Norwood. *Medical aspects of crime* (London, 1936). Eighteenth and nineteenth century prints of the Fleet, King's Bench Prison, the treadmill at the Brixton House of Correction, and Shrewsbury Gaol.

Gordon, Charles. *The Old Bailey and Newgate* (London [1902]). Newgate throughout its history as well as famous inmates such as Jack Sheppard and Jonathan Wild; also Elizabeth Fry and her room at Newgate.

Griffiths, Arthur. *The chronicles of Newgate* (2 vols., London, 1884). The prison as well as events and criminals associated with Newgate and the Old Bailey.

Griffiths, Arthur. *Memorials of Millbank, and chapters in prison history* (2 vols., London, 1875). Drawings of Millbank Prison, a cell with loom, female prisoners at exercise, the female pentagon, convicts embarking and at work, and hulks at Woolwich.

Griffiths, Arthur. *Secrets of the prison-house, or gaol studies and sketches* (2 vols., London, 1894). Drawings of a convict train as well as English, French and Chinese convicts.

Hooper, W. Eden. *The history of Newgate and the Old Bailey ...* (London, 1935).

Horsley, John William. *How criminals are made and prevented: a retrospect of forty years* (London, 1913). Engravings of the House of Detention at Clerkenwell and of an old-fashioned and a modern prison chapel.

Howard, John. *The state of the prisons in England and Wales ... and an account of some foreign prisons and hospitals* (2nd ed., London, 1780). Detailed plans of prisons, e.g. Newgate, the Bastille, La Maison de Force at Ghent, the House of Correction at Rome, Milan and Breda; prisoners at work (male and female) in Bern. Howard's 4th ed. (1792) contains additional plates of the prison at Moscow, and the House of Correction at Zwolle and Amsterdam.

Johnson, W. Branch. *The English prison hulks* (rev. ed., London, 1970).

Judges, Arthur Valentine (ed.). *The Elizabethan underworld* (London, 1930). Front entrance of Newgate (1650), gallows and pillory (sixteenth century).

Klare, Hugh. *People in prison* (Pitman, 1973). Modern prisons.

Mayhew, Henry, and others. *London labour and the London poor: those that will not work comprising prostitutes, thieves, swindlers, beggars* (1861–62). Boys exercising, crank labour, visiting prisoners, liberation of prisoners.

Mayhew, Henry, and Binny, John. *The criminal prisons of London and scenes of prison life* (London, 1862). Numerous nineteenth century engravings some of which include Pentonville (cells, chapel, exercise); the female prison at Brixton (cells, wash house, nursery, chapel, silent hour); hulks at Woolwich; Millbank Prison (work-shop under the silent system, chain room, prisoner in refractory cell); House of Correction, Coldbath Fields (friends visiting, oakum room under the silent system, treadwheel, dormitory); House of Correction, Tothill Fields (workshop, boys' and girls' school rooms, dining hall, mothers with children); Surrey House of Correction, Wandsworth (female prisoner, crank labour, adult school); City House of Correction, Holloway (treadwheel and oakum shed, kitchen); Newgate Jail (condemned cell); House of Detention, Clerkenwell; and Horsemonger Lane Jail.

O'Donoghue, Edward Geoffrey. *Bridewell Hospital, Palace, Prison, Schools from the death of Elizabeth to modern times* (London, 1929).

Potter, J. Hasloch. *Inasmuch: the story of the police court mission, 1876–1926* (London, 1927). Photograph of children's prison dress before *Children's Act 1908*.

Tickell, Tom. *Prisons: time and punishment* (Economist, 1969). Illustrated pamphlet.

Tobias, John Jacob. *Against the peace* (London, 1970). Repro-ductions of original eighteenth and nineteenth century illustrations of prisoners exercising, women at work in Brixton Prison, prison chapel, a prison visit, a hulk, and a photograph of Dartmoor during the mutiny of 1932.

Vaux, James Hardy. *The memoirs of J.H.V. including his vocabu-lary of the Flash Language*, ed. Noel McLachlan (London, 1964). Illustrations of convicts departing from England and in Australia.

FRENCH PRISONS AND PRISONERS

Alhoy, Maurice. *Les bagnes* (Paris, 1845). Illustrations of prisons and prisoners at work, sick-bay, execution, punishments, recreation.

Dauban, C. A. *Les prisons de Paris sous la Révolution* (Paris, 1870).

Guillot, Adolphe. *Les prisons de Paris et les prisonniers* (Paris, 1890). Drawings of prisons and prison life: warders, men, women and children.

Hell beyond the seas: a convict's own story of his experiences in the French Penal Settlement in Guiana, retold by Aage Krarup-Nielsen (Garden City, N.Y., 1938). Photographs of convict life.

Hopkins, Tighe. *The dungeons of Old Paris: being the story and romance of the most celebrated prisons of the Monarchy and the Revolution* (New York, 1897).

Lepelletier de la Sarthe. *Système pénitentiaire: la bagne, la prison cellulaire, la déportation ... en Bretagne ...* (Le Mans, 1853). Illustrations of convicts.

Le monde criminel: histoire des prisons d'état des prisons criminelles, des galeres, des bagnes et de leurs habitants (Paris, 1845). Drawings of convict punishment (bastonade) and execution; and of convicts in hospital, chapel, cells and at work.

Savant, Jean (ed.). *Le procès de Vidocq* (Paris, 1956). Illustrations of and documents dealing with Vidocq.

Vidocq, Eugène François. *The life and extraordinary adventures of Vidocq* (London [18—]). Illustrations of his career.

FAMOUS CRIMES AND CRIMINALS

Annals of Newgate or, the Malefactor's register (4 vols., London, 1776). Plates of Jonathan Wild, Jack Sheppard, Jack Ketch, the execution of the Rebel Lords at Tower Hill, Dr Cameron, Earl Ferrers, etc.

Fitzgerald, Percy. *Chronicles of Bow Street Police-Office, with an account of the magistrates, 'runners', and police* (2 vols., London, 1888). Eighteenth and nineteenth century illustrations of James Mackcoull, housebreaker; Charles Price, swindler; Richard Patch, murderer; view of hayloft (Cato St. conspiracy); the Fieldings; Sir Richard Birnie; interior of Bow St. Court, etc.

Howson, Gerald. *Thief-taker general: the rise and fall of Jonathan Wild* (London, 1970).

Macdonald, Arthur. *Hearing on the bill (H.R. 14798) to establish a laboratory for the study of the criminal, pauper and defective classes ...* (Washington, D.C., 1902). Measuring instruments for physiological detection of criminals.

Palmer, William, *defendant. The Times report of the trial of W.P. for poisoning John Parsons Cook, at Rugeley* (London, 1856). Engravings of figures associated with the crime and the trial.

Pelham, Camden (pseud.). *The chronicles of crime; or, The new Newgate calendar, being a series of memoirs and anecdotes of notorious characters who have outraged the laws of Great Britain from the earliest period to 1841* (2 vols., London, 1887). Drawings by 'Phiz' of famous crimes and criminals.

Rayner, J. L. and Crook, G. T. (eds.). *The complete Newgate Calendar* (5 vols., London, 1926). Eighteenth and nineteenth century illustrations of Edward Oxford shooting at Queen Victoria; Bellingham murdering the Speaker of the House of Commons; Jonathan Wild on his way to the gallows; Lord George Gordon and the attack on Newgate; the execution of Earl Ferrers; Dick Turpin shooting a man; Jack Ketch arrested; execution by 'The Maiden'; etc.

Scott, Sir Harold (ed.). *The concise encyclopedia of crime and criminals* (New York, 1961). Photographs and illustrations of famous criminals and figures associated with crime, e.g. Count Cagliostro; Burke and Hare; the trial of the Duchess of Kingston; the Fieldings; John Howard; Judge Jeffreys; Constance Kent; Jack Sheppard; Jonathan Wild; Earl Ferrers; Mary Read and Anne Bonny; William Palmer; etc.

Seccombe, Thomas (ed.). *Lives of twelve bad men* (2nd ed., London, 1894). Illustrations of Simon Lord Lovat (from etching by Hogarth), Lovat in female attire, Jonathan Wild, James Maclaine, Ned Kelly, G. R. Fitzgerald, Judge Jeffreys, etc.

Tobias, John Jacob. *Against the peace* (London, 1970). Reproductions of original eighteenth and nineteenth century illustrations of a thieves' public house, Maclaine, a highwayman, Turpin, Jack Sheppard.

West port murders: or an authentic account of the atrocious murders committed by Burke and his associates ... (Edinburgh, 1829).

Wilkinson, George Theodore. *The Newgate Calendar improved* (6 vols., London, [183–]). Sarah Malcolm, Jonathan Wild, Jack

Sheppard, interior of Newgate (seventeenth century), Cold Bath
Fields Prison, John Bellingham, John Thurtell, etc.

PUNISHMENTS AND TORTURES

Andrews, William. *Old-time punishments* (Hull, 1890). Illustrations
of ducking stools, branks, pillory, jougs, stocks, etc.

Atholl, Justin. *Shadow of the gallows* (London, 1954). Famous
hangings and hangmen.

Birkett, Sir Norman (ed.). *The Newgate Calendar* (London, 1951).
Engravings from *The malefactor's register*, e.g. pressing, branding,
hanging.

Bleackley, Horace. *The hangmen of England* (London, 1929).
Hangmen and hangings.

Claver, Scott. *Under the lash: history of corporal punishment in
the British Armed Forces* (London, 1954).

Cooper, William. *Flagellation and flagellants: a history of the rod
in all countries from the earliest period to the present time*
London [18—]).

Earle, Alice Morse. *Curious punishments of bygone days* (Chicago,
1896). Woodcuts of early punishments, e.g. drunkard's cloak, the
bilboes, stocks, ducking stool, etc.

Famous crimes (ed. Harold Furniss, London, 1903–). Issued
weekly? Drawings of tortures and forms of punishments regularly featured.

Helbing, Franz. *Die Tortur: Geschichte der Folter im Kriminal-
verfahren aller Völker und Zeiten* (3.Aufl., Berlin [1909]). Woodcuts and drawings of tortures and punishments.

Howard, John. *The state of the prisons in England and Wales ...*
(4th ed., London, 1792). Prisoner wearing a 'Spanish mantle'.

Judges, Arthur Valentine (ed.). *The Elizabethan underworld* (London, 1930). Medieval woodcuts of gallows and pillory.

Marks, Alfred. *Tyburn tree, its history and annals* (London, 1908). Hangings at Tyburn throughout its history.

Mayhew, Henry and Binny, John. *The criminal prisons of London and scenes of prison life* (London, 1862). Whip and whipping post at Wandsworth (Surrey House of Correction).

O'Donoghue, Edward Geoffrey. *Bridewell Hospital, Palace, Prison, Schools* ... (London, 1929). Ducking stool; harlot beating hemp in Westminster Bridewell (from 'The Harlot's Progress', by William Hogarth).

One who has suffered (pseud.). *Revelations of prison life* (London, n.d.). Nineteenth century flogging cell.

Pritchard, John Laurence. *A history of capital punishment* ..., by J. Laurence (pseud.). (London [1932]). Executions in Great Britain.

Saint-Edme, B. *Dictionnaire de la pénalité dans toutes les parties du monde connu* (5 vols., Paris, 1824–28). Punishments, executions and torture.

Scott, George Ryley. *The history of capital punishment* (London, 1950). Forms of capital punishment: e.g. death penalty on a sow in medieval times, execution in old Smithfield, condemned cell in Newgate, breaking on the wheel, etc.

Scott, George Ryley. *The history of corporal punishment: a survey of flagellation* ... (London, 1954).

Scott, George Ryley. *The history of torture throughout the ages* (London, 1959).

Swain, John. *The pleasures of the torture chamber* (London, 1931).

Tobias, John Jacob. *Against the peace* (London, 1970). Reproductions of original eighteenth and nineteenth century illustrations of a treadmill, a crank, whipping, pressing, a pillory, stocks, and torture with iron bars and collar.

Whitaker, Ben. *Crime and society* (London, 1967). Illustrations from seventeenth and eighteenth century prints of branding, a pillory, treadmill, trial by ordeal.

13

Official publications

John E. Pemberton and *Martin* Wright*

BRITISH

Her Majesty's Stationery Office publishes for sale some 6500 different items each year and offers a comprehensive catalogue service which facilitates access to them. Unfortunately, not all official publications pass through HMSO. Government departments issue varying amounts of literature themselves, usually free of charge, which is not covered by the official catalogues. Certainly the Home Office, whose publications are of especial interest to the criminologist, produces a good deal in this way. A common misconception is that a search through the HMSO indexes will reveal the sum of official publishing in a particular topic. It is important at the outset to dispel this notion and, by way of emphasis, to note that the volume of material issued independently by a department can exceed that which it channels through the Stationery Office.

Certain categories of official publications are, however, invariably published by HMSO. With each new parliamentary session the Controller of the Stationery Office is reappointed Printer and Publisher to Parliament and thus becomes responsible for the publication of bills, select committee reports, returns made to Parliament, papers required to be laid before the House under statute, minutes of proceedings of standing committees, debates and a wide variety of reports which originate in government departments but which are presented to Parliament 'by Command of Her Majesty'. The

* Martin Wright has contributed the sections on official publications in the USA and on publications of international organisations.

Controller is also Queen's Printer of Acts of Parliament.

It follows that familiarity with HMSO's bibliographical apparatus is invaluable to anyone whose work requires a knowledge of the findings and recommendations of official advisory bodies, of the activities of government departments and of the legislation affecting their subject. This applies not only to matters of the day but also to their antecedents. The great blue books of the second half of the nineteenth century, for instance, are primary source material for the study of social conditions of the time, and in order to find one's way about them one has to know the indexes which are available and how they are arranged.

Official lists

All new publications issuing from HMSO are announced in the *Daily List of Government Publications from Her Majesty's Stationery Office*. Parliamentary papers are listed first followed by non-parliamentary publications in an alphabetical arrangement of departments. Details are also given of reprints of earlier publications and of documents sold but not published by HMSO—for example, those of UNESCO and the International Court of Justice. Finally, there is a list of new statutory instruments. The *Daily List* is undoubtedly the best source for keeping abreast of official publishing, although it excludes (with very few exceptions) those items which are published independently by departments. If posted daily (Monday to Friday), the annual subscription is £6.80; but if posted in weekly batches, the annual rate is reduced to £1.80.

Entries from the *Daily List* are cumulated in the *Monthly Catalogue*. Parliamentary papers are listed under the headings House of Lords Papers and Bills, House of Lords Parliamentary Debates, House of Commons Papers, House of Commons Parliamentary Debates, House of Commons Bills, Command Papers, Public General Acts, Local Acts, and General Synod Measures. The second part is a Classified List in which publications, both parliamentary and non-parliamentary, are listed under their issuing bodies; and again publications for which HMSO acts as sales agent are included. Each monthly catalogue concludes with an index of names, titles and subjects. A major exclusion is statutory instruments, for which separate cumulative indexes are compiled, as will be noted later.

The next cumulation is the annual *Catalogue of Government Publications*, whose arrangement is virtually the same as that of the monthly catalogue. An extra feature is a list of periodicals, while, as regards items sold but not published by HMSO, the annual catalogue includes only those issuing from public bodies in the UK—the rest being listed in a separate catalogue entitled *International Organisation and Overseas Agencies Publications*. A separate *Annual List of Publications* is issued by HMSO, Belfast.

These are the basic guides for use with official publications of the last half-century. Over the years the internal arrangement and the indexes of the annual catalogues have improved, although a little imagination and an allowance for inconsistency in indexing are both necessary on occasion. The annual catalogues in fact started in 1922 and since then there have been quinquennial indexes covering, respectively, 1936–40, 1941–45, 1946–50, 1951–55, 1956–60, 1961–65 and 1966–70.

Another approach to currently available publications is through the sectional lists, whose purpose is to constitute a check list of documents which are in print. In the main they cover non-parliamentary publications, although some lists also include a selection of parliamentary papers. Exceptionally—for example, with certain historically important documents such as treaties and other national archives—out-of-print material is included. Sectional lists may cover publications on a given subject or by a given department, and revised editions are issued as necessary. All are available free of charge. Examples, giving the sectional list number in each case are: 12 Medical Research Council; 26 Home Office; 11 and 49 Department of Health and Social Security; 53 Central Office of Information; 56 General Register Office.

Other indexes to official publications exist—some published by HMSO, others by commercial publishers—and these will be mentioned, as appropriate, in the course of the chapter.

Royal Commissions, committees and advisory councils

Legislation is frequently preceded by an investigation carried out by an advisory committee, whose report, incorporating recommendations, may form the basis of Government policy. The majority of such investigations are undertaken by departmental committees; a smaller number are the work of Royal Commissions, which, although more prestigious, do not necessarily deal with subjects of sions are always published as Command Papers: that is to say, correspondingly greater importance. Reports of Royal Commissions they are presented to Parliament 'by Command of Her Majesty' and ordered to be printed by the House of Commons. Departmental Committee reports may or may not be so presented, although if legislation is anticipated they normally are. It is worth noting that much useful information is collected in the *Appendices* of reports; an index to these would be of enormous value.

Command Papers are designated by serial numbers preceded by an abbreviation of the word 'command'. Different abbreviations have been used at different times (at first within square brackets), and it is important when citing such papers to give the correct form. The series are as follows:

1833–69	[1] – [4222]
1870–99	[C. 1] – [C. 9550]
1900–18	[Cd. 1] – [Cd. 9239]
1919–56	[Cmd. 1] – Cmd. 9889
1956–	Cmnd. 1 –

If only the serial number is known, the document may be further identified by consulting the numerical lists at the beginning of the HMSO catalogues. This does mean that one has to have some idea of the paper's date of publication, and in this connection the concordance of Command Papers in Pemberton's *British Official Publications* (Pergamon, 2nd ed., 1973) is useful.

An added complication in using Command Papers is that in many large libraries they are bound into the so-called 'sessional volumes' of parliamentary papers, which also contain bills and House of Commons Papers (accounts, annual reports, and so forth). Having identified the parliamentary session in which the required paper was issued, one has then to consult the appropriate sessional index to ascertain its location within that session's set of bound volumes. To ease the task when only the number is known and when one is further faced with finding it in a library of sessional volumes, the *Numerical finding list of British Command Papers published 1833–1961/2*, compiled by E. Di Roma and J. A. Rosenthal (New York Public Library, 1967), may be used.

Often the reports of advisory commissions and committees are referred to by the names of their chairman or, confusingly, of the chairman of the sub-committee which drafted a particular report. One speaks, for example, of the Barry Report (on preventive detention) and the Mountbatten Report (on prison escapes and security). In order to identify a report cited in this way, one may use *British Government Publications: an index to chairmen and authors*, ed. A. Mary Morgan (The Library Association, 1969), for the period 1941–1966, or *British Official Publications*, by John E. Pemberton

(Pergamon, 1971), for the period 1900–1972. The HMSO catalogues do include chairmen in their indexes—and have to be used for the period since 1972—but the two volumes mentioned are more convenient when the date of the report is not known.

So far this century there have been about two dozen Royal Commissions which have some bearing on criminology and related matters. In chronological order they are:

1903 Poisoning by Arsenic (Lord Kelvin), Cd. 1848
1908 Care and Control of the Feeble-Minded (Lord Radnor), Cd. 4202
     Duties of the Metropolitan Police (D. B. Jones), Cd. 4156
1909 Poor Laws and Relief of Distress (Lord Hamilton), Cd. 4499; Ireland, Cd. 4630; Scotland, Cd. 4922
     Whiskey and other Potable Spirits (Lord Hereford), Cd. 4796
1910 Selection of Justices of the Peace (Lord James), Cd. 5250
1912 Divorce and Matrimonial Causes (Lord Gorell), Cd. 6478
1913 Delay in the King's Bench Division (Lord St. Aldwyn), Cd. 7177
1916 Arrest and Subsequent Treatment of Mr Francis Sheehy Skeffington, Mr Thomas Dickson and Mr Patrick James McIntyre (Sir J. Simon), Cd. 8376
     Rebellion in Ireland (Lord Hardinge), Cd. 8279
1926 Lunacy and Mental Disorder (H. Macmillan), Cmd. 2700
1927 Court of Session and the Office of Sheriff Principal (Scotland) (Lord Clyde), Cmd. 2801
1929 Police Powers and Procedure (Lord Lee), Cmd. 3297
1933 Lotteries and Betting (Sir S. Rowlatt), Cmd. 4341
1936 Private Manufacture of and Trading in Arms (Sir John Eldon Bankes), Cmd. 5292
1948 Justices of the Peace (Lord Du Parcq), Cmd. 7463
1951 Betting, Lotteries and Gaming (H. U. Willink), Cmd. 8190
1953 Capital Punishment (Sir Ernest A. Gowers), Cmd. 8932
1955 Marriage and Divorce (Lord Morton of Henryton), Cmd. 9678
1957 Law Relating to Mental Illness and Mental Deficiency (Lord Percy of Newcastle), Cmnd. 169
1962 Police (Sir Henry Willink), Cmnd. 1728
1966 Penal System in England and Wales (Viscount Amory). Wound up, but Minutes of Evidence and Written Evidence (4 vols.) published in 1967
     Tribunals of Inquiry (Sir Cyril Barnet Salmon), Cmnd. 3121
1969 Examination of Assizes and Quarter Sessions (Lord Beeching), Cmnd. 4153 (and Written Evidence, 1971, and Special Statistical Survey, 1971)

There have been many more departmental committees and working parties during the same period, and the following have been selected as being of interest to the criminologist. As explained earlier, not all departmental committee reports are issued as Command Papers. In the list, therefore, many items appear without a serial number. All the reports have, however, been published by

HMSO. Those produced by the Advisory Council on the Treatment of Offenders or its successor the Advisory Council on the Penal System, the Advisory Council on the Employment of Prisoners, or the Advisory Council on Drug Dependence are indicated by the initials of those bodies.

1900 Scottish Prisons (Earl Elgin of Kincardine), Cd. 218
1906 Vagrancy (J. L. Wharton), Cd. 2852
1910 Probation of Offenders Act 1907 (H. Samuel), Cd. 5001
1911 Prison Libraries (M. L. Waller), Cd. 5589
1920 Juvenile Delinquency (J. H. Lewis)
1921 Alterations in Criminal Procedure (Indictable offences) (Sir A. H. Bodkin), Cmd. 1813
Detention in Custody of Prisoners Committed for Trial in England and Wales (Mr Justice T. G. Horridge), Cmd. 1574
1923 Insanity and Crime (Lord Justice Atkin), Cmd. 2005
1925 Sexual Offences against Young Persons (Sir R. Adkins), Cmd. 2561
1926 Morphine and Heroin Addiction (Rolleston)
1927 Treatment of Young Offenders (Sir E. Cecil), Cmd. 2831
1928 Legal Aid for the Poor (Mr Justice Finlay), Cmd. 3016
Street Offences (H. Macmillan), Cmd. 3231
1932 Persistent Offenders (Sir J. C. Dove-Wilson), Cmd. 4090
1933 Courts of Summary Jurisdiction (Sir W. F. K. Taylor), Cmd. 4296
1935 Employment of Prisoners (Sir I. Salmon), Cmd. 4462 and Cmd. 4897
1936 Social Services in Courts of Summary Jurisdiction (S. W. Harris), Cmd. 5122
1937 Courts of Summary Jurisdiction in the Metropolitan Area (Sir A. Maxwell)
1938 Corporal Punishment (E. Cadogan), Cmd. 5684
1943 Detention Barracks (Mr Justice Oliver), Cmd. 6484
1945 Legal Aid and Advice in England and Wales (Lord Radcliffe), Cmd. 6641
1946 Legal Aid and Advice in Scotland (J. Cameron), Cmd. 6925
Report of the Care of Children Committee (Miss M. Curtis). Cmd. 6922
1949 Scottish Legal System (C. W. G. Taylor)
1950 Children and the Cinema (K. C. Wheare), Cmd. 7945
1951 Review of Punishments in Prisons, Borstal Institutions, Approved Schools and Remand Homes, 1948–51 (H. W. F. Franklin), Cmd. 8256 and Cmd. 8429
1953 Discharged Prisoners' Aid Societies (Sir A. Maxwell), Cmd. 8879
Supreme Court Practice and Procedure (Sir R. Evershed), Cmd. 8878
1954 New Trials in Criminal Cases (Lord Tucker), Cmd. 9150
1955 Summary Trial of Minor Offences (Sir R. Sharpe), Cmd. 9524
1957 Alternatives to Short Terms of Imprisonment (Earl of Drogheda) (ACTO)
Homosexual Offences and Prostitution (Sir J. Wolfenden), Cmnd. 247

1958 After-Care and Supervision of Discharged Prisoners (B. J. Hartwell)

Proceedings before Examining Justices (Lord Tucker), Cmnd. 479

Remuneration and Conditions of Service of Certain Grades in the Prison Services (Mr Justice Wynn-Parry), Cmnd. 544

1959 Treatment of Young Offenders (Mr Justice Barry) (ACTO)

1960 Children and Young Persons (Visc. Ingleby), Cmnd. 1191

Corporal Punishment (Mr Justice Barry), Cmnd. 1213 (ACTO)

Custodial Sentences for Young Offenders (H. R. Leslie) (Scottish ACTO)

Youth Service in England and Wales (Countess of Albemarle), Cmnd. 929

1961 Business of the Criminal Courts (Mr Justice Streatfeild), Cmnd. 1289

Drug Addiction (Sir Russell Brain)

Magistrates' Courts in London (C. D. Aarvold), Cmnd. 1606

Remand Homes (R. W. B. Ellis), Cmnd. 1588

Work for Prisoners (Sir W. Anson) (ACEP)

1962 Custodial Training of Young Offenders (Sheriff W. J. Bryden) (Scottish ACTO)

Non-Residential Treatment of Offenders under 21 (Mr Justice Barry) (ACTO)

Preventive Detention (R. C. Mortimer) (ACTO)

Probation Service (Sir R. P. Morison), Cmnd. 1650 and Cmnd. 1800

Work and Vocational Training in Borstals (England and Wales) (Sir W. Anson) (ACEP)

1963 Legal Aid in Criminal Proceedings (R. R. Pittam)

Organisation of After-Care (B. J. Hartwell)

1964 Children and Young Persons (Scotland) (Lord Kilbrandon), Cmnd. 2306

Organisation of Prison Medical Service (E. H. Gwynn)

Organisation of Work for Prisoners (Sir W. Anson) (ACE?)

1965 Alcoholics (A. K. M. Macrae)

Court of Criminal Appeal (Lord Donovan), Cmnd. 2755

Drug Addiction, 2nd report (Lord Brain)

1966 Legal Aid in Criminal Proceedings (Mr Justice Widgery), Cmnd. 2934

Prison Escapes and Security (Earl Mountbatten), Cmnd. 3175

Residential Provision for Homeless Discharged Offenders (Marchioness of Reading)

1967 Criminal Statistics (M. Perks), Cmnd. 3448

Organisation of After-Care (Mr Justice Barry)

Place of Voluntary Service in After-Care (Marchioness of Reading)

Police Manpower, Equipment and Efficiency (D. Taverne)

The Sheriff Court (Lord Grant), Cmnd. 3248

1968 Crime Recording: the Scottish Criminal Statistics (A. Thomson), Cmnd. 3705

Detention of Girls in a Detention Centre (K. Younger; sub-c. Rt Rev. R. Mortimer) (ACPS)

Regime for Long-Term Prisoners in Conditions of Maximum Security (K. Younger; sub-c. L. Radzinowicz) (ACPS)

Rehabilitation of Drug Addicts (Sir E. Wayne; sub-c. A. Blenkinsop) (ACDD)

1969 CS (Sir H. Himsworth)
Cannabis (Sir E. Wayne; sub-c. Baroness Wootton) (ACDD)
Forensic Psychiatry (J. Harper)

1970 Amphetamines and LSD (Sir E. Wayne; sub-c. Baroness Wootton) (ACDD)
Better Provision of Legal Advice and Assistance (Baroness Emmet), Cmnd. 4249
Detention Centres (K. Younger; sub-c. Rt Rev. R. C. Mortimer) (ACPS)
Non-Custodial and Semi-Custodial Penalties (K. Younger; sub-c. Baroness Wootton) (ACPS)
Powers of Arrest and Search in relation to Drug Offences (Sir E. Wayne; sub-c. Rt Hon. W. Deedes) (ACDD)
Reparation by the Offender (K. Younger; sub-c. Lord Justice Widgery) (ACPS)

1971 Habitual Drunken Offenders (T. G. Weiler)
Physical Brutality in Northern Ireland (Sir Edmund Compton), Cmnd. 4823

1972 Court Proceedings—Recording (S. P. Osmond)
Homicide Penalties (Lord Emslie), Cmnd. 5137
Interrogation of Persons suspected of Terrorism—Authorised Procedures (Lord Parker of Waddington), Cmnd. 4901
Misuse of Drugs in Scotland (J. A. Ward) 2nd Report
Probation Officers and Social Workers—Work and Pay (J. B. Butterworth) Cmnd. 5076
Rehabilitation (Sir Ronald Turnbridge)
Terrorist Activities—Northern Ireland—Legal Procedures (Lord Diplock) Cmnd. 5185

White Papers and Green Papers

Royal Commissions, departmental committees and working parties are advisory bodies. Their reports include recommendations, but it is up to the Government of the day to decide whether or not—or to what extent—it will accept them and adopt them as its own policy. It is usual for the Government to issue policy statements in the form of 'White Papers'. (This designation can be rather misleading, as many in fact have tinted covers.) Policy White Papers are always presented as Command Papers and when one is citing them the Command number should form part of the reference. The following are some examples from the last decade, all originating in the Home Office:

1961 Compensation for Victims of Crimes of Violence, Cmnd. 1406
1964 Compensation for Victims of Crimes of Violence, Cmnd. 2323
War against Crime in England and Wales, Cmnd. 2296

1965 The Adult Offender, Cmnd. 2852
   The Child, the Family and the Young Offender, Cmnd. 2742
1968 Children in Trouble, Cmnd. 3601
1969 People in Prison, Cmnd. 4214

Reports of inquiries, if they are published at all, are also issued as Command Papers—for example:

1953 Mrs Beryl Evans and Geraldine Evans (J. Scott Henderson), Cmd. 8896
   Case of Timothy John Evans (J. Scott Henderson), Cmd. 8946
1960 Disturbances at the Carlton Approved School on Aug. 29 and 30, 1959 (V. Durand), Cmnd. 937
1966 Case of Timothy John Evans (Mr Justice Brabin), Cmnd. 3101
1967 Administration of Punishment at Court Lees Approved School (E. B. Gibbens), Cmnd. 3367

This is a convenient point at which to mention two further sets of indexes—one official, the other non-official. The first consists of two volumes of cumulated references to sessional papers: the *General Alphabetical Index to the Bills, Reports and Papers printed by Order of the House of Commons and to the Reports and Papers presented by Command, 1950 to 1958–59* and its companion, the *General Index ... 1900 to 1948–49*. The second comprises three volumes of digests of official documents produced by P. and G. Ford, entitled *A Breviate of Parliamentary Papers 1940–1954; ... 1917–1939; ... 1900–1916*. Entries are grouped by subject under such headings as 'Prisons, prisoners, punishment and probation', and each volume has a full index and useful appendices. With Diana Marshallsay the Fords have also produced a *Select list of British parliamentary papers 1955–1964*.

In recent years a new term, 'Green Paper', has come into fashion. Green Papers are consultative documents in which the Government sets out tentative policies for the purpose of inviting comments thereon. An ideal flow would therefore be: Royal Commission or departmental committee report → Green Paper → White Paper → Legislation. The first Green Paper was published in 1967. Some appear as Command Papers, while others are non-parliamentary publications. An even more recent tendency, and one which is much to be regretted, is that of government departments to publish consultative documents independently of the Stationery Office. This means that pre-legislative literature which ostensibly is intended to foster public participation fails to gain the publicity afforded by the catalogue service of HMSO.

The legislative process

What initiates the legislative process itself is the announcement of a bill in Parliament (known as 'First Reading') and the publication of its text. There may be several versions of a bill printed as it passes through both Houses. All are given serial numbers. In the case of Commons bills, these are printed within square brackets; and of Lords bills, within curved brackets. Both series begin afresh each new session, so that it is essential when citing a bill always to indicate the relevant session. Thus, the *Misuse of Drugs Bill* of 1970 is properly cited as H.C. Bill 1970–71 [15].

The progress of any bill may be followed in the *Votes and Proceedings* (the daily minutes of business in the House of Commons) and the *House of Lords Minutes of Proceedings*—both of which are available on subscription from HMSO. At the end of the parliamentary session there appears a *Return Relating to Public Bills* which gives the number of bills which became Acts during the session and the stage at which those which were not enacted were dropped, postponed or rejected or had their progress ended by the closure of Parliament. There is a corresponding *List of Private Bills* for each session which is published as part of the House of Commons *Order Paper* (the House's daily agenda).

In a library whose parliamentary papers are bound into sessional volumes, bills are rather easier to find than Command Papers, since they are simply arranged in alphabetical order in the beginning of each sessional set. If only the bill's serial number is known, it is necessary to locate it through the appropriate sessional index.

Debates on every bill in both Houses of Parliament are fully reported in the *Official Report of Debates*, popularly known as *Hansard*. Up to 1908, Commons and Lords debates were printed in the same volumes, but from 1909 onwards they have been issued separately. Early sources of debates are documented in a publication of the House of Commons Library entitled *A Bibliography of Parliamentary Debates of Great Britain* (HMSO, 1956). William Cobbett began his reports in 1803, since when there have been five series. The name *Hansard* derives from Thomas Curson Hansard, who took over reporting from Cobbett in 1811.

Both Commons and Lords debates are currently published daily, weekly and in bound volumes. The Commons *Hansard* has a *Weekly Index*, an index in every bound volume, and a consolidated index covering each session. In addition, the Lords *Hansard* has had since 1965–66 a *cumulative* index published about nine times a year.

As there is usually no debate when a bill is introduced, the first debate to be looked for in *Hansard* is that which takes place on Second Reading, when the whole House considers the principles of the proposed legislation. One has next to turn to the *Standing Committee Debates*, which are issued quite separately from *Hansard*. They appear in separate parts, covering the various sittings, and then in bound volumes. To locate the debates on a particular bill, one has to know the designation of the committee which considered it (A, B, C, etc.), and this can be ascertained from the HMSO annual catalogues. Further debate comes when the standing committee reports back to the House. Both this Report Stage and any debate on Third Reading are again reported in *Hansard*. In the indexes, the various stages are indicated as 1R, 2R, 3R, Amendt. (Amendment), Com. (Committee) and Rep. (Report). Thereafter, one turns to the Lords' *Hansard* to follow the bill's passage through the Upper House, which is similarly recorded except that the Committee Stage is generally included in the ordinary *Hansard*. At each stage the Bill, if amended, is reprinted; if new clauses are inserted, the numbering is changed. An example of an extensively amended Bill is the *Criminal Justice Bill 1971–72*.

It should be noted in using *Hansard* that the columns in the body of each volume are numbered in ordinary arabic numerals and that at the end of the volume written answers to parliamentary questions are gathered together in columns denoted by numerals in italic type. References in the index are similarly distinguished. Thus an index entry in the form 726 *23* signifies a written answer which appears in the last section of Vol. 726 in the column numbered *23*.

A bill which successfully passes the scrutiny of both Houses receives the Royal Assent to become an Act of Parliament; and unless the Act itself contains a specific statement to the contrary, it becomes law from that moment. This date is given in square brackets after the full title. One of the last sections of an Act frequently contains a provision, however, that either the whole Act or part of it will come into force on an 'appointed day' to be specified by the Minister by means of a Statutory Instrument. To find out, therefore, whether an Act containing such a provision has come into force, one has to check for the issuance of the relevant instrument (or instruments, since more than one may be necessary for different parts of the Act).

Even the experts can have difficulty in keeping *au fait* with developments: Baroness Wootton found it necessary to ask a Parliamentary Question on 6 December 1972 to ascertain which sections of the *Children and Young Persons Act 1969* had come into force (and Lord Colville's answer is given in the Lords' *Hansard* for that date).

Statutory Instruments are first issued as separate items and then in bound volumes, and each has a unique reference which is cited as 'S.I. serial number: year'. There is also a 25-volume set of *The Statutory Rules and Orders and Statutory Instruments Revised to December 31, 1948*. First notification of issuance occurs in the HMSO *Daily List*. Then there is a *List of Statutory Instruments for the Month of* . . . , which includes the very useful feature of an index which cumulates in each successive issue, and an annual *List of Statutory Instruments year* provided with subject and numerical indexes. Beyond these are an annual *Table of Government Orders*, which lists S.I.s issued since 1949 along with notes of amendments and revocations, and a biennial *Index to Government Orders*. An alternative source of textual and bibliographical information is the non-official, multi-volume *Halsbury's Statutory Instruments*, published by Butterworths, which is kept up to date through a loose-leaf service. *Halsbury's Statutes of England*, another multi-volume work, also provides references to commencement orders made under Acts. For example, under Section 44 of the *Criminal Justice Act 1961*, Halsbury notes the various *Criminal Justice Act 1961* (Commencement) orders, and cites the relevant Statutory Instrument.

Should Halsbury, or a set of Statutory Instruments, not be available, a journal devoted to the relevant field of law may give the answer; to take the above example, an article in the *Criminal Law Review* for March 1965 (about 18 months after the Statutory Instrument concerned) begins with 'on August 1, 1963, those sections of the *Criminal Justice Act, 1961*, which restrict the power of the courts to sentence young offenders came into force'.

To return to the Public General Acts themselves, they too are first issued as separate documents and then in bound volumes. Since January 1963 they have been given serial or 'chapter' numbers, starting at 1 each year, and citation is made by indicating the year and chapter number. The *Criminal Justice Act* of 1967, for example, is cited as 1967 c. 80. For Acts promulgated prior to 1963 it is necessary to quote the regnal year in which they were passed, plus the chapter number. Thus, references to Acts issuing between 6 Feb. 1961 and 5 Feb. 1962 would begin '10 Eliz. II' (i.e. the tenth year of the reign of Queen Elizabeth II).

Annual volumes of Statutes have been published since 1831, while for the earlier period various editions of the *Statutes at Large* are available. Annotated editions such as *Current Law Statutes* are invaluable for those having to deal with criminal law, and the multi-volume *Halsbury's Statutes of England* conveniently arranges the section of Acts in force into subject sections and offers an excellent loose-leaf updating service. Halsbury also has a separate index volume. There are two official indexing publications, namely, the annual *Index to the Statutes* and *Chronological Table of the Statutes*. More recent Acts are listed in the daily and monthly HMSO catalogues.

Before leaving parliamentary publications, brief mention should be made of a series called House of Commons Papers. They are important to the criminologist because they include such documents as select committee reports (including those of the Estimates Committee) and most of the annual reports of government departments. As with bills, the numbering starts afresh each session, so it is essential to include the session when citing them. Unlike bill numbers, however, H.C. numbers are printed without brackets. Typical citations are:

> Estimates Committee. Eleventh Report: Prisons, Borstals and Detention Centres. 1966–67, H.C. 599
> Estimates Committee. Fifth Special Report: Prisons, Borstals and Detention Centres. 1967–68, H.C. 87
> Estimates Committee. First Report: Probation and After-care. 1971–72, H.C. 47

Non-parliamentary publications

Turning to non-parliamentary publications, the criminologist is clearly primarily concerned with those emanating from the Home Office. When they are published by HM Stationery Office, there is little difficulty either in keeping abreast of new titles or identifying those of earlier years. All that is required is access to the indexes and catalogues described at the beginning of the chapter. Sectional List No. 26 gives details of all the HO titles which are still in print, including, for example, those of the important series of *Studies in the Causes of Delinquency and the Treatment of Offenders* (1955–69) and *Home Office Research Studies* (1969–).

Non-parliamentary publications are largely a product of the present century. As regards official publishing, therefore, students of historical criminology are almost exclusively concerned with parliamentary papers; and while the indexes which cover them have their own idiosyncrasies, they are quite comprehensive. As the following list shows, they also overlap to some extent.

General Alphabetical Index to the Bills, Reports, Estimates, Accounts, and Papers, printed by Order of the House of Commons, and to the Papers presented by Command, 1852–1899 (HMSO). Since this compilation fails to indicate the serial numbers of papers, it is frequently necessary to use instead the cumulative index for 1852–53 to 1868–69 and the three decennial indexes which cover the last three decades of the century

Ford, P. and G., *Select List of British Parliamentary Papers 1833–1899* (Blackwell, 1953)

General Index 1801–52 (HMSO). This is in three volumes: (i) General Index to Bills; (ii) General Index to Reports of Select Committees; (iii) General Index to Accounts and Papers, Reports of Commissioners, Estimates, etc.

Hansard's Catalogue and Breviate of Parliamentary Papers 1696–1834 (Blackwell, 1953). An augmented reprint of H.C. Paper 626 of 1834

Catalogue of Papers Printed by Order of the House of Commons from the year 1731 to 1800 in the Custody of the Clerk of the Journals (HMSO). Arranged in three parts: Bills, Reports, and Accounts and Papers, with separate indexes to each

Lambert, Sheila, *List of House of Commons Sessional Papers 1701–1750* (List and Index Society, 1968). Contains a valuable introduction to eighteenth century papers

Nineteenth century parliamentary papers are being reprinted by the Irish University Press. Documents relating to particular subjects are bound together, making it possible for researchers to bypass some of the tedious job of identifying relevant papers in the indexes and locating them in long sets of sessional volumes; although of course many have a bearing on more than one subject, so some cross-checking is still necessary.

Documents which are published independently of HMSO present greater difficulty, since there is no single source of information devoted to them. Selected titles are recorded in the *British National Bibliography*, which is issued weekly and then cumulates into quarterly and annual volumes, and some are picked up by the professional and national press. Examples of non-HMSO publications are prison standing orders, ministerial circulars, the Chief Psychologist's research reports and publications of the Home Office Prison Department. Furthermore, a good deal of statistical information which is too specialised to be incorporated into the regularly published series is available from the Home Office and other government departments.* The most complete collection of this

* Criminal statistics are dealt with in Chapter 10.

kind of material is in the library of the Home Office itself. A good deal of hitherto unlisted material in the libraries of government departments is catalogued in *Guide to government data* (Political Reference Publications, 1973).

For more information on the sometimes perplexing but generally rewarding subject of official publishing the following texts may be consulted: P. and G. Ford's *A Guide to Parliamentary Papers* (Blackwell, 1956), J. E. Pemberton's *British Official Publications* (see p. 220) and F. Rodgers and R. B. Phelps's *A Guide to British Parliamentary Papers* (U. of Illinois School of Librarianship, 1967).

A NOTE ON OFFICIAL PUBLICATIONS IN THE UNITED STATES

In a short section it is impossible to go far into the complexities of US Government publications, but a few starting points may be useful.

Federal publications are obtainable from the United States Government Printing Office, Washington D.C. 20402 (referred to in this volume as US GPO). Price Lists of publications in print on specific subjects are available free; for example, *PL 10, Laws*; *PL 54, Political science* (which includes crime); *PL 71, Children's Bureau*. The lists contain details of the cumbersome system of payment in advance, on which the US GPO insists: it is best to order through a good bookseller who has experience of the GPO, and to be prepared for orders to take months rather than weeks.

For material published since the latest list, consult the *Monthly catalog of United States Government Publications*, available on subscription.

Among the most important publications are the reports of Presidential and other Commissions of Inquiry, which are often published with full supporting research reports, reports of 'Task Forces' and other material. The most substantial of these were perhaps the President's Commissions on Law Enforcement and Administration of Justice (the Katzenbach Commission, 1967); on Obscenity and Pornography; and on the Assassination of President Kennedy (the Warren Commission, 1964). It is worth remembering that the US GPO claims no copyright, and so reports on controversial subjects, such as sex and violence, are often available from commercial publishers, sometimes in paperback, within days of publication, and in this form can be obtained much more quickly than through the GPO.

Many publications relevant to criminology and the treatment of offenders are produced by departments of state such as the Bureau of Prisons and the Children's Bureau, and the library of an organisation with a direct interest in this field may find it possible to obtain them direct.

Further guidance may be found in *The Government Printing Office*, by Robert E. Kling (Praeger, 1970), and *Government publications and their use*, by L. F. Schmeckebier and R. B. Easton (2nd ed., Washington: Brookings Institution, 1969).

For the social scientist, J. B. Mason has compiled *Research resources: Vol. 2—Annotated guide to the social sciences* (Oxford: European Bibliographical Center and Clio P., 1971). This covers US Government official publications since 1789, and also lists publications of the United Nations and related agencies, other international organisations, and statistical sources. The basic criminal statistics for the US are published under the title *Crime in the United States: uniform crime reports* (US GPO, annual).

Publications of the Federal Government are regularly distributed to a network of depository libraries, and details are given, with much other information which should be useful to non-depository libraries, in Sylvia Mechanic's *Annotated list of selected United States Government publications available to depository libraries* (Wilson, 1971). For historical material there is a *Checklist of United States public documents 1789–1909*, of which only Vol. 1 was ever published (3rd ed., US GPO, 1911; Kraus Reprint, 1962).

In addition to the Federal Government, the individual states publish an enormous range of material, from tourist leaflets to scientific research reports. This is listed in the Library of Congress *Monthly list of State publications*; the main interest for criminologists lies in the research reports and possibly annual reports from Departments of Corrections and Parole Boards of a few states, such as California; but since the arrangement is by state and issuing body, rather than by subject, searching these lists requires great devotion to duty and is not recommended if the information can be obtained in another way. Data about each state, including governmental services and finance, are given in *The book of the States* (1313 E. 60th St., Chicago, Ill. 60637: Council of State Governments; biennial with supplements on elective and administrative officials). There are sections on Judiciary and Corrections.

For more general information about the USA, a large annotated bibliography has been compiled by the General Reference and Bibliography Division of the Library of Congress: *A guide to the study of the United States of America: ... the development of*

American life and thought (the L. of C., 1960). General statistics, which may be required as a basis for the interpretation of criminal ones, are summarised in the annual *Statistical abstract* of the Bureau of the Census; back numbers (1878–1928) are now available in reprint (Johnson Reprint, 1971). Sources of information on vital statistics, education, climate, offences, persons under custody and many other topics are listed, with a subject index, in the *Directory of Federal statistics for local areas*, compiled by the Department of Commerce and the Bureau of the Census (US GPO, 1966).

SOME PUBLICATIONS OF INTERNATIONAL ORGANISATIONS

United Nations

In addition to J. B. Mason's *Research resources: Vol. 2* (see pp. 231–2), United Nations publications are explained in *A guide to the use of United Nations documents* (*including . . . specialized agencies and special UN bodies*), by B. Brimmer and others (Oceana, 1962). For some time the UN provided only two main activities relating to criminology. One was the quinquennial Congresses on the Prevention of Crime and the Treatment of Offenders, of which the fourth was held in Kyoto, Japan, in 1970. Proceedings of these are published, in addition to a large number of supporting documents prepared for participants by governments and non-governmental organisations. It is difficult to obtain a comprehensive collection of these except by finding a person who attended the conference and does not wish to retain the literature. The other UN contribution is the publication of the *International Review of Criminal Policy* (1952–   ), of which issues Nos 1/2, 4, 6, 9, 11, 13, 15, 17/18, and 19, and a supplement to No. 23, contained an international bibliography, in classified order with index by author but not by subject, which is a valuable source for foreign material of the period. The bibliography, however, appears to have been discontinued.

In 1971 the UN set up a new Committee on Crime Prevention and Control, whose first session is recorded in Document E/5191 (1972); this was followed by *Crime prevention and control*, a worldwide review of the problem of crime, including some sources relating to the 'third world'. Further publications are to be expected from this committee in due course, including a revision of the *Standard minimum rules for the treatment of prisoners and detainees* (1957; reprinted in Britain by Amnesty).

The main listing of UN publications is the *United Nations Documents Index* (1950–), which includes a subject index.

Council of Europe

The Council of Europe holds Conferences of Directors of Criminological Research Institutes, for which criminologists are invited to prepare reports. These often take the form of comprehensive re-reviews of the literature, with bibliographies. Their advance circulation in mimeographed form is restricted, but many are subsequently published in the series *Current Trends in Criminological Research* by the European Committee on Crime Problems. The Council also publishes the lists of research mentioned in Chapter 1 (p. 13).

Another agency of the Council is the European Commission of Human Rights, which has published a series of *Case-law Topics*. These include 'Human rights in prison' (No. 1, 1971) and 'Bringing an application before the ECHR' (No. 3, 1972).

Index